ALSACE

Other books by James Bentley

Albert Schweitzer
Between Marx and Christ
The Blue Guide to Germany and Berlin
A Calendar of Saints
A Children's Bible
A Guide to the Dordogne
A Guide to Tuscany
Languedoc
Life and Food in the Dordogne
The Loire
Martin Niemöller
Oberammergau and the Passion Play
Ritualism and Politics in Victorian Britain
Secrets of Mount Sinai
Weekend Cities

ALSACE

James Bentley

Aurum Press

In memory of Alida Silver

Copyright © James Bentley 1988

First published 1988 by Aurum Press Limited
33 Museum Street, London WC1A 1LD

Maps by Richard Natkiel Associates
Illustration by Joy FitzSimmons

ISBN 0 948149 86 8

Typeset by Bookworm Typesetting, Manchester
Printed in Great Britain by
The Bath Press Ltd, Avon

Contents

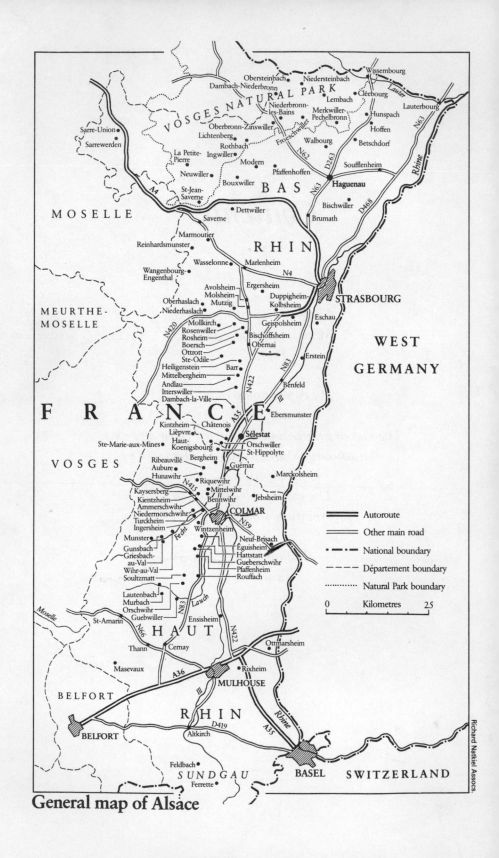

General map of Alsace

Autoroute
Other main road
National boundary
Département boundary
Natural Park boundary

0   Kilometres   25

Richard Natkiel Assocs.

Map of the wine route

Preface

Early one summer evening, while the local clock with its two bells chimed every quarter of an hour, I sat on the balcony overlooking the courtyard of the hotel Chez Lucien at Wintzenheim in Alsace, just outside Colmar on the main road to Gunsbach. By Alsatian standards Wintzenheim is not the greatest of towns. By any other standards it is exquisite. Its origins date back to Roman times. The Holy Roman Emperor threw defensive walls round Wintzenheim in 1275 to protect the local vintners whose wines he much treasured. Wintzenheim town hall was once a château belonging to the knights of Malta. The town fountain topped by a statue of the Virgin Mary dates from 1726.

Today the little town is guarded by two ruined châteaux: that of Pflixbourg, which the emperor built at the beginning of the thirteenth century, and that of Hohlandsbourg, which Rudolph von Habsburg built in 1279. And the hotel where I was sitting is one of many lovely half-timbered vintners' houses which grace Wintzenheim. It boasts a staircase tower, an oriel window and three other windows whose leaded lights are perfect, each lozenge exactly dissected by the horizontal iron bars. That summer evening chopped wood was piled neatly in the courtyard under plastic covers. The *patronne* was planting troughs with the begonias she had stored against the winter frosts. First she raked up the weeds of the courtyard and placed their chlorophyll-packed selves in the troughs, covering them with earth and then peat, into which she tucked the plants.

It was time to eat. There was no menu, but Alsace is gastronomically astounding. That evening my wife and I ate a set meal beginning with an hors-d'oeuvre of pâté, tomatoes, peas and lettuce, garnished with a mayonnaise that we saw the *patronne*'s husband mixing beforehand. The hors-d'oeuvre was followed by a guinea-fowl served in its own sauce, accompanied by noodles. Arranged on top of the dining-room panelling were large pieces of a honeycombed substance which, the *patron* explained as he poured out his own white wine, came from the sediment from the vats. After dinner he took us down to his cellar to see those same ancient carved vats.

It was my first introduction to Alsace, the land of *savants* of the rank of Albert Schweitzer, of that extraordinary artist Mathias Grünewald and the scarcely less brilliant Martin Schongauer, of Romanesque churches and baroque organs, an endlessly varied country comprising mountains and valleys, pastures and hops, a region of France which leans towards Germany but refuses to be swallowed up by either country. Its castles inspired Walter Scott. The cathedral at Strasbourg made Goethe dizzy with ecstasy.

Alsace is a delicious blend of city, town and village, of gentle hills, vineyards and river-washed countryside. As Victor Hugo put it half a century after Goethe, balancing in his mind Strasbourg cathedral and the heights through which he had passed on his journey there, 'Mountains and cathedral, vying with each other in grandeur, represent man's work for God and God's work for man.'

James Bentley
JANUARY 1988

My cup runneth over

Whenever I find myself in Alsace I instantly begin to think about the African jungle.

Not that Alsace is remotely like the African jungle. On the contrary: with its feudal and Renaissance castles, its wine routes, the splendid city of Strasbourg, its gentle rivers and the mighty Rhine, Alsace is a region of immense charm and seductiveness. Situated on the borders of France and Germany, it boasts half a dozen lovely wines as well as beers far choicer than the usual mean stuff found in French cafés.

So renowned is Alsace wine that you drink little else miles away in the typical Paris restaurant. Ask for a white wine around the Gare du Nord and likely as not they'll offer you an Edelzwicker from Alsace. And if not an Edelzwicker, a Gewürztraminer. These are fine wines, but incontestably the king of Alsace is Riesling, a Riesling quite different from those of Germany.

To sit in the half-timbered inns of the medieval villages of Alsace, drinking such wines, listening to the talk in either German or French and then wondering what on earth they are saying in the Alsatian dialect itself, is altogether adorable. Certainly the locals must be praising their drink. *Hesch e Fried, so trinksch; un trinksch, so hesch e Fried*, runs a bizarrely delightful Alsatian saying, roughly translated as 'If you are happy, drink; and if you drink, you are happy.' Divided from the rest of France by the lovely Vosges mountains and from

Germany by the Rhine, this delightful region has a quality all its own, into which are blended the gastronomic and vinous delights of its two neighbours. *Coq au vin* in my view is totally transformed when it becomes *coq au Riesling*.

This is also the land of that extraordinary artist Mathias Grünewald, whose tortured saints and gruesome crucifixion are the treasure of Colmar's art gallery. Here are ancient monasteries, geranium-decorated villages and charming walled towns. Their ramparts and fortresses, today a tourist attraction, served a grim purpose in the past. At Turckheim, for example, the redoubtable Turenne in 1675 fought off 60,000 German troops determined to march on Paris. Today Turckheim, though still surrounded by defensive walls, is crammed with medieval and Renaissance houses, boasts fountains and taverns and is a centre of the Alsace paper industry, making the rest of its solid living mostly from tourism and wine.

Tourism and the wine trade enrich many other towns and villages of Alsace. Not surprisingly the Alsatians themselves (the citizens of Turckheim among them) laud their own local wines at the expense of rival vineyards. One rhyme, which appears in Mathias Mérian's *Topographia Alsatiae*, published in 1644, runs:

> *De Thann im Rangen,*
> *In Gebweiler in der Wannen,*
> *In Turckheim im Brandt,*
> *Wächst der beste Wein im Land.*

> (From Thann in the Rangen,
> From Gebweiler in the Wannen,
> From Turckheim in the Brandt,
> Come the best wines in the land.)

They also have a dialect proverb neatly putting down wine snobbery: *E güet elsässer Winie isch besser as e Tritt from a Esel* ('A good little Alsace wine is better than a kick from a donkey').

So (to return to my original question) why in this hospitable land muse on the African jungle? My unfortunate dilemma began long ago when I was a schoolboy knitting blankets to send to Dr Albert Schweitzer's jungle hospital at Lambaréné in Gabon. For Schweitzer, the world's most celebrated missionary, a brilliant organist, Bach scholar and jungle doctor, was an Alsatian.

The Great White Doctor is by no means forgotten today. But thirty years ago Albert Schweitzer, Nobel prize-winner, seemed a Colossus among men: not simply a profound philosopher and student of the world's religions but also one of the greatest ever interpreters of the organ works of J. S. Bach. And not only that: having made two world-wide reputations – as musician and theologian – Schweitzer had turned his back on it all, trained as a physician and set up a hospital in Africa, in reparation, as he put it, for the sins of white civilization against the coloured races.

The world pressed a track to his jungle hut. Society women sent him money, sometimes delivering it personally. At Lambaréné Schweitzer was surrounded by beautiful nurses and brilliantly gifted doctors. Some people called him a heretic; most called him a saint. By day he operated on the strangled hernias of his black patients; by night he wrote profound books. And in between he practised on a piano specially constructed with organ pedals and made to withstand the rigours of the jungle climate.

Now Gabon, in those days, was French Equatorial Africa. And when war broke out in 1914 the French proceeded to arrest this great humanitarian and confine him and his wife in a concentration camp in Provence, the reason being that his native Alsace, though today part of France, belonged at that time to the Kaiser. As an Alsatian, Schweitzer was considered an enemy alien and that was enough for the French. This aroused Schweitzer's fury and caused him considerable mental distress.

After the war he decided he needed his own refuge back in Alsace, in case such a dreadful occurrence happened a second time. With his Nobel prize money he built a home in the little village of Gunsbach, where his father had once been pastor to the tiny flock. Schweitzer continued to return to Europe, giving superb organ recitals to raise funds for his jungle hospital. The last time he visited Britain some of us went from school to hear him – we shook his hand and gave him money.

So when my wife and I first went to Alsace we naturally visited Gunsbach. To our delight, after Schweitzer's death two of his former nurses had transformed his home (No. 8, rue Munster, Gunsbach, Haut-Rhin) into a Schweitzer shrine. Here are his piano-organ, his iron bed, portraits, ancient photographs of the jungle hospital and masses of letters. The two nurses were still there. (Alas, one of them, Schweitzer's devoted friend Miss Alida Silver, has since died.) Each day the house welcomes up to a thousand visitors. There's no charge. People are expected to pay what they wish. Often they give gifts as well as money.

We were entranced. Settling into a hotel at a delicious nearby village (where the beer was plentiful and the wine made from the landlord's own grapes), we revisited Gunsbach. The two nurses were invigorating and welcoming. They showed us everything we wished to see, rejoicing at a visit from two English admirers of their own revered Dr Schweitzer.

Then – as an enormous treat – we were asked to dinner. At table were a learned German organ scholar from Osnabrück, some Japanese guests (as a resolute opponent of atomic warfare Schweitzer is still adored in Japan) and a couple of other researchers. The talk ranged over the great days of the hospital at Lambaréné. But I perceived one sad fact: clearly the Great White Doctor drank only water in his jungle home. Only water is served in the maison Schweitzer at Gunsbach. Had we been able before dinner to slip out to the nearby hostelry for a mere half-hour to quench our thirst on some of the finest drinks in the world, the evening would have been perfect. As an ancient Alsatian dictum has it, 'To eat and drink well keeps love and the soul together' (*Güet esse un trinke, hebt Lieb un Seel zusammen*).

The following evening at Gunsbach we were once more supremely honoured: would we care to eat with the company again? My throat grew instantly dry, and my wife was suddenly inspired. 'Yes,' she replied, 'but my husband always takes an apéritif before dinner. Could we come back in half an hour?'

The effect on the nursing sisters was electrifying. 'Oh, Dr Bentley,' they cried. 'Oh, Mrs Bentley! Visitors give us so much drink that we don't know what to do with it.' In a trice chairs and a table were set out in the garden and vast amounts of booze appeared. On the tray stood Cointreau and malt whisky, as well as several bottles of plum liqueur and even a rare beaker of liqueur made from holly. Someone had given the maison Schweitzer a fine white Burgundy. But I simply drank a bottle of Alsatian Sylvaner.

The same ritual happened punctually at six the following evening. And again and again and again. We stayed an extra week researching at Gunsbach. Since those heady days we have returned to the maison Schweitzer many times. I know we shall go again.

Naturally, on these visits (where neither those who, like myself, are researching nor those who are merely visiting are asked for any specific amount of cash, but all are rightly expected to pay their way) I still drink mostly the wines of Alsace, all six lovely white varieties and one *rosé*: Sylvaner, Muscat d'Alsace, Riesling, Pinot gris, Pinot blanc, Gewürztraminer and Pinot noir. Two centuries ago the celebrated Dean Aldridge of Christ Church, Oxford, wrote a poem suggesting five excellent reasons for taking a drink of wine:

> If all be true that I do think,
> There are five reasons we should drink:
> Good wine, a friend, or being dry,
> Or lest we should be by and by;
> Or any other reason why.

In Alsace there are seven reasons – the seven great Alsatian wines. All take their names from the grape that creates them.

Riesling and Gewürztraminer indicate the magical uniqueness of Alsace, for here we taste the gentle loveliness of German wines and the stronger, though still delicate, French viticulture. Alsace is divided from Germany and the wines of the Rheingau, Rheinhessen and the Palatinate only by the great River Rhine. Even so, the Alsatians have become happily French, albeit determinedly retaining their own quiddities, and this they display in their wine.

Here, as in Germany, they produce both *Spätlese* wines (i.e. those pressed from grapes that have been allowed to remain on the vine longer than usual, thus producing an unusually ripe and rich wine) and exquisite *Beerenauslese* wines (pressed from even more succulent, individually selected overripe grapes). But instead of describing them as *Spätlese* and *Beerenauslese,* words understood by every Alsatian and many other Frenchmen, they dub these wines, in French, respectively *vendange tardive* and *sélection de grains nobles*.

On the Alsace side of the Rhine, running in complementary symmetry with the river, stretches the far from menacing range of mountains known as the Vosges, and on its slopes have been planted over a hundred kilometres of vineyards. Here vines are grown on something like 13,000 hectares of land. Though the major grapes produced are all white, their gamut is remarkable.

Technically Alsace is divided into two French *départements*, Bas-Rhin (lower Rhine) and its southern neighbour Haut-Rhin (upper Rhine). Bas-Rhin is the principal home of the light, fruity Sylvaner, the most prolific of Alsatian wines, the cheapest save for Edelzwicker but by no means for that reason inadequate. When Ali Silver and Toni van Leer first opened their vats for me, Sylvaner (as I have said) was the first I drank, not wishing to appear either greedy or discourteous. Greed would have chosen a dearer bottle first; discourtesy would have selected the cheapest, as if doubting my hosts' generosity. Sylvaner, I soon decided, was my favourite lunchtime wine when wandering around Alsace, a refreshing and agreeable accompaniment to a picnic salad on the edge of a field just off the main road.

At the maison Schweitzer, however, I soon moved over to a bottle of Muscat d'Alsace, partly because it was the only one of that *appellation contrôlée* to be seen when the maison Schweitzer wines appeared on the second evening, partly because I knew it to be an increasing rarity among Alsatian wines. Muscat I had drunk in the Languedoc, in that inhospitable countryside known as the Minervois. There it is rich and yellow, not as good as Sauternes, lesser than the late-harvested sweet Monbazillac grown near where I live in France (from grapes that have matured so long that the French call their essence 'noble rot').

The Muscat of Alsace is utterly remote from these wines, and I do not really know why. Far sharper and drier, yet somehow still mature, it quite entranced me. In spite of the Schweitzer wine cellar being apparently totally at my disposal, my wife and I drove away to buy some more (which proved difficult) and drank it quietly in our bedroom as a nightcap, as we leafed through the papers we had gleaned from the Schweitzer archive.

Would the great doctor have approved? I think so, for he cherished everything about his native Alsace. Even with regard to the less salubrious effects of too much alcohol, traditional Alsatian wisdom rudely sets them to one side. 'If I drink, I stumble and limp,' runs one proverb, ruminatively continuing, 'but if I don't drink, I limp none the less. Why not drink and limp, rather than limp sober?' (The dialect original is worth transcribing: *Trink i, so hink i. Trink i net so hink i doch. Liewer trinke und hinke, als nit trinke und doch hinke.*)

Whatever Dr Schweitzer's views might have been, I certainly felt much better that evening for drinking the Muscat d'Alsace of his Gunsbach home. The habit displayed my ignorance of the ways of the Alsatians themselves, for on later visits I discovered that they prefer drinking it not after a meal but as an apéritif.

How I wish Pinot gris retained its former name, banished by the French wine authorities in 1984! For one thing, the adjective *gris* suggests to non-Frenchmen that it is a milky-white wine, whereas it is a strong, heady white (though just as able to match meats and rich dishes as any red). For another, Pinot gris's former name, Tokay d'Alsace, which appears in the wine records of Alsace only in 1750, gives an erroneous but romantic impression that somehow the moody, doomed Hungarians penetrated into this exquisite region of France (tradition said in the mid-sixteenth century). They never did, and the grape in truth is a descendant of the old French Furmint variety – though later I shall be unable to resist repeating the legend that a Habsburg general introduced it here after his campaigns in Hungary! Pinot gris (may I please call it Tokay d'Alsace for nearly the last time?) is glowingly golden. Once tasted, it is unforgettable – sharpish as well as offering a hint of sweetness, quite powerful. Too much of it leaves one's nose a trifle redder the following morning than it should be.

Its sister wine, Pinot noir, again bears a misleading adjective from the point of view of foreigners: Pinot noir is not black but a *rosé* wine whose delightful paleness may make it look innocuous but whose dryness masks some potency. Paleness does not preclude opulence, and Pinot noir (also known as *rosé d'Alsace*) is certainly opulent. I relish it more than its delicate white sister, Pinot blanc, which the Alsatians also dub 'Klevner'. Beware though: much *rosé* wine from Alsace is not the product of Pinot noir, but spuriously made by lightly fermenting red grapes.

Riesling is the third most prolific grape in Alsace. Of Alsatian wines I like it best of all. The French describe it as virile and proud, as well as fresh and elegant. Here we are drinking a wine made from one of the greatest German grapes and showing its German mettle, albeit with a flavour unique to Alsace, where it grows on sunny and unusually chalky slopes. It adds its own charm not only to oysters and Alsatian cheese but also to the ubiquitous Alsatian *Sauerkraut*. I adore peering at its delightful strawy colour before taking my first sip of the day.

Finally, Gewürztraminer (sometimes also known as Traminer-Gewürztraminer, for it is a descendant of the ancient Traminer grape) is the grape that creates one-fifth of Alsatian wines, the majority of these grapes planted in Haut-Rhin. Experts who argue that the wines of the Haut-Rhin *département* are finer than those of Bas-Rhin clinch the argument with this uniquely fragrant, sharply piquant wine. The first time I tasted it was not in Alsace but in Paris, in a little café in the rue de Surène, opposite the hôtel de la Madeleine. The place was smoky. In typical French fashion the customers were bankers and postmen, single women and old codgers, office workers, garage mechanics, plus in this case me and a Scots television producer.

He and I chose to eat the dish of the day. The house wine – the

cheapest on offer – was Edelzwicker, the one Alsace variety mixed
from various vines. *Edel* means noble; and the Alsatians dub four of
their grapes noble, namely Riesling, Muscat, Gewürztraminer and
Pinot gris. If grapes creating Edelzwicker were not in fact among the
noblest, then the cheaper variety of wine produced used to be named
simply Zwicker. The name Zwicker does not seem to appear on
bottles these days, but the memory of its far from unacceptable taste
was evoked by the white wine which this café served in its carafes.

Since our TV budget was tight but not too tight, we sometimes
rejected the house wine for that extraordinary, almost bullying wine,
Gewürztraminer: spicy; sweeter, as I now know, than the usual
Alsace wine; instantly recognizable by its strong bouquet; utterly
able to match, if not overpower, the pungent Parisian working-man's
dish we were eating; and (as it turned out) utterly able to overpower
me. Gewürztraminer is a wine with a 14 per cent alcohol content. I
did not know it then. I knew it the following morning.

Is this why my friend the Scots television producer still in my view
owes me £1,000, a fact he strenuously denies? Did I put in
appallingly inadequate work the following morning? If so, I blame
him for introducing me to the entrancing, dangerous Gewürztraminer. Too much of it puts a thief in your head to steal away your brains.
There are days in Alsace when, in spite of my need to earn an honest
living as a sober writer, I have been content for this wondrously evil
effect to put me to sleep. And the Parisians, who sometimes spurn
their own cuisine for curries, rightly hold that a Gewürztraminer can
match the spiciest.

Although (apart from the Champagne country) Alsace is the most
northerly of French wine regions, the slopes of the Vosges mountains
to the west perfectly shelter the vineyards from harsh winds and too
much rain. Over 30,000 of the inhabitants of the region earn their
living mostly by growing vines and creating fine wines. Today almost
half the wines drunk in France come from Alsace. Alsatian wines are
exported (in order of quantity) first to Germany, then to Holland and
Belgium, with the British coming a poor fourth just in front of the
USA. Why are these obviously relished wines not more renowned
among English wine-lovers? For an answer look to history, the
history of human greed and oppression, as well as a history showing
an Alsatian determination to succeed against all the odds.

Vines have been grown here certainly since Roman times. And as
elsewhere in France, Germany, Austria and Italy, the fact that the
puritanical Christian St Paul fortunately instructed his followers to

take a little wine for their stomachs' sake meant that among the ancillary blessings brought by the Church were monks who lovingly cultivated and improved their grapes. By the twelfth century monastic vineyards in Alsace were often so renowned that their wines were highly prized. The monks developed a nose for deciding which fields and slopes were best suited to various types of vine. As they increased the quantity of their wines, they managed also to increase their quality.

In consequence we can read documents 500 years old or so, already speaking of some of the major grapes used in today's fine Alsace wines. The monks were weeding out poorer varieties, conscious that for over a century they had been profiting from the fact that wines created in their region were relished as some of the most sought-after in the world. Using the great river to export their wines, these medieval monks built up a flourishing trade with Scandinavia and the English.

By Shakespeare's time Englishmen and women had come to appreciate and even fear the potency of these wines from the Rhine valley. Shakespeare's alcoholic German suitor in *The Merchant of Venice* behaves 'very vilely in the morning, when he is sober; and most vilely in the afternoon, when he is drunk'. To render him drunk (and thus unfit for success) Portia arranges to have a glass of Rhenish wine placed within his reach, knowing he will drink it and incapacitate himself. The wine I take to be a white Alsatian, for later Salarino, the friend of Bassanio and Antonio, insults Shylock with the remark that there is more difference between his flesh and his daughter's than between jet and ivory, 'more between your bloods than there is between red wine and Rhenish'. Shylock is deeply offended.

Almost immediately the Thirty Years' War, which lasted from 1618 to 1648, brought the first set-back to the quality and profitability of this trade. Refugees and soldiers pillaged with equal rapacity. Vintners abandoned their vines and fled to hide in the forests from the vengeful armies, mercenaries from Spain and the Empire, from Sweden and Croatia. Whole villages were destroyed (twenty, historians have computed, for ever), and the vineyards surrounding them ravaged.

The eventual French participation and successes in this war brought new skills to Alsatian vignerons after the Peace of Westphalia in 1684, when France gained suzerainty over much of the region. Gallic clarity soon regulated for the better the wine trade of

Alsace. 'Wine magistrates' were appointed to inspect its quality, to improve local methods of harvesting, to regulate the varieties of grapes grown and to oversee the type of soil in which they were planted. Casks of wine were rigorously labelled. The renown of Alsatian wines picked up again, and Switzerland and Austria became new conquests alongside their older trading countries.

But if Christian monks had initially brought Alsatian wine to a peak of quality and repute, their Christian gospel condemned greed as one of the seven deadly sins. Condemnation, however, does not mean automatic extirpation. Now rapacious Alsatian vignerons were exploiting the huge renown of Alsatian wines in a way that inevitably led to disaster. Inferior vines were increasingly planted on inadequate land. Far more wine was produced than could possibly be consistent with quality. Yet throughout the next century lessons were not learned.

With the French Revolution of 1789 appeared a temporary but huge market. Napoleon's soldiers were thirsty men. Inferior Alsatian wines seemed good enough to slake their thirst. Then the revolutionary armies disappeared, leaving behind suddenly impoverished vignerons weighed down with a reputation for producing little better than alcoholic rubbish. And the revolution brought other dangerous changes. The religious orders were soon expelled, and new property laws broke up great vineyards into vulnerable smallholdings, run by individual and often impoverished families.

Such wine-making families frequently could not afford to replace their poor stock with noble vines. For the next fifty years Alsatian vineyards remained poor and Alsatian wines unpalatable, only to suffer a further blow in 1870–1 when the soldiers of Bismarck routed the French troops of Napoleon III. Alsace was annexed to Germany, and Germany had no intention of allowing her former French neighbours to compete with her own lucrative wine trade. Instead, the Germans decided to exploit the inadequate vines of their newly annexed citizens for their own profit.

Until this time (as Shakespeare's remarks reveal), Alsatian wines were dubbed wines of the Rhine. To safeguard their own wines from this river valley, the Germans forced the Alsatians to use a new *appellation* – one that is still in use today, *vins d'Alsace*. Alsatians were encouraged to give up their former noble vintages and start producing low-quality table wines that would not vie with the German wines of the Rhine. To their delight, these dubious wines found a ready market, since their own poor-quality products were still better than contemporary poor-quality German wines. It seemed an excellent notion to profit by producing and selling inferior alcohol.

The notion was a disastrous one. Just as the quality of Alsatian wines was reaching its lowest ebb, in 1918 the allied victory in World War I liberated Alsace from the Germans. She became once more part of France. Alas for Alsace, its vignerons suddenly found themselves competing again with the world's largest producer not only of high-quality wines but also of cheap ones. Existing producers of low-quality French wines had no intention of letting these newcomers from Alsace shoulder their way into the market place.

Yet the Frenchman's nose for a fine wine weakened this resolve. Alsatian wines slowly crept back into favour. For their part the Alsatians themselves, recalling their ancient skills, set about replanting fine varieties of vine, conscious that nowhere else in France but in their own Rhine-washed land could be found the unique combination of northern soils and sheltered dry vineyards.

Although France's early capitulation in World War II protected for a time the economy and viticulture of Alsace, the end of the war proved a savage blow to this enterprise. During 1944 and 1945 vicious fighting between the Germans and the army of liberation in the region once more devastated both Alsatian agriculture and viticulture.

Small wonder, then, if the wines of Alsace have taken time to recoup their former prestige. Yet once again the vine-growers remembered their centuries of tradition and began replanting. They still remain for the most part smallholders, often earning only part of their living from wine. The co-operatives constituting the *Union Vinicole pour la Diffusion des Vins d'Alsace* comprise no more than 15 per cent of the whole Alsatian wine trade. But the trade has reached a new peak of prosperity and the quality of its wines matches this peak.

As soon as Alsace was liberated, its ancient brotherhood of wine lovers, dedicated to St Stephen, revived itself. Numerous *confréries* of wine connoisseurs have existed in France since the Middle Ages. The origins of the *Confrérie Saint-Étienne* of Alsace stretch back in written history at least as far as the fourteenth century, when its members are found meeting at Ammerschwihr to savour fine wines and to elect new members worthy of worshipping the noble grape in their exalted circle. And the hierarchies embodied in its constitutions derive from the medieval corporations. Postulants are first admitted

as 'apprentices', then 'companions', then 'masters of wine', each rank
honoured by increasingly sumptuous robes of office. Only persons of
great renown, whose service to and love of wine has been truly
exceptional, may be admitted as *confrères d'honneur* without
passing through these probationary ranks.

After the war Alsace was once again French – but in its own special
fashion, as the very wine-bottles themselves indicate. A decree of
1959 laid down that only the now traditional slender, green, almost
flute-like bottles should carry the wine of the region. The dimensions
of this *flûte d'Alsace* are jealously specified: the height over the
diameter of the base should be in a relationship of five; the
relationship of the main bottle to its total height should be three.

Now *appellation contrôlée* status was granted to the great Alsatian
wines, but again with a difference from the rest of France (save for
Champagne). In Alsace *appellation contrôlée* refers not to the place
of origin, but to the type of grape from which each wine is pressed. In
addition, by a decree of 1972, every Alsace wine must be bottled in
the region where it is produced.

As wine production was refined still further, the words *grand cru*
were next allowed on Alsace labels to indicate wines designated as
having a higher alcoholic content and, perhaps, a higher quality than
the rest. Soon this *grand cru* designation was to break through a
traditional Alsatian rule: that individual vineyards are less important
than vines. In 1975 ninety-four vineyards suggested themselves as
specially worthy of *grand cru* status. The Alsace wine authorities
thought different. No more than twenty-five were accepted, though
new ones have been added since then. In the production of *grand cru*
wines only the noble grapes are acceptable; but the exacting label
appellation Alsace grand cru contrôlée is clearly here to stay.

To these fine wines must be added Alsace's own sparkling wine, *le
crémant d'Alsace*. Light, luminous, elegant, only discreetly bubbly, it
is made from Pinot blanc grapes (for the white *crémant*) and Pinot
noirs (for the *rosé*), with a judicious addition of Riesling or Pinot
gris. Thus, unlike the other fine wines of Alsace, *le crémant d'Alsace*
is not made 100 per cent from one grape.

Once the wine is fermented, production of this sparkling wine
follows the traditional method of nearby Champagne. The bottles
are placed in racks, leaning downwards, and turned each day by
hand, in cellars traditionally lit by candles. They are sold under
various descriptions: in ascending order of quality, *bruts blancs de
blancs, blancs de noirs, millésimés* and *cuvées*. Unlike most Alsatian

wines, which can and probably should be drunk fairly soon after they are created, *le crémant d'Alsace* can be kept for up to four or five years, provided it is kept bottled in racks and at a stable temperature between fifty and sixty degrees Fahrenheit (ten and fifteen degrees Centigrade).

Those who make this wine insist that it should be drunk even colder – between forty and forty-five degrees Fahrenheit (five and seven degrees Centigrade) – not in a virtually flat glass such as champagne is often foolishly poured into, but in a fluted glass that allows you to enjoy its pale golden colour and preserves the wine's sparkle till the moment you drink it. *Le crémant d'Alsace,* like champagne, is a favourite in its own region for weddings, festivals, birthdays, first communions and New Year's Day, as well as offering itself as a partner for fish, entrées, birds and seafood.

Alsatians also use it as the basis for cocktails. One and a half centilitres of curaçao poured into a fluted glass, topped up with *le crémant d'Alsace* and decorated with a slice of orange produces the cocktail known as *bleu crémant.* A measure of tangerine juice topped up with the wine and lightly stirred creates *crémant mandarine.* Orange juice instead of tangerine creates *crémant orange.* The locals also make an infusion of verbena tea and let it go cold before adding to it very cold *crémant d'Alsace* to make *crémant verveine.* Save for the first mentioned, such cocktails are not lethal and are infinitely refreshing, as is *le crémant d'Alsace* mixed either with syrup of strawberry or else with blackcurrant *(cassis).*

Unusually among sparkling wines, *le crémant d'Alsace* is sometimes used in cooking. Antoine Westermann, chef of the restaurant Buerehiesel in Strasbourg, offers the following recipe for '*crémant d'Alsace* in a chef's hat' (*crémant d'Alsace en toque blanche*):

Ingredients for four people: four escalopes of turbot, each weighing 150g (5½oz); eight fine prawns (taken out of their shells); 120g (5oz) butter; 20g (1oz) shallots; salt, pepper and some twigs of chervil.

Method: Reduce the *crémant d'Alsace* with the shallots. Salt and pepper, and add small quantities of melted butter. Keep the mixture warm.

Cook the turbot for five minutes in steam made from water and seaweed (this is my timing: Antoine Westermann decrees three minutes; please choose for yourself), adding the prawns for two minutes. Garnish the bottom of four plates with the butter that is now enriched with the *crémant d'Alsace,* and serve in this butter the turbot decorated with the prawns and the chervil.

Naturally enough the best wine to accompany *crémant d'Alsace en toque blanche* is a cold *crémant d'Alsace*.

Now as if this were not enough, Alsace is also rich in two other drinks: beer and liqueurs. 'An Alsatian will change his religion before changing his beer,' runs the local proverb. The religious comparison is apt. Michel Debus, president of the brewers of Alsace, once put it thus: 'Between religion and drinking there is a concordance. The wine of unbridled carnivals corresponds to the gaiety of Catholicism. By contrast, beer, which produces not so much merriment as a communal feeling, finds itself more in accord with the mentality of a Protestant.'

Beer in Alsace, as elsewhere, represents a sometime heretical drink. Medieval monks devoted themselves to producing wine in part at least because the Christian eucharist demanded that each Mass involve a repetition of Jesus's comparison of bread and wine to his own soon-to-be broken body and shed blood. Beer has no such spiritual and theological connotations.

Not surprisingly then, the first Alsatian brewer to appear in history was not a monk or priest but a layman, Arnoldus Cervisarius, who set up his brewery in Strasbourg in a cul-de-sac still called the ruelle de la Bière. Alsatian Protestants, who often minimized the Catholic sacraments (though never entirely dispensing with them) found brewing beer an extremely congenial occupation and, like their master Martin Luther, they found drinking it equally congenial. They also brought to the art of brewing their unique capitalistic energy. After the Protestant Reformation, Alsatian brewing prospered. By the eighteenth century, not a single Catholic brewer could be found in Strasbourg. The Protestants had taken over the beer-trade.

God, it seems, blesses Protestants and Catholics alike in Alsace. Devout Catholic monks were provided with the climatic wherewithal and a fastidious terrain to produce marvellous wines. Beer, in its turn, needs exquisite water, and Alsace possesses in abundance fine waters flowing from the Jura mountains. Beer cannot profitably be brewed where hops do not flourish, but they do so in Alsace – and nowhere else in France. Beer needs a coldish temperature to ferment properly, and Alsace has been granted just such a temperature. The result is a round, delightfully satisfying brew, a light, gay and refreshing drink. Some Frenchmen take thirty-three centilitres of beer as their daily breakfast, and who is to say they are wrong?

Alsace is virtually unique in consecrating its territories to producing these two rival drinks. On average each one of its citizens drinks twice as much beer as anyone else in France, a total of ninety-one litres per head each year. This achievement by no means matches the beer-quaffing abilities of the British, Germans or Belgians; but of these three races, only the Germans produce a wine to rival their beer. If we British are to consume our own native drink, we have few wines to compete with our beers.

A celebrated event in the history of Alsatian beer was the opening of the Basel-Paris railway. The first beer-bearing train from Alsace reached Paris in 1855, and the Parisian market submitted to the onslaught of this Protestant thirst-quenching drink. Scarcely fifteen years later the effects of the Franco-Prussian War were transforming Alsatian brewing just as they had affected Alsatian wine. Strasbourg experienced most of the changes. Whereas elsewhere in Haut-Rhin and Bas-Rhin small, charmingly decorated pubs persisted, in Strasbourg were built huge beer halls, some of which survive to this day.

This Prussian Protestant impulse, albeit harming the small brewer, was ultimately beneficial to Alsatian breweries, even though it had hampered the Alsatian wine-trade. Between 1872 and 1903 brewing amalgamations reduced the fragmented Alsatian beer industry from 270 large breweries to forty-five. Yet these breweries were soon producing over 150 per cent of the Alsatian beer sold ten years earlier.

World War I failed to destroy the industry. Instead Alsace beers simply penetrated farther into the French market. The boss of Kronenbourg (Jérôme Hatt) made a brilliant innovation, introducing from the USA thirty-three-centilitre bottles – a stroke of genius because many connoisseurs were increasingly aware that most of the beers sold in litre bottles were undistinguished, tasteless and soon went flat. Today 50 per cent of French beer is brewed by this one Alsatian company, Kronenbourg.

Yet Kronenbourg has not utterly displaced or destroyed all the smaller breweries. People describe the suburb of Strasbourg which is dominated by the Schiltigheim brewery as a *Bierstadt* (beer town). Obernai beer, by its very quality, forces itself on today's French supermarket shelves. Beers nowadays are described as 'sumptuous' or specially luxurious (*bières de luxe*). Incredible though it may seem, today nearly 100 per cent of Alsatian beers are officially designated *bières de luxe*. So fearful have German brewers become of the competition from Alsatian beers that in spite of the European Common Market's commitment to eliminating trade barriers, in the 1980s they managed for a time to prohibit the importation of French beer.

To add liqueurs to this plethora of Alsatian drink is almost embarrassing, yet they flourish here in Alsace, created by the climate and the fruits of this astoundingly beneficent region. The liqueur of the cherry is known in Alsace by its German name of Kirsch. Odd though this may seem, the best Kirsch is said to derive not from sophisticatedly cultivated cherries but from the wild cherry which grows between the summits of the Vosges mountains and the Alsace plain. Kirsch has an alcohol content of at least 50 per cent, as does strawberry liqueur, which again is often made from wild strawberries (though these are nearly always supplemented by cultivated ones). Alongside these is distilled Quetsche, the bizarrely attractive regional damson liqueur.

Can one drink more than a thimbleful of such heady alcohols? If so, no one can drink pure Alsatian raspberry liqueur and live for very long afterwards. Undeterred, the Alsatians macerate their raspberries in a less potent alcohol and thus offer (in my opinion) an entrancing yet still deadly drink.

I sometimes have a nightmare that there is nothing which the fanatically dedicated distiller will not put into his pot, be it pigs' trotters or old shoelaces. The Alsatians almost prove my wild dreams true. From the roots of the yellow gentian they create a liqueur known as Enzian. Apricots, blackberries, peaches, myrtles are all grist for their stills. The distillation of greengages is a much sought-after liqueur. And on the slopes above Ammerschwihr grows holly from whose berries the Alsatians distil Houx, the most expensive and rarest liqueur in the world.

Alsace is so narrow and tiny compared with the other wine regions of France that its great vineyards are compressed in a wine route stretching barely 120 kilometres from Thann in the south to Obernai in the north. The route winds through hilly country and valleys, with the Vosges mountains a constant shelter to the west, through tiny walled towns, past magical châteaux and ancient inns and always alongside vineyards and wine taverns.

One problem of this wine route is that you need four people, preferably five, capable of driving for part of the trip, since its purpose is to enjoy not only buying wine but also tasting it *en route,* and the French police are commendably strict about those who drive with their faculties impaired by strong drink. The crime could easily come about, for along the route wine merchants have set up their stalls, and in magnificent cellars you are invited to sample endless glasses before buying.

A second happier problem is that the villages and towns through which it passes are often so exquisite that an hour is scarcely enough to sample merely the finest of their treasures. Here I set out only the most superlative sights, leaving the magical rest for my gazetteer in the chapter 'Gems of Alsace'.

Thann sets the whole scene, a picturesque old town overlooked by the ruined château of Engelbourg. This château was partly razed in 1673 on the orders of Louis XIV, and its single keep, staring bleakly to heaven, is known to the locals as the witch's eye (*Haxenoïg* in the Alsatian dialect). Louis had inherited Thann at the end of the Thirty Years' War, before which the town had been invested alternately by the Swedes and the forces of the Holy Roman Emperor. Its charming sleepiness today belies such a turbulent past. Yet in our own century it has also suffered, annexed by Germany in 1870 and much bombed in both the 1914–18 and the 1939–45 wars.

Before setting out, see the church of Saint-Thiébaut, a superb example of the fourteenth- and fifteenth-century style which the French call flamboyant. The west doorway was sculpted towards the end of the fourteenth century and is one of the masterpieces of Alsatian Gothic. The north doorway dates from the next century, as does the choir whose carved stalls are realistic and sometimes offer merry caricatures.

Now, the Christian world contains many magnificent churches with merry caricatures; but the church of Saint-Thiébaut in Thann is, to my knowledge, unique in one respect: part of it was literally built with wine. In 1431 the chronicle of the Franciscan monks of Thann records that the wine-crop that year was so abundant that no one possessed enough barrels in which to keep it. So instead it was used to make mortar, and used here in the building of this church.

Ultimately the bones of St Theobald ('Thiébaut' in French) and not the wine are what made possible such a building in this quietly spoken spot. He was never a bishop, in spite of local legend, but a nobleman turned hermit. After his death his relics worked miracles and brought to Thann increasing numbers of pilgrims, eager for more wonders and healings. Thanks to the opening of the St Gotthard Pass around 1220, the pilgrims were international. Their gifts paid for this sumptuous house of God. As the inhabitants of Thann will tell you:

> The bell-tower of Strasbourg cathedral is taller;
> the steeple at Freibourg is bigger;
> but ours at Thann is the most beautiful.

Thann wine not only built a great church; it also reputedly gets one drunk. Oddly enough, the *Little Chronicle of Thann* of 1766 seems proud of the fact, describing its wine as beguilingly soft as milk, insinuating itself amicably inside you, and then producing 'such deplorable and shaming effects that it is better not to describe them here'. Well, here I set myself against the eighteenth-century chronicler. I have drunk my share of Thann wine without the slightest ignoble effect, and my friends will surely agree.

Drive from Thann east to Cernay, where the valleys of the Thur and the Doller meet, a village much wounded in two World Wars, yet preserving some of its ancient fortifications (the porte de Thann dates from the thirteenth century and now houses a museum of local history). Because of its situation as a crossroad, Cernay has developed industrially. Today two sad, beautiful military cemeteries, one German, one French, mutely testify to the hatreds of the past.

From here the route runs north along the D5 as far as Guebwiller. Guebwiller instantly confirms the happy problem of driving along the wine route of Alsace: that to sample every architectural treasure would take days and days. Whereas Thann boasts one magnificent church, Guebwiller boasts three, the late-twelfth-century Romanesque church of Saint-Léger; the fourteenth- and fifteenth-century Dominican church (with its frescos dating from its foundation); and the mid-eighteenth-century church of Our Lady – not to speak of a town hall dated 1514 and possessing a lovely oriel window and a monumental staircase, and of many ancient houses and a couple of former châteaux.

Guebwiller and its valley from the Middle Ages to the revolution belonged to the abbots of Murbach. Casimir de Rathsamhausen, the last prince-abbot, paid for the church of Our Lady when he decided to forsake monastic seclusion and come to live here. His predecessors were those who first laid out the great terraces of vines overlooking the town and its valley. To sample all the wines, mostly varieties of Riesling (and especially those of the celebrated Wannen vineyard), would take just as long as to explore this town and its environs. Obviously one must come here again.

Pleasingly the Alsace wine route is here well-signposted, by way of Bergholtz (whose name means wooded mountain and which boasts not a military but a medieval cemetery). Bergholtz was founded in the eighth century by Irish monks, who next founded the abbey of Murbach. Its neighbour is Bergholtz-Zell, where Pope Leo IX consecrated a church in the eleventh century whose Romanesque pillars are built into the present church of 1874.

Drive on through the terraced village of Orschwihr as far as Soultzmatt. If you have strength of mind enough resolutely to ignore Orschwihr's ruined fifteenth-century château and its vintners' houses, I defy anyone not to pause at Soultzmatt. Nearby are planted the highest vineyards in Alsace, those named the Zinnkoepfle. The château of Wangenbourg (sole survivor of three) dates from the sixteenth century, the town fountain from 1663, and many of the houses from the same century. As for its parish church, the bell-tower is a mighty Romanesque construction and inside the nave is cool and Gothic. If you have already drunk too much, try the waters of the nearby Nessel spring. They are reputed to restore overworked livers, despairing bladders, depressed kidneys and complaining stomachs.

The road leads east now to Rouffach by way of Westhalten, a village surrounded by vineyards and, because it is cradled by the three celebrated hills known as the Zinnkoepfle, the Strangenberg and the Bollenberg, a site specially protected by the French from despoliation by incompetent builders. Rouffach itself is even more delightful, though its loveliness means that it is usually filled with tourists. The church of Notre-Dame de Rouffach took basically four centuries to build, although after it was finished in the late-fifteenth century more bits were being added for another 400 years. The result is a masterpiece. Its stones are palely beautiful, some grey, some light brown, some pink. Inside is an exquisite pink font, dated 1492, and a fifteenth-century Madonna. But what makes Rouffach so fine is not just one building but the whole ensemble of Renaissance and classical houses, the former home of the Teutonic knights, the former bishop's palace, delicious oriel windows, remains of the thirteenth-century synagogue (even though the Jews of Rouffach were savagely persecuted in the same century).

The women of Rouffach, if history teaches anything, are to be approached with temerity. In 1106 the future emperor Henry V lived in the château here, and his servants made the lives of the citizens miserable. Men and women alike retaliated by throwing him out and confiscating his royal insignia. Henry, humiliated and enraged at having his crown and sceptre lifted from him not only by the menfolk of Rouffach but also by mere women, returned and set fire to the town, whereat the women, now scorning their timid menfolk, again drove him away. In consequence, ever since, women have occupied the right-hand seats in the church, an honour usually reserved for the males of Alsace. Moreover, whenever Rouffach celebrates one of its annual feasts, women take pride of place.

From Rouffach drive north through Pfaffenheim to Éguisheim. Both are worth a pause. Anyone with a nose for etymology will know that at Pfaffenheim there will be fine wines, since the word means 'the home of the clergy'. In fact, most of the religious buildings, though attractive, have lost their medieval and Renaissance origins through rebuilding. The neo-Romanesque church is huge, a nineteenth-century exuberance. But what primarily draws one here on the wine route are the lovely vintners' houses, nearly all of them in the Renaissance style, and all selling excellent wines, usually Gewürztraminer. Note the scratches on the outside wall of the church. Vintners made them, sharpening their pruning knives on this holy stone to keep the devil away.

Éguisheim from the eleventh century was the home for a hundred years of the most powerful family in Alsace, the counts of Nordgau. They came and went. When the counts died out in 1225, the bishops of Strasbourg took over, fortifying the place in the 1290s with ramparts that in part still remain. In consequence, although Éguisheim is today but a village with no more than 1,500 inhabitants, in its centre it boasts the ruins of an octagonal château dating (it is said) from as far back as the eighth century, and it is dominated by the three splendid châteaux of Haut-Éguisheim, set on a summit outside the village.

You can walk around the thirteenth-century fortifications of Éguisheim and perceive that the village is designed as a perfect circle. Many of its houses are entrancing, often tiny, some half-timbered, others constructed entirely of stone. Here are two sixteenth-century fountains. The White Horse Inn (auberge du cheval blanc) was built in 1613 and the vintners' houses mostly a century or so later. When the church of St Peter and St Paul was rebuilt in the first decade of the nineteenth century, the villagers kept the splendid late-Romanesque doorway of the old church (dating from around 1225), which depicts Jesus between St Peter and St Paul, as well as the wise and foolish virgins.

Its most celebrated citizen was Bruno, son of Count Hugo IV of Éguisheim, born to his wife the Countess of Dagsburg in 1002, and Pope Leo IX from 1048 until his death six years later. Leo IX longed to reunite the Eastern and Western branches of the Catholic Church. Alas, during his pontificate the Eastern Christians split yet farther away from their Western brethren and sisters. If you arrive at the village of Leo's birth on the last Sunday in August you will run into the wine festival; and on the last weekend of March you will find the whole village riotously drinking and selling its *vin nouveau,* both Riesling and Gewürztraminer.

Properly speaking, the wine route should now take us south-west again, along the valley of the River Fecht by way of Turckheim as far as Wihr-au-Val. It is an entrancing trip, but if we took it we should never reach the end of our journey in a day. Again, having driven back from Wihr-au-Val, we ought to set off north-west to Kaysersberg. I should love to do so, for there in 1875 was born Albert Schweitzer, who (from beyond the grave, so to speak) introduced me to the wines of Alsace and whose birthplace still stands; but instead I suggest we drive directly north-east from Éguisheim to Colmar, the very heart of the finest (or nearly the finest) Alsace wine country. Colmar is so marvellous that we must return to explore another day; but its wines, famous throughout Europe since the fourteenth century, can be sampled without delay.

Long ago Colmar was renowned for its wine-bibbing clubs, groups of discerning topers who, as they drank, clustered around their stoves or *poêles* and thus came to be known as precisely that: *poêles*. Clubbing together, they could command the finest products of the local vintners. Here, in an historic centre of Alsatian wines, dare we use the prayer of the *Confrérie Saint-Étienne?*

Let us pray, my brethren, to honour the Lord in his creation and to sing his greatness, above all in giving us wine, created by the divine hand and through the work of men becoming the finest of gifts – one too which gives us poor humans a ladder to heaven and to the pleasures of the celestial feasts.

Give thanks to the God of the holiest joys, found in drinking several quarts of this famous and delicious beverage which renders us joyous, garrulous and shrewd.

You, Lord, who have given us both wine and women: accept our common flame which permits us to laud at one and the same time your two masterpieces and the wisdom of your decrees.

Both woman and wine possess by their natures a generous, limpid and pure spirit, a spirit killed by the slightest brutality on our part, a spirit which would lose all its sparkle in such a fatal disaster.

Give us, Lord, the remarkable insight to experience joy and listen to reason, forgetting age, mood and season, the sole happy way of living to a good old age while waiting for the eternal happiness of heaven.

So be it.

Then, true to their medieval past, the brethren turn to dog-Latin:

Fratres, Primo mirate, deinde gustate, tandem gaudete ad magnum Dei gloriam in unitate sanctorum nostrorum Stephani, Vincenti et Urbanu. Amen.

Drive north from Colmar shortly to reach the town of Ingersheim, which lies at the confluence of the Munster and Kaysersberg valleys. Although much damaged during World War II, Ingersheim still possesses an eighteenth-century town hall, some fine vintners' houses dating from the Renaissance and a baroque church: Saint-Barthélemy. But our purpose is to continue speedily north by way of the little wine village of Mittelwihr (where both Protestant and Catholic churches had to be rebuilt after the bombs of World War II), and to turn west as far as exquisite Riquewihr.

Unlike Mittelwihr, this medieval town has been wondrously preserved, its former mid-sixteenth-century château now a postal museum, its fortifications of 1291 intact, with the upper gate (Obertor) dating from the thirteenth and sixteenth centuries. Riquewihr in truth boasts a double ring of fortifications. The Grand'Rue is unmissable, packed with fifteenth-, sixteenth- and seventeenth-century houses. Scarcely less remarkable are the side streets, the rue de la Couronne, the rue Latérale, the rue des Écuries and the rest. Read the dates of the houses on their heraldic plaques. Admire the courtyards and the oriel windows. Sample the wine, for around Riquewihr grow 300 hectares of vines, producing an unmatched Riesling, especially that grown on the sunny slopes of the Schoenenberg and the Sporen.

Here it was in the sixteenth century that the wine growers of Alsace first sagely determined that only seven fine grapes should produce the wines of their region. And a few kilometres north-east we reach Hunawihr, with a park filled with storks, its church of Saint-Jacques frescoed in 1492 with the legend of St Nicholas, and its Renaissance fountain that once reputedly flowed with wine when the vintners of Hunawihr were experiencing a bad year. It must have been good wine, for the inspired drink created here today is rivalled in France only by the finest vintages of other regions.

The village of Hunawihr lies half-way between Riquewihr and Ribeauvillé, a town dominated by no fewer than three ruined châteaux, the thirteenth-century château Haut-Ribeaupierre, the thirteenth- to fifteenth-century château Girsberg and the altogether splendid château Ulrichsburg which boasts a thirteenth-century keep and knights' hall.

Augustinian monks not only built at Ribeauvillé the Gothic parish church, with its massively fortified bell-tower, but also presumably helped to develop the town's vineyards, and today on the second weekend of July you can enjoy an unequalled wine festival. On the first Sunday in September occurs here the strange feast of Pfifferday, which re-creates the time when minstrels would come to pay homage to the lords of Ribeauvillé. The Pfifferhaus (also known as the maison de l'Ave Maria), deriving its name from these minstrels, is a splendid building dating from 1660, with a lovely oriel window.

In the sixth century St Huna not only gave her name to Hunawihr but also dug the well which in the Middle Ages (if legend is to be believed) flowed with wine instead of water, like the one at Riquewihr, when the vintage was bad. Hunawihr belonged to the house of Wurttemberg from 1324 to the French Revolution, and on its town hall you can descry the coats of arms of the house, carved there in 1517.

Drive north-east to the wine town of Bergheim, where the apparently medieval château de Reichenberg was in fact rebuilt around 1900, where the fourteenth-century double ring of walls is genuinely medieval (as are the nine towers and the gateway), where little bridges are needed to cross some of the wide, open gutters; where the apse and choir of the parish church date from the same century as the walls, and where the vintners' houses are both Gothic and Renaissance. Vines have been cultivated at Bergheim since Roman times, and here today you should quaff Gewürztraminer made from a grape known as Kanzlerberg de Bergheim.

Directly north of Bergheim you reach Saint-Hippolyte. The village is lovely enough: vestiges of the old ramparts; an entrancing medieval church; half-timbered houses; a Renaissance fountain (it dates from 1555). But its greatest gift, apart from its unusual red wines, is a view of the château du Haut-Koenigsbourg, lying to the north-west 753 metres above sea-level. The château du Haut-Koenigsbourg dominates three valleys as well as the River Rhine. Basically fifteenth-century, it had fallen into ruins and was rebuilt in an architecturally questionable but brilliant style between 1900 and 1908 on the orders of Kaiser Wilhelm II. Here then is a stunning example of fifteenth-century military architecture as seen through the eyes of early twentieth-century German Gothic architects.

From Saint-Hippolyte drive north to Kintzheim, which is not to be confused with Kientzheim, the place where the *Confrérie Saint-Étienne* in 1977 found a new headquarters and established a fascinating wine museum (fittingly enough in the château which once belonged to Lazarus von Schwendi, the general who led the Holy

Roman Emperor's troops against both the French and the Turks and is said to have introduced the Tokay vine to Alsace). Unlike the beautifully restored château at Kientzheim, the twelfth- to fourteenth-century fortress perched on a wooded 280-metre-peak at Kintzheim remains but an imposing ruin, for the Swedes captured and demolished it at the beginning of the Thirty Years' War. If you visit Kintzheim in summer, do not miss the daily demonstrations of flights by half-tamed birds of prey, including eagles (see p. 125). Kintzheim has also become a major centre for restoring a more peaceful bird to Alsace, the stork, symbol of good fortune to the Alsatians.

The D159 leads north-east from Kintzheim to Sélestat, and Sélestat is frankly delightful, once you penetrate the boring environs to the intimate, intricate centre. The brilliant military architect Vauban rebuilt its fortifications in the late-seventeenth century, and inside his gates you find two fine churches (one Gothic, one Romanesque), a clock tower, a former arsenal, a nineteenth-century corn hall, not to speak of a Jewish cemetery and a restored synagogue. Sélestat was the birthplace of the celebrated humanist Beatus Rhenanus and the yet more celebrated Reformer Martin Bucer.

Leave Sélestat by the north-west for Châtenois, where storks nest in the witches' tower of the ruined thirteenth-century chapel and where the piquantly baroque church boasts a Romanesque tower and, inside, a splendid eighteenth-century Silbermann organ.

From here the Alsace wine route follows the D35 north to Barr, a village decked with flowers, surrounded by vineyards planted in perfect chalky soil, crammed with lovely buildings and hosting an annual fair on the first Sunday in October to celebrate the wine harvest. So brutal was an attack on the castle of Barr by the town's enemies in 1295 that the citizens later attributed its destruction to the devil; and here at the end of November 1944 German and American troops fought viciously; yet today the peacefulness of the village seems to have set past conflicts aside. The wines prove to be predominantly Sylvaner, but with an excellent sprinkling of Riesling. By a pleasing accident of bibulous history, the first document in which the name 'Barr' appears is one of 788, celebrating the presentation of vines to the abbey of Fulda.

Due north of Barr along the N422 lies Obernai, where the Alsace wine route ends. If you are at Barr to celebrate the wine harvest, you can sleep off the effects for a week before visiting Obernai, where the celebration takes place on the second Sunday of October. Obernai lies on the Ehn, a tributary of the River Ill. Here is an old well, but little water gets into the wine. Obernai's splendid half-timbered houses, thirteenth-century bell-tower (the rest of the church has disappeared), the beautiful fifteenth-century stained glass of its main parish church and its town hall dating from 1523 make this small town a fitting end to the wine route.

Or not quite. I still feel guilty at not having found time to visit the very special wine town of Kaysersberg. Dr Schweitzer himself, that great theologian, also cherished wine (though not, as I surmise, at his jungle hospital at Lambaréné). Kaysersberg was also the birthplace, the ecumenical Schweitzer recalled, of a great Catholic preacher named Geiler, who died in 1510. As for drink, at Kaysersberg a dialect rhyme runs:

> *Drinks tu Wasser in dem Kragen,*
> *über Disch es kalt bin magen;*
> *Drink Masig alten subtiln Wein,*
> *Dath ich ud las nuch Wasser sein.*

> (Wrap up well to drink water,
> In case it freezes your stomach at the table;
> In my view, set water to one side,
> And moderately quaff old, subtle wine.)

The year of Schweitzer's birth, the Great White Doctor himself recalled, was also the year of a superb vintage of Kaysersberg wines. 'As a boy I used to pride myself not a little,' he wrote, 'on having been born in the town where Geiler von Kaysersberg had lived, and in a famous wine-year, for the season of 1875 was an extraordinarily good one for the vines.'

Alsace à table

If you are lucky enough to take the Alsace wine route when the grapes are still on the vines, take care to relish their plump ripe colours. Pinot noir, the begetter of *rosé d'Alsace*, finally explains its own name, for its colour is blue-black amid the wide green leaves. Then the colours of the grapes gradually lighten: the Gewürztraminer grape a smoky red against its vine's yellowing leaves; Pinot gris a sharper red; Muscat d'Alsace definitely white; Riesling a greener white with some red skins; Pinot blanc yellow-white, again with some red skins; and finally the lightest grape of all, Sylvaner.

Late autumn, then, is in my view one of the finest seasons to follow this route, just before the grapes are picked in early October, just as the trees higher up the slopes of the Vosges mountains are about to shed their leaves. Best of all is to combine the two seasons: the moment when the grapes are finally ripened and the harvest time itself. Although the Alsatian vignerons are as mechanized as any in France, the harvesters still carry on their backs the picked grapes in cone-shaped baskets, as they have done for centuries, pouring them into tubs on the wagons at the side of the vineyards.

If you must visit Alsace at another time of the year, do not miss a trip to the museum of viticulture and Alsatian wine at the château de la Confrérie Saint-Etienne in Kientzheim, which I have already in part described, the château that was once the home of the counts of Lupfen zu Kientzheim. (It opens daily from June to September between 10.00 and noon and between 14.00 and 18.00, and if you are with a party you can telephone outside the season to arrange a personal visit.) Here you can see the old-fashioned harvest wagons of yesteryear, with the cone-shaped baskets that are still in use. Here is a mobile wine-press, once upon a time wheeled from house to house. Here too is revealed the art of the rustic vintner, an art itself sometimes far from rustic: woodcuts depicting monks and their helpers tying up vines and gathering grapes; barrels carved with mythological figures; exquisite wine-glasses and bottles dating as far back as the fifteenth century, when the glass-blowers of Alsace suddenly blossomed.

A key delight of such a small region is the intense variety of its terrain, almost instantly accessible by car from wherever you start. As Matthew Arnold astutely put it in 1859, 'The plain of Alsace is to me one of the pleasantest anywhere, so genially productive, so well cultivated and so cheerful, yet with the Vosges and the Black Forest and the Alps to hinder its being prosaic.' Alsace is tiny by contrast with other French provinces, less than 8,500 square kilometres in all, but its charms are inexhaustible.

It comprises two French *départements*, created in 1790, Bas-Rhin and Haut-Rhin. Nearly every segment of the western part of Bas-Rhin verges on the Alpine Vosges mountains, part crystalline, part sandstone – especially where these rise from the Bruche valley. At the foot of these mountains the slopes that nurture most of Alsace's vines decline into the Rhine plain (as Hilaire Belloc expressed it, 'like sloping cliffs above a sea'). Here the climate is half warmly Spanish, half north-Atlantic, depending on whether you are in the plain or on the hills. Although this is one of the most prosperous regions of France, partly because of its industries, you would scarcely guess the fact. Factories for the most part are tucked away, and a good third of the *département* is clad with forests.

The Haut-Rhin is equally varied and picturesque. Consisting chiefly of a long plain between the Vosges and the Black Forest, it also boasts to the south the chalky soils of the Jura, as well as the southern region of the Sundgau, at once hilly and blessed with richly fertile plains. Orchards and vineyards blossom in the sun. Although the winters in the Sundgau are long and cold, its rains encourage polyculture, with cereals and hops and fruits and vegetables thriving in the hot (and frequently stormy) summers.

Nature has divided Alsace into three distinct parts and blessed each one of them. To the west rise the lower slopes of the Vosges.

Flanking them is the Rhine plain, some thirty to forty kilometres wide and washed from south to north by the waters of the River Ill. Thirdly, bordering the Rhine plain to the south and the west you can see the peaks of the Alsatian Jura and the upper Vosges mountains. These three regions produce that abundance of crops and livestock which has enabled the people of Alsace to create their own distinctive, unusual and succulent cuisine as well as their celebrated beers and wine.

To divide this region into three parts is, however, crudely to ignore the much richer variety of its terrain. The Alsace plain has over the centuries been enriched with silt and loam able to support an intensive mixed agriculture. By contrast, closer to the Rhine the low-lying, once unfruitful marsh land has been drained to create grazing for Alsace cattle. The forest of Haguenau in Bas-Rhin teems with game. The Kochersberg in the same *département* is an almost unknown territory which, since the sixteenth century, Alsatians have dubbed their granary, where farming families live in opulent houses and drink and chatter of an evening in the most sumptuous of *Weinstube*. The Vosges mountains are themselves far from homogeneous. Forests alternate with pastures. For up to eight months of the year these pastures are snow-covered and the cattle must stay in their byres. Then the snow melts and rich grazing appears.

The peaks of the Vosges are known as *ballons*, and the ballon d'Alsace at 1,250 metres above sea-level is the highest outside Lorraine. Its neighbour is the 1,178-metre-high ballon de Servance. This is winter sports country and above all hiking country. A day's hike along well-signposted tracks from the ballon d'Alsace to the ballon de Servance takes you through forests, by lakes, along open pasture and then plunges you once again into fir and elm trees. Half-way there you reach Wesserling, where in the sixteenth century the abbot of Murbach built a château (to be replaced in 1780 by the one that stands there now). On the way to Wesserling you skirt the Sternsee or 'lake of perch'.

The connection between monks and fishing is not fortuitous. Fish was enjoined by the church on religious and laity alike throughout Lent and on Fridays. Monks willingly obeyed the law of their religion, yet were unwilling to eat badly. They learned to cook subtly, with spices and wine. They passed their learning on. One of the earliest Alsatian cookbooks was written in the 1580s by Bernardin Buchinger, abbot of Lucelle. He called it *A Cookery Book for*

Religious Houses and also for the Laity. The perch and eel, carp and pike, bream and tench of the rivers and lakes of Alsace were then, as now, available for all. As the humanist Jerome Guebwiller wrote at the beginning of the sixteenth century, 'Strasbourg market abounds in both expensive and common fish, so that the rich may satisfy their greed and the poor their hunger.'

Since the River Rhine has recently been savagely polluted, I can only suppose that the abundant and superb perch, pike, tench and eel you are served here are these days fished from the Rivers Ill, Fecht, Lauter and the rest, as well as from the lakes. At any rate, the fish dishes of Alsace remain miraculously succulent and healthy. Whenever you find yourself by a riverside, ask for *la matelote*, Alsace's unique fish stew. If it is billed as *la matelote au Riesling*, your treat will be delightfully enhanced. Part of the cunning of the chefs of this region lies in their fine appreciation of the different lengths of time needed for cooking different varieties of fish, and the recipe for *la matelote au Riesling* illustrates this perfectly. In Alsace this is how they prepare it:

Ingredients for six people: trout, pike, perch and (the most important ingredient) eel, adding up in weight to 2kg (4lb 6oz); onions, carrots, parsley, thyme, a bay leaf and laurel; one-quarter of a litre (9fl oz) fresh cream; 100g (4oz) butter; six Paris mushrooms (*champignons de Paris*); four eggs; 50g (2oz) flour; three leeks; a cup of *court bouillon*, and half a litre (18fl oz) of Riesling.

Method: Slice the cleaned fish into 5-cm (2-in) pieces. Cut up the leeks, and place in a large pan with the onions (also sliced), the carrots, seasonings and wine. Add the eel and simmer for ten minutes on a low heat, after which you add the trout and pike, simmering for another five minutes. Now add the perch, simmering for a further ten minutes.

Meanwhile, prepare a sauce by melting the butter in another pan, removing from the heat and beating in the eggs and flour, followed by the cream and the *court bouillon*. Finally, add the mushrooms, cooking them delicately for one and a half minutes.

Now arrange the pieces of fish in a serving dish, and pour over them the sauce.

La matelote by no means exhausts the fish dishes of Alsace. I was once there for no more than a week and as an experiment decided to see if I could eat nothing other than fish dishes as a main course before returning to the *foie gras* of the Dordogne. Without abandoning my vow, I could have stayed in Alsace for at least a fortnight. Take the carp which swims in the rivers of the Sundgau region. They are hooked out of the river and then often set to swim in tanks in the restaurants, since the Alsatians of the Sundgau believe that carp should be killed at the very last moment before they are scaled, washed and cooked. They are served sliced junkily, often while the oil is heating. Meanwhile potatoes are boiling and a lemon is being sliced. The cooks then dip the carp into the beaten eggs that have been seasoned with salt and pepper. Next they coat them with flour. Finally and speedily the *carpe frite du Sundgau* is fried in the oil till it is brown, to be triumphantly served alongside the boiled potatoes with a slice of lemon.

The River Ill also nourishes a delicious pike (or *brochet*), which is cooked sliced, in a greased dish, on a base of chives and quartered shallots. Half a litre (18fl oz) of cream and one-quarter of a litre (9fl oz) of Riesling enrich the dish as the pike is poached. Throughout the cooking, water, butter and sometimes more wine are added to prevent any dryness in the finished dish. I have many times wonderingly watched Alsatians cook *le brochet de l'Ill à la crème* and then tucked into it with scant regard for the subsequent effect on my health and digestion. So far, I have never failed to sleep soundly after eating it.

In spite of the great variety of the Alsatian landscape, one unifying element is that scarcely 6 per cent of the territory is uncultivated, taken up by towns and villages, roads and rivers. Although vines deck almost all the lower reaches of the Vosges, protected from harsh winds by the heights to the west, the higher slopes of these mountains and of the Jura are covered in forests, with breaks for pasture whose grazing herds give the region its milk and cheese.

As you drive and drink a little, exploring ancient villages and martial châteaux, you also need to eat. The happy truth is that gastronomically Alsace is unique, possessing a taste all of its own, and blending recipes and ingredients from France, from nearby Germany, and brought to this region from as far away as Algeria and China. No one can in his own home far away from Alsace create the superb wines of this region; but I have collected and successfully tried out many Alsatian recipes, for the ingredients nowadays travel far and wide, appearing in many supermarkets in Britain as well as in France. And where a recipe demands an Alsatian wine, that too can usually be found nestling on the shelves.

Discerning palates have long appreciated the unique quality of the food of Alsace. In 1580 Michel de Montaigne, who came from the gastronomic heaven called Périgord, paid the cuisine of this region a generous compliment, as he passed through the land on his way to

Italy. The people, he said, 'care more about their dinners than they do their dwellings'. He noted that they cooked fish excellently, as well as enjoying a great abundance of meats. He found that they served food in a fashion quite different from the way he ate in Périgord. Alsatians would mix and serve together several well-prepared meats. They would eat as many as six or seven courses, two by two. And they took time over their food. 'The smallest meals,' Montaigne observed, 'take three or four hours because of all these courses; and in truth they eat far less hastily than we do, and more healthily.' Finally, he added, 'They never mix water with their wine, and they are probably right.'

I came across the unusual essence of Alsatian food on one of my early days in Alsace, sitting with my friend Frau Sybil Niemöller (widow of Adolf Hitler's most celebrated opponent, about whom I had just written a biography). Onions abound in the vegetable gardens of the region, and in the place Gutenberg at Strasbourg I and Frau Niemöller sat eating warm onion pie while drinking a glass of white Sylvaner and meditating on the delightful bizarreness of this region of France. Onion pie is an Alsatian speciality. It is delicious, and the Alsatians serve it either as a starter or as a main course. This is how I have learned to make it as a starter for eight people:

La tarte à l'oignon, also known in Alsace as *Ziwelkueche*

First bake your pie crust. For this you need: 150g (6oz) flour; 50g (2oz) butter, plus the same amount of shortening.

Method: Blend the flour, the shortening and the butter. Slowly add enough water (not too much) until the dough is malleable. Roll half of it out, and place it in the greased bowl in which you plan to bake your onion pie. Keep the rest of the dough for the covering.

For the *Ziwelkueche* itself you now require: 100g (4oz) sliced bacon; six large onions; a tablespoon of butter; a cup of rich cream; four eggs; salt, pepper and ground nutmeg.

Method: Crisply cook the bacon, then cut off its fat and crumble the rest. Slice the onions thinly, melt the butter in the pan and add to this the onions and the crumbled bacon. For no more than fifteen minutes cook the mixture until the onions are soft. Then season with salt and pepper, remove the pan from the heat and sprinkle on a tablespoon of flour. Blend in the cream and then add the eggs, one by one, mixing everything together. Now pour into the pie crust, adding (if you wish) the top crust, sprinkling on some nutmeg and baking for about forty minutes in an oven preheated to 400°F (200°C). When the top of the dish is browned, serve immediately.

You can often taste the sad fact that as a short cut, instead of blending in the cream and the eggs, many Alsatian chefs today make do with a béchamel sauce, which I think is a pity.

Alsatians adore onions, cooked delicately and inventively. An onion fondue here is called *Kachelmues*, often served with jacket potatoes.

Ingredients: 500g (1lb 2oz) onions (after they have been peeled); 50g (2oz) butter; two large tablespoons of fresh cream; two hard-boiled eggs; milk, salt and pepper.

Method: Slice the eggs, none too thinly. Chop the onions into cubes and then fry them in the butter. Salt and pepper, and then add one tablespoon of flour and a little milk to the mixture. Cooking slowly, mix in the cream. Add the sliced eggs and serve.

Is *Kachelmues* really a French dish? Ask a more basic question: is Alsace really French? Strasbourg is as good a place as any to try to answer these questions. The city itself became French only in 1689. Mulhouse, at the bottom end of Alsace, stayed German even longer – till 1793. Bismarck, as we have seen, decided to annex the province when the Prussians beat the French in 1871. The French took Alsace back in 1918. Hitler disapproved of this and marched in. Alsace rejoined France again after World War II.

So it should be no surprise to find this 120-kilometre-long region of the French countryside crammed with delightful villages with scarcely pronounceable Germanic names such as Wissembourg, Merkwiller-Pechelbronn, Guebwiller, Geispolsheim and Gueber-schwihr. Nor should anyone be surprised at eating onion pie here and drinking absolutely superb white wines, with German names like Riesling and Sylvaner, vying with equally superb beers.

One Germanic trait is that Alsatians cook in beer as well as in wine. *Biersupp* is an extremely cheering starter to a meal, made from a chopped onion, one and a half litres (53fl oz) of chicken stock, breadcrumbs, fresh cream, *croûtons* and a third of a litre (12fl oz) of light ale. And a change from *coq au Riesling* is *coq à la bière*. Beware when you order it: a moderate-sized chicken will be cooked in and served with sauce that has been made not only from a third of a litre of beer but also a glass of potent Alsatian liqueur.

Another Germanic influence can be instantly perceived in the traditional cafés of Alsace – not the typical French bistros but the *Weinstube* (or *Winstube*, as the Alsatians call them): carved mahogany seats, decorative barrels everywhere, heavy wooden chandeliers, sometimes an ancient tiled stove (what the Germans call a *Kachelofen*) and even a host's table where only his treasured guests may sit. But suddenly a French element intrudes. In the *Winstub* you can usually consume not just onion tart but pungently cooked snails.

Alsatians rate their *escargots* as finer than those of Burgundy (though they also import them from the USA). They prepare them with extreme care. If they catch the snails alive, they starve them for several days. Then they clean them for a couple of hours in salt, vinegar and a pinch of flour. Next the snails are blanched, that is plunged into boiling water for five minutes, then taken out of their shells and the black part is cut off. Finally the snails are put back into the shells and topped up with garlic butter. At this point an exceedingly useful utensil appears, one so far unobtainable in Britain but found in every French supermarket: the *escargotière*. Simply an ovenproof dish with holes for six, or preferably twelve, snails, it enables you to pop the shells into the holes and cook them without spilling any of the garlic butter. The snails in their *escargotière* are put into an oven preheated to 450°F (230°C) and, after ten minutes or so, when the garlic butter is foamy, served hot as *les escargots à l'alsacienne*.

To eat French snails in a Germanic *Winstub* is a rare experience. It takes time to accustom oneself to all the German aspects of the gastronomy of this unique part of France. This is, for example, also a land of dumplings. *Les spätzle à l'alsacienne* are made with 300g (11oz) flour, two cups of milk, three eggs, 50g (2oz) butter, some *croûtons* and salt and pepper. To make them whip the flour, eggs and milk in a bowl with a little salt and pepper to produce a very smooth dough, while setting salted water to boil. Then the dough is rolled out on a board and cut into strips with a knife that has been dipped in the boiling water. Next these strips are boiled in the salted water until they rise to the surface. Rinsed in cold water, drained and then sautéed in the butter, the finished *spätzle* are garnished with *croûtons* fried in the same butter. These dumplings make the perfect partner to Alsatian jugged hare.

If the Germanic *Winstube* are a revelation to the first-time visitor, what also astonishes is the often sensationally beautiful Alsatian countryside. On my second trip to Alsace I came into the country from the west, from Gérardmer in its sister province Lorraine, crossing the Vosges mountains and reaching Colmar along the so-called route des Crêtes – a route which runs spectacularly along the mountain ridge itself. Matched in beauty by the northern part of Alsace (the lower Rhine or Bas-Rhin) this is a region of splendid forests and enchanting, sometimes quite savage natural parks, criss-crossed with solitary nature trails and well-marked hiking routes.

This is game country, and although game is fairly rare on Alsatian menus, when it appears don't pass it by. As well as jugged hare with *spätzle*, try for example *le faisan à l'alsacienne*. What makes this dish specially Alsatian is its use of dried sausage, *Sauerkraut* and white Sylvaner wine.

Le faisan à l'alsacienne

Ingredients for four people: two pheasants; 450g (1lb) *Sauerkraut*; a large onion; 225g (8oz) bacon; one dried *saucisson*; a tablespoon of butter; plus salt, pepper and a few juniper berries.

Method: Slice the bacon into fairly wide strips. Finely chop the onion. Put both of them, with the *Sauerkraut*, the *saucisson* and the juniper berries in a pan. Salt and pepper, add a bay leaf and two glasses of Sylvaner. Cover the pan and cook over a low heat for half an hour.

In another pan, delicately brown both sides of the pheasants in butter. Then add them to the other mixture, and cook till the pheasants are tender. (Take care not to overcook: this should take scarcely thirty minutes.)

Since we are entertaining four people, cut each pheasant in half; place one half for each guest on a plate and surround it with *Sauerkraut*, serving immediately.

The southern Alsatian district known as the Sundgau, beyond Mulhouse and bordering on the Jura, is also game country, blessed with lakes and rural valleys as well as some lovely villages and towns. From its hill-top site, perched over the River Ill, Altkirch, for instance, the former capital of the Sundgau, commands fine panoramas, especially from the garden of its former château (which was destroyed in the eighteenth century). Ignore the industrialization that has beset part of Altkirch and follow the Grand'Rue to the main square, which has a fountain that seems to come from the fifteenth century but was built in 1850 to support a genuine sixteenth-century statue of the Virgin Mary. Here stands the eighteenth-century town hall, and next to it a fine fifteenth-century building now housing the museum of the Sundgau.

An even finer panorama of the Sundgau is offered by the town of Ferrette, which stands almost on the Swiss border and is rendered yet more picturesque by two ruined châteaux. The huge polygonal one with a vast keep dates from the twelfth century and was partly demolished by Swedish invaders in 1633. The second château at Ferrette was built in the sixteenth century and demolished by the

French Revolutionaries in 1789. From this second ruined château you can see not only the Jura, the Vosges and the great Rhine plain but also across the river as far as the Black Forest. You see the abundant Alsatian forests, the haunt of wild boars, deer, partridge, wild duck, rabbit and hare. Hunting is strictly limited in Alsace, but all of these in season appear on Alsatian menus. If you want to try wild boar, look out for the word *marcassin*, which technically ought to mean that the beast is a young one.

Jugged hare makes a more frequent appearance on Alsatian menus (eaten often, as we have seen, with *spätzle*). If this sounds a simple dish, try cooking it. Here in Alsace the French influence on the local gastronomy is apparent, especially in the careful use made in the kitchen of the animal's blood. For once, too, Pinot noir comes into its own, for jugged hare needs red wine. When the cook cuts up the hare, its intestines are thrown away, but care is taken to keep not only its liver but also its blood. Then the hare is marinaded for a whole day and night in red wine made yet more powerful with brandy or some other local liqueur, into which has been stirred a glass of oil or goose fat, some sliced onions and a few cloves of garlic, not to mention thyme, cloves, a bay leaf and salt and pepper.

The following day, strips of bacon are fried in oil, to which are added the pieces of hare which have been dried. Next the marinade is poured in, followed by a *bouquet garni*, and the whole is cooked over a gentle heat for about an hour and a half. Towards the end of this cooking time you fry the liver in a separate pan. Fry a few sliced onions, add them to the hare just before it is finally cooked. Lastly, a few minutes before the hare is ready to be served, thicken the sauce with its blood. Serve the jugged hare in a pre-warmed dish, pouring over it the sauce and decorating the dish with the fried liver.

If the forests of Alsace teem with game, the Rhine plain is also rich in corn, potatoes and beetroot, as well as alfalfa and clover. Oddly enough, sugar beet, flourishing in the 1830s, had almost disappeared from Alsace by the 1890s, until a new refinery was built in 1893 at Erstein near Obernai. Erstein is certainly worth a visit simply for its twisting old streets and half-timbered houses, though I found its nineteenth-century neo-Romanesque church simply too overwhelming. What would I think if ever I arrived at the end of August in time for its sugar festival?

In this region too are grown the hops that produce the Alsace beers, as well as the tobacco plants which will create the deadly Gauloises cigarettes. Tobacco has been grown here since the sixteenth century. When the Germans owned the region, they relished Alsatian cigars, though today French cigarettes consume most of these leaves. One major centre of the industry is Lauterbourg, a mere three kilometres from the Rhine and named after the River Lauter, where the Romans built a fort and where the walls constructed by Vauban after the revolution still partially encircle the town. No doubt many citizens, brought to a premature death by smoking, have journeyed to their last resting place by way of Lauterbourg's fine early eighteenth-century parish church, with its polygonal choir which dates from 1467. Happily, at the beginning of July the town annually celebrates not a feast of tobacco but the *fête* of roast chicken!

By contrast with the tobacco plants, beetroots and potatoes are used to make the healthiest of Alsatian salads. Beetroot salad the natives call either *Gullerilappelsalad* or *Rotrahnesalad*. The washed and peeled beetroot is cooked in salted water before being cut into thin slices and left for several days in a mixture of vinegar, salt, pepper, chopped onion and chopped garlic. When you serve it, add some onion rings and sprinkle on a morsel of oil. Marinaded beetroot complements the richest meats.

Potatoes spread throughout Alsace almost as soon as they were introduced into Europe. In the seventeenth century poor families high up in the Vosges mountains often lived on nothing else. In the regional tongue the potato is known as the *Hardaepfel*, and *Hardaepfelsalad* is a more subtle dish than beetroot salad. Again it is prepared with vinegar, and the baked potatoes, like the beetroot, are sliced thinly. But the vinegar mixture (one glass to a kilo (2lb 3oz) of potatoes) is enriched with a small carton of cream, some stock, salt and pepper and a little mustard, as well as the chopped onions used for beetroot salad. This is poured over the potatoes, and the whole is then sprinkled with chopped chives and parsley, to create a traditional accompaniment to Alsace *charcuterie*.

The potato is also an essential ingredient of an extraordinary Alsatian stew known as *le bäeckaoffa*. To serve half a dozen people with *le bäeckaoffa* you need:

Ingredients: 1 kilo (2lb 3oz) of potatoes; 500g (1lb 2oz) shoulder of lamb, boned; 500g (1lb 2oz) lean beef; 500g (1lb 2oz) *échine de porc* (i.e. pork cut from the region of the backbone) or, as second best, shoulder of pork; 250g (9oz) onions; three cloves of garlic, as well as thyme, salt and pepper; and half a litre (18fl oz) of Pinot blanc.

Method: Cut up the meat into cubes and let them marinate overnight in a *bouquet garni* enriched by the wine, onions, garlic, salt and pepper. Next day in a greased casserole lay alternate tranches of potatoes and onions, followed by the meats, followed by the potatoes and onions, and so on. Then the marinade is poured over the dish, which is cooked, covered, until the meats are tender, in an oven preheated to 350°F (180°C). Cooking *le bäeckaoffa* should take something in the region of an hour and a half.

In the Rhine plain, market gardens around Strasbourg and Colmar were long ago intensively developed, raising rich crops of high-quality vegetables: not only onions but also cabbage, tomatoes, spinach, lettuce and salads. Since the 1930s increasingly convenient transport systems have enabled the farmers to extend the production of these crops farther and farther away from the main market centres.

The town of Krautegersheim, some ten kilometres outside Strasbourg, had become the centre of the all-important cabbage plantations by the sixteenth century. It was then that the German word for cabbage, *Kraut*, was added to the original name of the village, Egersheim. Along with Krautegersheim, the lovely village of Blaesheim which lies some seven kilometres away at the foot of the Gloeckelsberg, and the fortified old town of Geispolsheim another four kilometres nearer Strasbourg today house some seventy producers who grow no less than 15 per cent of all the cabbage of Alsace – amounting to a massive 10,000 tonnes from these farmers alone.

Choucroute, or *Sauerkraut* (i.e. cabbage pickled in vinegar) is the Alsatians' winter dish. Their own dialect word for it is *Sürkrüt*, though it used to be the even more delightful *Gumbostkrüt*. Historians of the delicacy believe that the plant originated in China, created to sustain the builders of the Great Wall and brought to Europe by Tartar invaders. Alsatians may revere their religion more than they love their national winter dish, but perhaps only a little more. At any rate, if you are in Geispolsheim on the feast of Corpus Christi you will be rewarded with costumed processions and much gaiety. But so you will if you arrive there in September for the festival of *Sauerkraut*. I do not think that Blaesheim holds a similar festival, its own chief annual celebration being a folklore festival known as the *Messti* and held at the end of August. But at the end of September and the beginning of October the quintessential *choucroute* town of Krautegersheim goes wild with its annual cabbage festival.

La choucroute garni à l'alsacienne is an unmatchable way of repleting and also warming yourself on a cold winter's day. Oddly

enough, the posher restaurants tend to disdain it. In smaller ones it
may not be the cheapest dish, for cooking *Sauerkraut* properly
demands care. You can, of course, prepare it yourself, but in Alsace
today you can also buy *Sauerkraut* in tins. Take care if you do so to
wash the vegetable in running water and set it aside to drain, for
tinned *Sauerkraut* is overwhelmed with salt. To make *la choucroute
garnie à l'alsacienne* (serving six people or so) you will need:

Ingredients: 2 kilos (4lb 6oz) *Sauerkraut*; four German sausages (*Knock-
wurst* are a suitable variety); a large onion; 250g (9oz) white sausages; two
black puddings; one shoulder of smoked ham; two knuckles of ham; half a
litre (18fl oz) Riesling; three cloves of crushed garlic; one quarter of a litre
(9fl oz) beef stock; a tablespoon butter; 100g (4oz) bacon; salt and pepper;
four juniper berries.

Method: Cut the bacon, the black puddings, the ham and the sausages
into small cubes. Slice the onion. Melt the butter in an oven-proof casserole
and add the onions. Brown them, before adding the cubed meats, with the
casserole removed from the heat. Now add the beef stock, the *Sauerkraut*,
the garlic and some pepper. Simmer over a low heat for an hour (or until the
meats are tender), with the casserole covered.

La choucroute garnie à l'alsacienne is usually served with boiled
potatoes. Since, as Montaigne noted long ago, nothing is stinted in
Alsace restaurants, *Sauerkraut* will be piled on to a hot plate. Pork
loins, sliced quite crudely, as well as the smoked shoulder of pork,
grilled sausages, bacon and the pungent Strasbourg sausages are next
heaped on the platter, almost smothering the *Sauerkraut*. And before
you have looked around in the restaurant or picked up your knife
and fork, a hugely satisfying glass of beer has been plopped down
beside you. The variety of sausages, ham and other meats, served
strewn over the *Sauerkraut*, are in fact what gives the dish its
different piquancy throughout the region – whether smoked bacon,
smoked pork chops, Strasbourg sausages, sausages from Mont-
béliard, fried sausages (these being mostly *Brotwürste*, i.e. made out
of bread and pork), and more rarely duck. As for wine, sometimes it
is cooked not with a Riesling (as I prefer) but with a Sylvaner.
Whichever wine you have used in the cooking, drink a glass or two of
the same with the dish. Often the menu in a restaurant serving
choucroute announces that you are eating *choucroute au Riesling*. If
it offers *choucroute royale*, then make sure you start with an empty
stomach, for *choucroute royale* is *Sauerkraut* served with what seems
like every conceivable meat and sausage.

Alsatians call smoked shoulder of pork *Schiffala*, and this too they often cook in the piquant pickled cabbage that is *Sauerkraut*. Since my French home is in the Dordogne and not Alsace, I find myself at once bemused and delighted by the remarkable similarities in the methods of cooking in these two gastronomic havens, in spite of the quite different tastes that finally emerge from their ovens. Chefs and housewives in both the Dordogne and Alsace prefer to cook, where possible, with goose fat rather than butter. A sister to *choucroute* is red cabbage and (once again) this will almost certainly have been cooked in goose fat, and is served with apples and chestnuts. If the chefs cannot find goose fat, they turn next to lard or oil. As for the differences, in Alsace the way restaurateurs serve their dishes can be powerfully overwhelming at first, though the sharp quiddities of Alsace food soon allow one to tuck in resolutely, richly and regardless.

After *Sauerkraut*, asparagus became a second national dish of Alsace only in the nineteenth century, introduced into the town of Hoerdt (in the *département* of Bas-Rhin) some twenty kilometres from Strasbourg by its Protestant pastor. This good man, named Heyler, had been a missionary in Philippeville in Algeria, where asparagus was a staple diet. Arriving at Hoerdt in 1873, he was deeply distressed by the poverty he found there, peasant farmers scarcely supporting themselves and their families on the produce they scratched from apparently inhospitable soil. Pastor Heyler perceived that they were forcing on to their land the wrong sort of crop. Diligently and lovingly he experimented, planting Algerian asparagus instead. You must go inside the church here where once he preached and seek quite hard to find the small monument to this great benefactor of his fellow-men and women.

In the *département* of Haut-Rhin, Horbourg-Wihr only three kilometres from Colmar is the centre of asparagus cultivation. Horbourg-Wihr dates back to Roman times, and excavations of the suburb that was once simply known as Horbourg have revealed Roman walls, as well as a Roman potter's factory. Horbourg became the seat of a count in the early twelfth century and was bought in 1324 by the counts of Wurttemberg, who held it until the revolution. Their castle today lies in ruins. The town, like Hoerdt, now prospers on asparagus.

Nothing could be simpler than to make an asparagus salad from *asperges d'Alsace*. You take two and a half kilos (5½lb) of asparagus, wash and peel them, tie them into bundles weighing about 500g (1lb 2oz) and cook them in salted boiling water. Make sure they remain firm, so the cooking time should not normally exceed twenty or twenty-five minutes. Then you drain them (usually on a cloth). What gives asparagus its particularly Alsatian tang is its sauces and its accompanying meats. Almost always you are given a choice of three sauces – vinaigrette, mousseline and mayonnaise – to dip your asparagus in, as well as either a white sauce or a *sauce hollandaise* to garnish smoked or boiled ham which the asparagus perfectly complements.

Driving through villages unchanged since the Middle Ages, with half-timbered houses direct from toytown and guest houses far more solid than any you expect in France (with beers correspondingly stronger), I used to stop and sit in the *Winstube* wondering whether the strong ale had gone to my head. Then I realized that the reason I didn't understand a word of the surrounding chatter was not drunkenness but the fact that the Alsatians have their own distinctive living dialect – neither French nor German – and a dialect spoken at home by 60 per cent of the population. Sometimes I think everybody speaks it in the *Winstube*.

Hilaire Belloc discovered the same phenomenon as he passed through Alsace on his path to Rome. One evening he arrived at an inn, the door opened at his touch, and there he saw a pleasant middle-aged woman frowning. 'She had three daughters, all of great strength, and she was upbraiding them loudly in the German of Alsace and making them scour and scrub.' Belloc tactfully turned his gaze to a great placard fixed to the wall, waiting till she had restored discipline in her family. The placard included an emblematic figure of a cock, and underneath the bird he read:

> *Quand ce coq chantera*
> *Ici crédit l'on fera*

which means:

> When you hear him crowing
> Then's the time for owing.
> Till that day –
> Pay.

The good woman then cooked him a ham omelette and gave him some brown bread and excellent beer, all the time speaking in what was 'the corpse of French with a German ghost in it'. Belloc paid up, and as he retired to bed all four women rose together and curtsied.

I too have found the same courtesy in Alsace. In the Kochersberg, in an inexpensive guest house with an ancient flowery courtyard, the housewife and landlady, learning that I was a writer, brought out old books, including some of those charming turn-of-the-century illustrated children's books by the Alsatian patriot who called himself Uncle Hansi. Preferring more than a ham omelette, I was delighted to learn that the menu was duck with red cabbage.

To prepare it must have taken most of the afternoon as I sipped wine, read, watched and wrote up some notes. She used (more or less) 100g (4oz) streaky bacon, 75g (3oz) thinly sliced carrots, a small sliced onion, two tablespoons of goose fat and 900g (2lb) of red cabbage leaves cut into small slices. First she removed the rind from the bacon and cut the rest up into thin strips, around 1cm (¼in) wide and 4cm (1½in) long. These were simmered in water for a quarter of an hour and then drained, before being added to the carrots and onions and cooked in fat in the covered casserole for another ten minutes. Nothing was allowed to brown, and my host stirred in the red cabbage leaves, making sure they too were well covered by the fat. The casserole was covered again and the dish slowly cooked for another ten minutes.

Meanwhile new ingredients appeared: 225g (8oz) sour apples cut into small pieces; a couple of cloves of crushed garlic; about 425ml (15fl oz) red wine; salt and pepper; and 550ml (2fl oz) stock. All these were stirred into the dish. The covered casserole was placed in a moderate oven and cooked for three and a half hours.

Only now did a 2 kilo (4½lb) duckling make its entrance. She seasoned it, pricked it all over and dried it. Next she browned it in hot fat, before placing it in the middle of the casserole, embedded in the cabbage, and cooking it for another hour and a half. Then she took the duck from the casserole and placed it on a hot serving dish. Next the red cabbage was taken out, drained and arranged around the duck. The juices in the casserole were speedily reduced over a high heat till they were quite thick. A little of this sauce was poured over the duck and the rest put into a gravy boat. Then it was time to eat.

The next evening I ate there half a goose and drank with it a wine powerful enough to match the splendid sauce: the rich white Pinot gris. I imagine both birds had been raised and killed by my host. Half a goose in Alsace is cooked in a fashion unique to the region. Sausage meat is mixed with thyme and parsley and then stuffed into the goose. The bird is roasted at 400°F (200°C) for a quarter of an hour, after which the oven temperature is reduced to 350°F (180°C) to allow it to cook more slowly. Using some of the goose fat, a finely chopped onion is cooked, with diced and mixed ham and bacon. *Sauerkraut* is added and then gently cooked for about an hour, when some Strasbourg sausages are also added. This mixture forms the base of the dish on which you serve the goose.

Such unusual mixtures, duck and red cabbage, goose and *Sauerkraut*, seem perfectly natural in the cuisine of Alsace. *Le délice du sandre* is another Alsatian fish delicacy, with its own special accompaniment. Usually cooked in Riesling, *sandre* means pike, though purists (I suppose) properly translate it 'pike-perch'. Mostly, I have found, it is cooked exactly as is *le brochet*, which I have already described, save for the fact that it is usually cooked whole rather than sliced. But then, so (often) is pike. What seem always constant are the noodles served with *le délice du sandre*.

Nouilles à l'alsacienne are made from dough created out of eggs, extra egg yolks and plain flour that has been kneaded twice, left for an hour or so, and cut into strips. Needless to say, they are filling. Incidentally, they came to Alsace from Italy, to complement a dish partly French, partly German.

Before I leave the subject of fish for a moment or two, I should warn that if you ask for *la truite au bleu* in Alsace, you will be served much the same dish as can be relished elsewhere both in France and Germany. I do not disparage it. My sole comment is that this dish is not peculiar to the region. It is perhaps absurd of me to recommend above the Alsatian *truite au bleu* other fish recipes, for I nearly always order it myself on first arriving in the region, as if to remind myself that here we are half-German, half-French, with a taste nevertheless unique. For delicately tuned consciences I should also add that there is a touch of brutality in preparing *la truite au bleu*: as the Alsatians remark, if you are to retain the unique bleu of *la truite*, keep your trout alive and swimming to the very final instant before cooking. Hit it firmly on the head and it dies swiftly. The fishermen of yesteryear (and many of their sons and daughters today) would instantly wrap a newly killed trout in the leaves of a stinging nettle, to keep it as fresh as possible on the way home.

There his wife would be preparing a *court bouillon*. In Alsace wine adds its own quintessence to the basic ingredient of countless dishes. My guess is that usually in restaurants it is created with the cheapest of Zwicker. Why not try making a powerful *court bouillon* with Gewürztraminer or at least a strong Riesling. In doing so I have aimed at and (I maintain) succeeded in producing *court bouillon* quite distinct from that used elsewhere in France. You need to place in a pan only a sliced carrot, a sliced onion, scarcely a tablespoon of vinegar and a cup of your chosen white wine. Simmer the pan for twenty minutes and then remove your vegetables. Left in the pan is a *court bouillon* unique to this region. Beware when using it for *la truite au bleu*: too much vinegar, an anodyne addition in other gastronomic regions, can here mar the delicacy of an Alsatian blue trout.

Now for the Alsatian recipe:

La truite au bleu

For each person clean one freshly killed trout, each weighing around 200g (7oz). While cleaning, hold them delicately by their fins, so as not to damage the skin and thus risk that your *truite au bleu* won't turn blue as you cook it.

Plunge them in the *court bouillon* and simmer for just over five minutes until they turn a sweet blue. Now drain the fish, before arranging them on plates, garnished with parsley and quarters of lemon. Boiled potatoes, served in butter, usually accompany this sophisticatedly simple dish. Subtle hosts and hostesses serve alongside it the same wine that has helped to create the *court bouillon*.

The Rhine reminds you that Alsace is border country, and border country requires massive defensive châteaux. That is why the little town of Ribeauvillé (where you are served free wine from the Renaissance fountain on the last Sunday in August) boasts no fewer than three. To eat a meal amongst such noble ruins is a joy (though one to my mind paralleled by the pleasures of eating in the far less well-known magical villages and towns of Alsace). Amongst the most powerful (and certainly the best restored) châteaux in Alsace is that at Haut-Koenigsbourg, dominating its valley from a height of nearly 800 metres. The restoration was done at the expense of Kaiser Wilhelm II, of World War I notoriety. Just before Germany was finally defeated in 1918, Kaiser Bill paid his last visit to Haut-Koenigsbourg. Over the mantelpiece of the main hall he dejectedly inscribed his own epitaph on four useless years of slaughter: 'I never wanted this.' You can eat traditional Alsace food in the fairly expensive but excellent hotel Clos de Vincent and look across the River Rhine as far as Kaiser Bill's own Black Forest.

Another mark of the turbulent past is that many of these villages, sitting peacefully today on the wine route, retain their ancient fortifications: Bergheim with its ramparts; Boersch, with its three defensive gates; medieval walls surrounding the ancient houses of

Dambach; Éguisheim with its guardian château, save that today it is in ruins. All offer their own gastronomic specialities. Dambach serves fish from its lake and hosts a wine fair in August, and at No. 3, place du Château, Éguisheim, is a restaurant in a former wine cellar where you can eat frogs' legs in Riesling.

Turckheim is another walled town of special renown. Here in 1675 the French General Turenne defeated a German army three times the size of his own. Today the villagers of Bergheim, Turckheim and the rest seem to have forgotten their often savage past and devote themselves to filling their villages with flowers and selling colourful (and also useful) pottery, made after ancient methods though usually in modern kilns. Here I have also eaten the humble turnip rendered royal by being cooked in white wine. And Turckheim, like much of Alsace, has forsaken warfare and re-dedicated itself to cherishing birdlife, especially storks. Did you notice at Kintzheim, just south-west of Sélestat, that the medieval château is now an aviary packed with birds of prey rather than men of war? At Turckheim, just in case the uncaged birds fail one year to return, the fortified fourteenth-century gateway has been topped by one of the delightful model storks' nests, worked mechanically and found perched on the rooftops in many another Alsace village.

At Turckheim I followed my vinous turnip with a *tarte flambée*. Nearly every other Alsatian delight pales in flavour beside the rich fruit tarts, almost all of them made from short-crust pastry to whose normal recipe has been added 15g (½ oz) castor sugar for every 100g (4oz) flour, and with luck also an egg. The abundant fruit of the region is rarely exported, some say because it is not in truth of the highest quality, or (as a chef told me in Strasbourg) because the Alsatians need it all for themselves and their tarts. Affectionately they dub them *tartes flambées*, or blazing tarts, and you see them advertised for sale everywhere. Outside cake shops often a long trestle is utterly laden with diverse, tempting *tartes flambées* of raspberry, apple, rhubarb, plum, strawberry. Their savoury cousin is the *Flammeküche*, a bread base covered with a layer of sliced onion, cream and bacon, cooked over a wood fire the way Italians cook a pizza.

Another version of *tarte flambée* is filled not with fruit but with cheese mixed with or covered by cream. To make cheesecake you need:

Ingredients: 300g (11oz) cream cheese; 125g (5oz) *pâté brisé* (the French equivalent of our short-crust pastry); two large eggs, separated; 100g (4oz) sugar; four tablespoons milk; 50g (2oz) flour; the grated rind of a lemon; and 125ml (5fl oz) double cream.

Method: Line a 22-cm (8½-in) flan ring with the *pâté brisé*. Sieve the cream cheese and beat in the egg yolks, sugar, milk, flour and lemon rind. Mix well together. Beat the egg whites until they form peaks and fold them into the cheese mixture. Pour into the flan ring. Bake in a moderate oven for one hour. Allow the cheesecake to cool. Whip the cream and spread it over the top of the cake.

Alsatians have taken to Gruyère and serve it in countless *Winstube* mixed with their salads. But their favourite and most renowned cheese is Munster, made in the Munster and Saint-Amarin valleys. Munster, no more than twelve kilometres from Turckheim, may not be one of the most entrancing of Alsatian towns, for its industries and the damage it suffered in World War I have detracted from the beauty of a spot where in 643 the Scottish Benedictine monk St Oswald founded a monastery (hence the town's name). Yet its situation at the heart of the Vosges mountains and at the confluence of the northern and southern Fecht rivers makes it a perfect centre for walking and exploring the hills and valleys, the Moenchberg forest and the chateau de Schwarzenbourg. This last was built in 1261 on behalf of the bishops of Basel, 520 metres above sea-level. Climb another fifty metres to reach the platform known as Napoleon's terrace, for a majestic view of the whole Munster valley.

The monks gave us Munster cheese, reputedly beginning to make it as early as the seventh century. Today 4,000 tonnes of Munster cheese are produced annually, 100 tonnes from small farms, the rest in factories. The cheese is legally guaranteed to come from this region, an equivalent status to that of *appellation contrôlée* wines. To my palate, farm Munster and factory Munster are indistinguishable. Usually it is eaten uncooked, sometimes garnished with cumin and served with jacket potatoes.

The tourist office at Munster will direct you along the *route du fromage*, a delightful cheese-discovering trek by way of farms, forests, fields and pastures. If you buy a chunk of Munster cheese, do not leave it in the boot of your car and then forget about it, as I once did. Three days later I opened the boot, to be attacked by a smell so pungent that I supposed a rat must have been trapped inside, died and rotted.

This region of Alsace offers holiday rooms of a kind unique in France. Local farming families take in paying guests in their *fermes-auberges* in the Vosges range, providing comfortable, simple rooms and mind-boggling traditional menus: potato soups, ham tarts, massive pork chops, fruit *tartes flambées* and Munster cheese. (For more information on these *fermes-auberges*, see the 'Information about Alsace' at the end of this book.) With luck you will also be offered *la tourte de la vallée de Munster*, a magical pie created from utterly simple ingredients: lean pork, garlic, bread, onions and eggs.

Once you have savoured Munster cheese, please do not neglect the other gastronomic curiosities of this region, such as white cheese mingled with myrtles, such as myrtle tart and the Munster roast potato (or *Roïgabraggelti*). Nearly every hotel in the Munster valley will offer you cream cheese enlivened with cream and Kirsch. As evening draws on, in the homes outside your hotel families will be eating damson jam with local cream cheese that has been flavoured with garlic.

We owe to the Church not only Munster itself and Munster cheese but also the traditional Alsace snail dishes, for the medieval monks in this region, judging that snails were not meat and therefore could be eaten with a good conscience throughout Lent, set about breeding them in earnest. So too must we thank the Christian year not just for Alsatian Christmas fruit loaves but also for Shrovetide doughnuts or *Fasenachtsküchle*. This is a time of bonfires and traditional processions, with children going from house to house in the village to collect their *Fasenachtsküchle*, a rich cake made richer still by a drop or two of Kirsch to pave the way for Lent.

At Christmas, as well as *petits fours* made either with butter alone or with the addition of almonds, the people of Alsace enjoy a traditional Christmas cake which I once ate in Strasbourg in a hotel where other guests kindly showered me with drinks. Crammed with fruit, rich with rum, it put me in a festive mood, and also reminded me and everyone else of the real reason for our rejoicing: for the Alsatian *Chrischstolle* is fashioned in the shape of the swaddling clothes that the New Testament tells us the infant Jesus was wrapped in at his birth.

Strasbourg's masterpiece is its massive red sandstone cathedral. The spire soars 142 metres above the city. (Inside there are 328 steps for the fit to climb.) The west end boasts a fantastic rose window and an equally superb galaxy of figures carved in biblical scenes and stories. This cathedral is in fact a stern Romanesque building, basically dating from the twelfth century and then wrapped around with a complex and beautiful Gothic skin.

Inside, the stained-glass windows are outrageously beautiful, some of them dating back to the thirteenth century. At noon Death strikes the hour on its astronomical clock, the cock crows once again to remind St Peter that he has betrayed his master, while the figure of Jesus forgives and blesses his apostles.

Despite its size, Strasbourg cathedral never seems to dominate the city, for you approach the great building along ancient, narrow, pedestrianized shopping streets, creating a cosy, unfussed intimacy. The city also boasts a quarter known as 'La Petite France', criss-crossed with canals and filled with gabled houses dating from the sixteenth century, many of them today transformed into excellent inexpensive restaurants. Here look out above all for *foie gras*.

Strasbourg is famed for its *foie gras*. *Foie gras* is native to the part of France where I live; that is to say, there geese are force-fed until their livers swell alarmingly for the bird and succulently for the gourmet. In Alsace, by contrast, *foie gras* is scarcely ever obtained from local geese, of which there are few, but usually imported, mostly from Hungary. *Foie gras maison* here means not that the chef has force-fed his own geese but that he has prepared it in his own fashion; it is none the less usually exquisite.

More than any other dish *foie gras* displays the French influence on the cuisine of Alsace. Initially the French had benefited from Alsatian skills, after taking over the region in the mid-seventeenth century. King Louis XIV ate so much that afterwards he frequently suffered pains in his stomach. His valet was delighted that these cramps could be relieved by judicious doses of the *eaux-de-vie* of Alsace.

Soon the upper classes in Alsace were importing French chefs, and the French officials who ran the province also brought their own cooks, adding their refinements to the regional cooking. One of them invented a culinary masterpiece. In 1780 Jean-Pierre Clause, *chef-de-cuisine* to the governor of Alsace, Marshal de Contades, made for his master a pie crust in the shape of a round box. He filled it with *foie gras*, topping the liver with a mixture of veal and chopped bacon, and baking it in the oven. He named it after the governor: *pâté de Contades*. Marshal Contades sent some to Versailles, where Louis XVI professed himself delighted with the dish. *Foie gras de Strasbourg* had been born.

To reach perfection the dish needed one further element – an ingredient from the land of Montaigne. During the revolution a chef named Nicolas François Doyen travelled from Bordeaux to Alsace and suggested adding to the pâté a Dordogne truffle. *Pâté de*

Contades became *pâté de foie gras de Strasbourg aux truffes du Périgord*. It is expensive and exquisite.

Its normal appearance in an Alsatian restaurant is in a kind of loaf (a *brioche*), whose pastry has been made from flour, butter and yeast. Today the *foie gras* itself, before being laid inside the pastry, will have been marinated overnight in sparkling wine, plus salt and pepper. After the dough surrounding it has been allowed to rise for another hour or so, that whole is baked in the oven for forty minutes. The *brioche de foie gras* is always served cold, sometimes laced with game stock.

This Strasbourg speciality, sometimes served there sliced, redolent not always of local wines but of Madeira, is worth anyone's money. Alsace restaurants serve a goose-liver pâté by no means insipid and second only to that of the Dordogne – there is nothing mealy-mouthed about this dish. *Quiche Lorraine* too, made here often with bacon as well as the usual eggs, cream and cheese, is in Alsace nothing like the feeble dish usually masquerading under that name in Britain. The pungently smoked ham transforms it. Ham, incidentally, is often incorporated by the Alsatians into that delicious crispy pancake, which they call *Flammeküche*.

Liver of course need not be *gras*, and a far less expensive dish is *Lewerknepfle* or liver dumplings, made from pig's liver or the liver of a cow. 200g (7oz) liver is minced with 100g (4oz) smoked bacon, 75g (3oz) breadcrumbs and 75g (3oz) onions that have been fried with garlic. Two beaten eggs and 50g (2oz) semolina are mixed with these ingredients, and then the dumplings are moulded with a couple of spoons which you repeatedly dip into hot water to prevent the mixture from sticking. Finally you simmer the dumplings for ten minutes in salted water.

Expensive too is the truffle, and I often wonder whether such a magical tuber should be wasted, so to speak, on pigs' trotters, which I personally dislike. Alsatians clearly disagree, as they tuck into a mountain of *Sauerkraut* alongside a huge boned trotter that has been stuffed with a mixture of minced veal and pork, breadcrumbs, beef marrow and truffle peel, and then baked in the oven.

Elsewhere in France you are rarely so overwhelmed with colossal amounts of food. For my part, the main course alone is frequently enough in an Alsatian *Winstub*. At this point I begin to realize that I am becoming too much of a tourist and not enough of an explorer of Alsace, for one course does not serve as a normal meal for the locals. Whence, after all, does the cuisine of the typical Alsatian restaurant derive but from the kitchens and stoves of innumerable homely, long or soon-to-be-forgotten families? The average family in Alsace spends much more time eating at home than in restaurants (however cheap these may be), and enjoys three meals a day: breakfast, often consisting of *Kougelhopf* and coffee; lunch, which probably consists of *Sauerkraut*, followed by a piece of cheese or a soufflé; and dinner, beginning perhaps with soup, followed maybe by *Schiffala* (smoked shoulder of pork), and topped off by a rich Alsatian cheesecake. The breakfast *Kougelhopf* could keep me going for a whole day.

Alsatian *Kougelhopf* is made in a specially moulded dish that produces a twisting jelly-like effect for what is a cake enriched with almonds, raisins, sugar and eggs and sprinkled with icing sugar. It is but the best known of a series of such rich cakes: Streusel cake, whose flavour comes from cinnamon; the admirable fruit loaf known both as *Hutlzelbrod* and *Bierewecke*, a Christmas cake that embodies remarkable amounts of candied lemon and orange peel, dried prunes, pears, figs, dates and raisins, not to mention hazelnuts, walnuts, almonds, aniseed, Kirsh and cinnamon; and *Schnecke-küche*, created out of Kirsh, almonds, raisins and cinnamon, as well as the pastry that holds them all together.

Cinnamon is the essential ingredient of a good number of Alsatian cakes, such as *Schenkele*, which in French are indelicately known as little ladies' thighs (*les petites cuisses de dames*, a tantalizing phrase to read on a menu) and cinnamon cakes or *Zimtschnoitte*, a fried pudding served with apple sauce and concocted by thrifty peasant housewives to use up stale bread.

My plan when I first followed the wine route south was to reach Colmar. The novelist Georges Duhamel called it 'the most beautiful city in the world'. It certainly must be among the most picturesque. Whereas Strasbourg has its 'Petite France', Colmar boasts its 'little Venice', watered by the River Lauch. In the rue Mercière in the sixteenth century Martin Schongauer the painter built himself a splendid gabled house, and in the same street the hatmaker Master Pfister built an even better one, with a tower, arcades and balconies. Nearby in the rue des Têtes is the even more remarkable maison des Têtes, its Renaissance façade covered with the carved heads that give both house and street its name.

Unlike any other Alsatian town, Colmar sits both at the foot of a hill and also on a river plain, where the River Fecht meets the Lauch. Multi-coloured tiles decorate the roofs, especially the one-time customs house, which dates from 1480. And in the Unterlinden

Museum you can see one of the most famous painted crucifixions of all time, that of Mathias Grünewald's Issenheim altarpiece.

But on my first arrival it was growing late in the evening and I had come to Colmar planning food before culture. The gastronomy of Colmar is esteemed, especially its *Süri Rüewe*, a mixture of smoked ham, onions and white turnips. You eat well there, as everywhere else in Alsace. So I think I shall never really get over arriving that day in September and finding myself taking part in the annual festival of *Sauerkraut*.

The kiss of France and the lure of Germany

On 14 August 1914 the French military commander Marshal Joffre drove the Germans out of Thann and there addressed the citizens of Alsace. Since 1871 they had lived under the rule of the Kaiser, their country ceded to Germany with Lorraine after the Franco-Prussian War. 'Your return to France is permanent,' Joffre now told them. 'You are citizens of France for ever. With those liberties that she has always stood for, France brings you respect for your own liberties, your Alsatian freedoms, your own traditions and your own ways.' Then Joffre added emotionally and grandiloquently, 'I am France. You are Alsace. I bring you the kiss of France.'

Marshal Joffre proved not quite correct in declaring that Alsatians would thenceforth remain for ever French. With the defeat of the Kaiser in World War I, Alsace was taken back from Germany by France, but this rich land was to be incorporated into Germany once again in 1940, before reverting to France after the collapse of the Hitler Reich.

Marshal Joffre was not even correct in supposing that Germany had been virtually defeated in Alsace in 1914. General Bonneau and his French forces had crossed the border into Alsace on 7 August, arriving at Mulhouse the next evening. Three days later the Germans had counter-attacked and the French ignominiously retired. Now Joffre was charged with retrieving the situation. Taking Thann, he did inflict a powerful blow on the Germans, following the valley of the Bruche as far as Urmatt and then the Munster valley as far as Wintzenheim. Colmar and then Mulhouse were retaken. Almost as speedily Mulhouse was once more abandoned, and under attack the French retreated a second time. Only Thann remained in French hands.

Yet most of Alsace enthusiastically welcomed Joffre's words. Created a German *Land* of Kaiser Wilhelm I's empire in 1871, the greater part of its people clearly preferred the French republic newly set up after the defeat of Napoleon III by Bismarck's Prussia.

They also had many sore wounds to lick, for the Franco-Prussian War had been initially savagely contested in this region. Alsace had suffered severely in 1870 and 1871. On 4 August 1870 the German Third Army had entered the province by way of Wissembourg, entirely driving French supporting troops out of lower Alsace within three days. French military strategy was virtually in ruins, and the Germans took brilliantly vicious advantage of this. Fortified towns and great cities such as Strasbourg were attacked, fiercely defended, and taken. Sélestat held out for a fortnight and surrendered only when its exquisite houses were burning to the ground. The German General Werder made military history by his bombardment of Strasbourg, a hitherto unparalleled military exercise in destruction which slaughtered 300 citizens, severely damaged the cathedral and destroyed 300,000 ancient and priceless volumes in the city library. Soon the Alsatians dubbed the general not Werder but *Mörder* – 'murderer'.

As soon as the Prussians had conquered enough of Alsace to assume control of the region, they displayed their future intention of taking over entirely, by issuing Berlin postage stamps, by staffing the railways with German officials, by garrisoning the major towns and by requisitioning goods and food that would be paid for at the end of the war by the vanquished. Herr von Bismarck-Bohlen was set up in Haguenau as governor-general. 'From today,' he decreed on 8 October, 'Strasbourg shall be and remain a German city.'

In 1871 the preliminaries to the peace treaty, discussed at Versailles, demanded the complete annexation of Alsace. The French statesman Thiers had no choice but to concede Otto von Bismarck's ultimatum, and the French government assembled at Bordeaux went along with his capitulation. In 1871 the Treaty of Frankfurt incorporated all of Alsace and half of Lorraine into Germany. The delegation from Alsace to the French government in Bordeaux protested in vain at the forcible transfer of their country to the

Kaiser's empire. In the words of Émile Keller, a leading delegate from Haut-Rhin, speaking, he said, 'as an Alsatian and as a Frenchman', the treaty was 'an injustice, a lie and a disgrace'. In England Mr Gladstone was incensed. He insisted 'that the transfer of territory and inhabitants by mere force calls for the reprobation of Europe, and that Europe is entitled to utter it, and can utter it with good effect'. Europe said nothing. Yet Gladstone's views were prescient. Alsace was to become a bone of contention between Germany and France for many years to come. Gladstone told his Foreign Secretary, 'I have an apprehension that this violent laceration and transfer is to lead us from bad to worse, and to be the *beginning* of a new series of European complications.' The annexation still took place.

Alsatians great and small were also incensed. Charles-Émile Freppel, a native of Obernai, had risen to become bishop of Angers and a French deputy. He wrote personally to remonstrate with the Kaiser over the annexation. He died in 1891, and his statue by Léon Maurice stands outside Angers cathedral, inscribed with his vow that his heart should never return for burial in his native land until Alsace was returned to France. Today his heart rests in its true home, a niche in Obernai parish church. One of Obernai's ramparts was gratefully renamed the rempart Monseigneur-Freppel, his birthplace (No. 44, rue du Général-Gourard) is a local show-piece, and a copy of Léon Maurice's statue of the bishop graces the place de l'Église.

For three years the German emperor and his federal council exercised supreme control over Alsace. The people were asked to decide by the end of September 1872 whether they individually wished to become German or remain French. No fewer than 45,000 in the two annexed provinces voted to remain French, packed their bags and left their native land. When Alsace was allowed to elect its own delegates to the imperial German parliament, these delegates, from the moment of their first election in 1874, continually protested against the rule of Bismarck and the Kaiser over their land.

Bismarck had hoped that these newly acquired citizens would soon be reconciled to membership of the German empire. He attempted in vain to molify public opinion by setting up a local committee with some legislative autonomy. This policy failed. Ernst Lauth, mayor of Strasbourg, followed by the entire municipal council, revolted against German *Diktat*, and were replaced by a German commandant (a former chief of police named Beck). Elsewhere the pattern repeated itself, and in 1879 Bismarck appointed as regional governor-general Edwin von Manteuffel, with power even to declare martial law. Happily, General von Manteuffel's nature was to conciliate and listen to his subjects. Not so the cold, distant and unsympathetic Prince Hohenlohe-Schillingfürst, who succeeded him as governor-general in 1885. Thus Alsace was ruled until 1902 .

Bismarck could also make propaganda mistakes, the worst in the case of Alsace-Lorraine occurring in November 1874 when he described the newly annexed land as Germany's 'buffer' against attack across the Rhine. The word he actually used was the military term 'glacis', which signifies a long, covered fortification sloping along the natural surface of the land, with every part of that land capable of being raked by defensive fire. 'Our warriors did not shed their blood for the sake of Alsace-Lorraine but for the German empire, for its unity, for the protection of its frontiers,' he unwisely declared. 'We took these lands so that in the next war the French should be unable to start invading us at Wissembourg because we should possess a glacis where we could defend ourselves long before they reach the River Rhine.' Naturally enough, the Alsatians, having suffered as a glacis for centuries, resented Bismarck's explicit reduction of their beautiful land to a mere military convenience.

But Bismarck was no fool. For a time his own policies in Germany included a savage attack on the papacy and its supporters. In Alsace he proceeded far more gingerly, well aware that the majority of its population was staunchly Catholic. France and the Pope had concluded a concordat in 1801 which the Iron Chancellor rigorously respected – a policy wisely followed by his successors.

By contrast, the French government itself for a time became increasingly anti-clerical, to the disgust of many Alsatians. Such trends in France itself tempered Alsace's resentment at German rule. The aftermath of the abominable Dreyfus case demonstrated the dominance of the French anti-clerical politicians. A new Pope now took them on. Elected in 1903, Pope Pius X, son of an Italian shoemaker and postman, declared, 'I was born poor, I have lived poor, and I want to die poor.' Two years later the French government proposed the separation of Church and State, setting up 'cultural associations' to administer Church property. Pius X's dedication to holy poverty was put to the test, and he boldly chose financial ruin for the French Catholic Church in order to secure its spiritual independence from the State.

The dominant Alsatian Catholics perceived such trends in French political life with abhorrence. By the turn of the century many of them were campaigning for a free Alsace-Lorraine that should still be part of the German empire. Alsace was prospering anew. German social security was keenly appreciated, and Alsatians and Germans were beginning to mix more easily, with over 200,000 of the former emigrating to Germany in the first quarter of the new century and a similar number of Germans crossing the Rhine to replace them.

In 1911 it seemed that the wishes of those who dreamed of an autonomous Alsace still loosely connected with Germany might be coming true. A new constitution set up an Alsatian parliament of two houses, offered the citizens a vote in the imperial council and made the province equal to the other members of the empire. Then the warlike successors of Bismarck proceeded to throw away all the sympathy these statesmanlike political moves had gained. Their Pan-Germanism possessed no emotional appeal for the resolutely independent Alsatians, and the increasingly punitive financial demands of the German army and navy proved even less attractive. Sandwiched between France and Germany, the people showed little relish for an imminent war that could only harm themselves, their homes, their families and their way of life.

Little events provoked huge emotional responses. Alsatian civilians continually clashed with German soldiers. At the end of 1913 a twenty-year-old German lieutenant named von Forstner provoked a riot by insulting Alsatian military recruits and denigrating the French flag. The German authorities acquitted him of all blame. Yet although Eugen Ricklin, president of the parliament of Alsace-Lorraine, was now passionately committed to the independence of his own people, Germany entered World War I with perhaps a majority of Alsatians still preferring her side to that of France. The mood changed. By 1916 so many of them had set their hearts against the empire that the German authorities even proposed partitioning the whole province, distributing sections of it to other German states.

Wiser heads prevailed in the councils of Germany, persuading their less cautious colleagues that what Alsace-Lorraine really needed was more, not less, autonomy. It was too late. The Alsace politicians and their Lorraine counterparts simply refused to form a cabinet.

Small wonder, then, that Joffre had so passionately embraced the citizens of Alsace when he reached Thann early in August 1914. 'France needs German elements, so long as they embrace French rule gladly,' as the English man of letters Walter Bagehot had put it, 'more probably than she needs any other element of the national life.' Small wonder too that many Alsatians rapturously received Joffre's embrace. Yet if these sorry affairs seemed to negate a whole Alsatian history of fruitful inter-relationships between Germany and France, they also represented a prolongation into the twentieth century of age-old disputes.

Battles are endemic to frontier states, and it is significant that the oldest extant Alsatian work of art is a statue of the God of war, sculpted here a hundred years before the birth of Jesus. What seems more remarkable, as the historians chronicle the many conquests of Alsace, is the way its citizens managed to develop a powerful spirit of independence that is today as strong as ever. Equally remarkable is their persistence in creating beautiful villages and towns, rebuilding them when enemies had partly destroyed them, and continually adding to their rich architectural heritage whenever a moment of peace and prosperity intervened. In addition, Roman vineyards, Irish monks inventing Munster cheese, Benedictines in Alsace deciding that snails were ideal Lenten food, German architecture, French, Italian, even Chinese dishes, Pastor Heysel bringing asparagus from Algeria, all bespeak an extraordinarily resilient people constantly triumphing over a turbulent past.

Moments of peace and prosperity were rare in much of Alsace's history. Two thousand years before World War I the Celtic Sequani and Rauraci tribes who lived here had been repeatedly invaded by Teutonic tribes from the other side of the River Rhine, only to be temporarily freed from this menace by another conqueror, Julius Caesar, who made the Rhine the eastern frontier of Gaul. For 500 years Rome ruled here, dividing the region into Maxima Sequanorum and Germany Superior.

Many towns and villages in Alsace are surrounded by rich archaeological legacies from these times. Habsheim in Haut-Rhin, for instance, is surrounded by Iron Age tumuli and the remains of an Iron Age farm. Here can be traced a Roman road and the foundations of a Roman staging post. Romans and Gauls built where Stone Age man had settled, as excavations at the tiny hamlet of Landserweg just outside Habsheim have revealed. At Houssen in the same *département* Bronze Age sculptures and a Gaullish treasure trove have been discovered.

Settling where men and women had lived for millennia, the Romans built upon Celtic achievements. Much of what they have left us in Alsace is fascinating, above all the so-called Pagan Wall (le mur des Païens) around Mont Sainte-Odile, created by Celts and fortified by Romans. At Mackwiller a second-century sanctuary consecrated to Mithras has been excavated, and its site and statues are now open to twentieth-century visitors. Today at Niederbronn-les-Bains we take the waters at the chief thermal baths in Alsace where springs combining healing chemicals (said to be specially therapeutic for arthritis, rheumatism and hypertension) were first exploited by the Romans.

The Romans eventually quitted France, but not before their rule had seen incorporated into Alsace more Germanic elements in the tribes known as the Triboci and the Alamanni. From the language of the Alamanni derives the tongue of today's Alsace. Then the Franks took over, under their ruler Clovis driving the Alamanni south.

Though the later Church regarded the version of the Christian faith Clovis espoused as heretical, his reign inaugurated a rich flowering of Christianity here, and one which included a long era of notably fruitful religious foundations. Clovis himself is responsible for the first church, built in 496, on the present site of Strasbourg cathedral.

Alsace became a duchy, ruled first by Duke Eticho and then by his descendants, who in turn have left us some powerful, mostly ruined castles as their memorial. The dukes also bequeathed to Alsace her patron saint. St Odile, daughter of the third duke, Adalric, was born blind, at Obernai around the year 670. Adalric had wanted a son and was determined to kill the handicapped girl. Her wet-nurse fled with the child, and she grew up in the convent of Palma, Beaume-les-Dames. When she was twelve Bishop Erhardt of Bavaria baptized Odile. At that moment she miraculously recovered her sight.

Her brother Hugh brought the girl back to Alsace, a foolhardy act since Duke Adalric in anger struck him dead. Momentarily chastened, the duke allowed Odile back into his home. Soon, however, he was forcing an unwelcome marriage on her. Once again Odile fled. Pursued by her father, she saw a rock miraculously open in the mountains and hid there to escape his wrath. The duke gave up the unequal struggle against heavenly powers and built for his saintly child the monastery of Hohenburg. There, and later in a second convent, Odile gathered around her young girls, as devoted as herself to the Christian life. She died in 720, was canonized by Pope Leo IX 400 years later, and in 1946 Pope Pius XII declared her patron saint of Alsace.

The convent of Sainte-Odile still stands on Mont Sainte-Odile (see the index to this book), though the present building is not that paid for by Duke Adalric. Most of the monastery buildings were totally destroyed in a fire of 1546. In the next century the Premonstratensian order set about rebuilding and restoring, a task taken up by the bishop of Strasbourg in 1853 and finished in our own century.

As the first religious house for women, the importance of this convent in the history of Alsace is immense. Frederick Barbarossa made one of his relatives abbess, and she introduced here the rule of St Augustine. In the late-twelfth century another abbess, Herrade de Landsberg, wrote the celebrated *Hortus Deliciarum* or *Garden of Delights*. Alas, the original copy of the book, with its exquisite miniatures, was destroyed when the Prussians bombed Strasbourg in 1870, though many fine copies remain. One such copy happens to be in the form of frescos on the convent chapel of the Cross on Mont Sainte-Odile itself.

After the death of St Odile, Christian monasticism continued to flourish in Alsace. The Benedictine abbey at Munster, the abbey founded at Murbach by St Pirmin in 727, and the still-extant abbey-church which a follower of St Columbanus founded at Marmoutier a hundred years later, all testify to a new and self-confident Christian civilization. Charlemagne himself found Alsace particularly attractive. We know he spent Christmas of 775 at Sélestat, and himself oversaw the extensions of Murbach abbey and established palatine counts at Colmar and Brumath. His unifying rule scarcely outlived him, and Alsace suffered as a result. In 833 his grandson was fighting on the battlefield of Lügenfeld outside Colmar against his own father, Emperor Ludwig the Pious.

When ten years later the empire established by Charlemagne was carved up, Alsace was consigned to what we today call the 'Middle Kingdom', an apt name for territories standing mid-way between Germany and France whose people lived partly under local rulers and partly under the sway of the Hohenstaufens and Habsburgs. In that year Alsace was officially incorporated into Lorraine (or 'Lotharingia') by the Treaty of Verdun, but soon the region was further broken up, divided among counts, among bishops and municipalities.

The unity of the region was re-established as a Hohenstaufen dukedom when the German King Heinrich I died. The Hohenstaufens remained dukes of Alsace from 1079 to 1268, presiding over a wealth of newly created Romanesque masterpieces – such as the late-twelfth-century church of Sainte-Foy, Sélestat, built on the site of a priory endowed by Princess Hildegarde of Hohenstaufen and her two sons. Charlemagne's own architectural legacy was not forgotten by these successors, witness the lovely Benedictine abbey at

Ottmarsheim, whose octagonal church, consecrated by Pope Leo IX in 1049, is an eleventh-century copy of the chapel endowed and founded by Charlemagne himself at Aix-la-Chapelle, itself a copy of the church of San Vitale in Ravenna.

Romanesque art came later to Alsace than to the rest of France. In consequence it is frequently more subtle, combining many diverse elements, though still nobly austere. In contrast to the Carolingian octagonal pattern of Ottmarsheim, Romanesque architects now developed basilicas with three lofty bays, such as the Dompeter at Avolsheim. Then they began adding transepts, such as you may find at Andlau and Rouffach. Anonymous sculptors carved leaves, animals, mythical beasts and quaint human figures on capitals. Ornamentation became richer and richer. The lovely sandstone of the region contributed its charm. And the peak of Romanesque architecture in Alsace was achieved in the mid-twelfth century with the masterpiece of Marmoutier.

In spite of the apparent political and social dominance of the Hohenstaufens, few of the local communities' hard-won rights were lost. Alsatians already displayed a streak of self-sufficiency and independence of their feudal lords, which surfaced in 1262, for instance, when the burghers of Strasbourg won a victory at Oberhausen over their prince-bishop and expelled him.

After 1273 the Austrian Habsburgs took over Alsace. Once again the country seemed resolutely Teutonic. Yet even the powerful Habsburgs, who frequently set up an imperial residence at Haguenau, were themselves not able totally to control their Alsatian subjects. First they divided the country into two landgraviates, upper and lower Alsace. In addition, fearful of the power of local nobles, they set up numerous free towns and cities with their own constitutions and governments. In 1354 ten cities – Haguenau, Colmar, Sélestat, Mulhouse, Wissembourg, Rosheim, Kaysersberg, Munster, Turckheim and Obernai – protected by the emperor's representative with a seat at Haguenau, formed a union known as the *Decapolis* and took the lead in politically and militarily defending Alsace.

Again the surviving architecture of these towns reveals their rich history. In such warlike ages inevitably they needed fortifying. The walls of Haguenau, alas, were half-demolished by the French in 1677 and totally pulled down by the Germans in 1871, but its town gates date from the time of Frederick von Hohenstaufen, duke of Swabia. He also began building the castle which his son, Frederick

Barbarossa, enlarged and made his favourite home. Here was another lover of Alsace who sought to combine Germany and France (in the form of Burgundy), and indeed Italy as well.

Barbarossa's son Heinrich VI continued building the castle of Haguenau and here in 1193 brought his prisoner Richard Coeur de Lion to appear before a regional assembly of princes. Alas, this castle too was destroyed in the seventeenth century. What still remains from the twelfth century is the Romanesque nave of the church of Saint-Georges, founded by the Emperor Konrad II, another legacy of German rule to Alsace's heritage.

Like all the towns of the *Decapolis,* the original foundation of Rosheim far predates this defensive alliance. Rosheim herself was probably established by Scottish monks in the seventh century. Kaysersberg lies on an old Roman road and derives its name from the Roman camp Caesaris Mons. As for the largest city of Alsace, Strasbourg first appears in written history as Strateburgum in the sixth century.

By the time of the Habsburgs she ranked as one of the finest cities in Europe, both intellectually and visually – her Gothic architecture pre-eminent in Europe (and created in part by masters hired from other great European centres), her inhabitants, according to the census of 1444, numbering an astonishing 18,000, her prince-bishop a mighty secular potentate with a string of fiefs. After expelling him in 1262, Strasbourg's rich citizens continued to contest his pre-eminence for another 200 years. They were equally prone to defy the emperor, refusing to supply him with troops when they thought it convenient and successfully establishing their own constitutions and rights. A senate of thirty elected members was its high court, but by the sixteenth century a yet more democratic government, known as the *Magistrat,* ruled the city. Strasbourg was wealthy, since she also minted her own coins and drew tolls from her strategic control of river traffic along the Rhine. Along with the towns of the *Decapolis,* the Habsburgs and later the Count Palatine of the Rhine, Strasbourg rose to dominate Alsace.

And for once the whole land had begun to prosper precisely because it was a frontier state. During the Hundred Years' War merchants desperately sought ways of avoiding travelling through France as they traded between Flanders and Italy. The Rhine plain was their answer, and in consequence in the fourteenth and fifteenth century this became a region of rich merchants and rising middlemen, whose families added to the architectural heritage of the land.

Alsace suffered and survived the Black Death, and (as did many other Christians) its citizens frequently blamed the plague on the Jews. In 1349 many of the lords and civic deputies met at Benfeld. In solemn assembly they accused the Jews of poisoning wells, and condemned them to expulsion and even death. Hundreds of innocent men and women were sentenced to the flames.

Within a couple of centuries Christians throughout Europe would be killing each other, as the Peasants' War and the Reformation were succeeded by the Wars of Religion and the Thirty Years' War. The people of Alsace needed their fortified towns and powerful châteaux. The Thirty Years' War in particular left its mark on Alsace. At Kaysersberg the mighty castle was partly ruined by the Swedes, though it remains impressive. At Turckheim, a town in the shape of a triangle, each corner is still guarded by a vaulted gateway set in a defensive tower, the three connected by remains of its still powerful fortifications. Obernai's yet more powerful stronghold repelled the Armagnacs in 1440, Charles the Bold in 1476 and the Peasants' War in 1525, even though 101 years later the Swedes managed to conquer the town and reduced the number of its surviving inhabitants to six. As for Rosheim, the town was fortified no fewer than three times: in the thirteenth, fourteenth and fifteenth century. From the first of these fortifications survive three massive gates.

The sixteenth century and the Reformation brought turmoil and political upheaval, as well as intellectual richness, to Alsace. Peasants had begun to rise against their masters at the very end of the fifteenth century. Led by a man from the Sundgau named Berner, in 1493 they attacked Jews, nobles and monasteries, a precedent of the Peasants' War of 1525. In that year Erasmus Guerber incited the workers of Strasbourg to rebellion and his countrymen followed suit. Guerber had been born at Molsheim and was a lowly servant in the employ of the bishop of Strasbourg. In Catholic eyes the rising he led displayed dangerous anti-clerical as well as social-revolutionary implications. The nobles responded savagely, executing rebels at Scherwiller, Ensisheim and Saverne. Mercenaries of the duke of Lorraine hanged Guerber himself at Saverne. Yet religious aspirations are not crushed so easily. Eventually it would take all the might of the anxious Habsburgs to suppress religious upheaval and restore Catholicism to Alsace.

Strasbourg's own traditions were entirely opposed to such religious intransigence. Its clergy had frequently sided with the laity against their overweening bishops. Humanists found themselves welcome and intellectually unshackled here. As early as 1519 the Strasbourg presses produced no fewer than four tracts of Martin Luther himself, who had just begun his attack on ecclesiastical corruption. A Dominican named Martin Bucer, a native of Sélestat, had met and been profoundly influenced by Luther, renounced his religious vows in 1521, took a wife and arrived at Strasbourg two years later, to be almost immediately appointed influential preacher at the church of Sainte-Aurélie. John Calvin himself was made pastor of the French church at Strasbourg in 1538 and stayed there until he moved back to Geneva in 1541. France and Germany thus combined to bring the Reformation to Alsace. Another bold Alsatian Protestant was the renowned Matthäus Zell, born in 1477 the son of a Kaysersberg vintner, ordained priest and soon preaching Christianity according to Martin Luther with such eloquence that the bishop of Strasbourg excommunicated him. Zell continued to preach and bear witness to the Reformation unabated, taking a wife in 1523 and the following year abandoning the Latin Mass to celebrate in his native German tongue.

Increasingly the bishops of the city displayed those worldly ambitions which so incensed these Protestant Reformers, alienating both laity and clergy alike. Bishop Guillaume de Honstein, whose episcopate lasted from 1506 to 1541, saw almost half his clergy and religious ally themselves with the new teachers. Elsewhere in Alsace Protestantism was flourishing. Mulhouse opted for Calvinism. Colmar became Protestant in 1557. Religious toleration seemed set to last. The canons of Strasbourg disagreed amongst themselves over the new teachings, but were by no means at each other's throats.

The Wars of Religion changed everything, and once again Alsace was a theatre of military savagery. Now the Protestant canons of Strasbourg sought the defence of the city government and the Catholic canons appealed to the dukes of Lorraine and Bavaria. The Catholics won. In 1599 Charles, duke of Lorraine, already cardinal bishop of Metz, was consecrated bishop of Strasbourg. At the same time the Habsburg Archduke Leopold of Austria, scarcely in his twenties, was appointed his coadjutor bishop. And the forces of the city government retreated before the forces of Lorraine. The Habsburgs now proceeded to tighten their grip on the rest of hitherto recalcitrant Alsace.

Only in the seventeenth century did the French begin to resume their sway, and paradoxically as a result of Protestantism, for the Thirty Years' War which began in 1618 cruelly harmed the land, as well as making it impossible for the Habsburg emperors to hold on to it.

Strasbourg fitfully tried to retain some religious freedom, soliciting the help of the tolerant French king Henri IV. But new disasters were about to overwhelm this beautiful city and the rest of Alsace. Gustavus Adolphus of Sweden led European Protestants in a counter-attack on the Counter-Reformation which resulted in the Thirty Years' War. Commanding the Rhine, cities such as Strasbourg and Brisach were prized by opposing armies and suffered deeply in consequence. As if this lot were not miserable enough, the Catholic French statesman and cardinal, Richelieu, had no wish to see the Catholic Spanish use the new conflict as a pretext for encroaching upon the lands claimed by France. Alsace, he perceived, was one of the most vulnerable of such territories. Richelieu sought the allegiance of Strasbourg, but Strasbourg was unable to resist an alliance with Gustavus Adolphus. In 1632 the Swedes crossed the Rhine at Strasbourg to advance on Ensisheim and crush all Catholic resistance in the countryside.

Since 1523 Ensisheim had been the chief town of the Austrian administration between the Vosges and the Black Forest. Here in 1570 the Habsburgs had set up a *Kammer* to tax and rule their Alsatian subjects; and the same year they also established at Ensisheim a mint. Now their *Landvogt* and his supporters fled from the Swedes to Brisach. But soon Gustavus Adolphus was killed in battle and Richelieu's forces were attempting to invest Alsace. The Catholics of Strasbourg cathedral gave them a relieved welcome. By way of Saverne the French retook Colmar from the disoriented Swedish army, followed by the rest of Alsace. Naturally their imperial Catholic allies from the other side of the Rhine were ill-pleased, suggesting instead that France might take over Franche-Comté and they themselves retain Alsace. Richelieu's successor Mazarin demurred, and by the Peace of Westphalia which ended the Thirty Years' War, Alsace, the bauble of the great powers, became French − or at least more or less French. The grateful French monarch created Mazarin count of Ferrette.

Wanting to be rid both of Habsburgs and Swedes, the Alsatians themselves had appealed to France for relief. Yet although the Peace of Westphalia in 1648 ostensibly ceded upper and lower Alsace to the French, along with ten free imperial towns, Alsatians still treasured their freedom. The French take-over was piecemeal, completed only a hundred years later. Initially, border towns declared themselves allied with France. Next the French expansionist king Louis XIV, at war with the empire, invaded Alsace. There were more battles to come, notably that at Turckheim on 5 January 1675.

The lovely fortified town of Turckheim, standing five kilometres west of Colmar in Haut-Rhin on the left bank of the River Fecht (close to where it is joined by the Logelbach), commands a major route from Haguenau to Lorraine. Strategically, by the end of 1674 it had become a crucial stronghold and prize in these vital campaigns, and the brilliant French general Henri de la Tour d'Auvergne, viscount of Turenne, perceived that soon he would be forced to defend it against some 60,000 Germans, ready to march by way of Turckheim and Lorraine to Paris.

Turenne chose a strategy of feigning to retreat into Lorraine. Deceived by this, the imperial troops failed to spot that the bulk of Turenne's army was marching by way of Ensisheim to Pfaffenheim, thirteen kilometres south of Colmar, while the French commander's spies were bringing information about the disposition of Austria's 35,000 soldiers. On the day of battle the imperial commanders were astonished to see Turenne's forces not only advancing south of the River Logelbach but also reinforced by thirty squadrons and twelve battalions from his allies. Turenne threw bridges over the Fecht and took Turckheim. That evening his infantry engaged the enemy. The following morning the imperial forces had been routed.

Yet at the Peace of Nijmegen in 1678 France failed to secure all its coveted Alsatian territories. Two years later Louis XIV claimed that the imperial princes had wrested from Alsace several towns and territories that were rightly his. These princes appealed in vain for help to the impoverished and now often defeated Habsburg emperor. With the active connivance (or, from the Habsburgs' point of view, treachery) of the bishop of Strasbourg, French soldiers took that city in 1681, and three years later the Treaty of Regensburg officially ceded it to Louis XIV, a decision ratified after further fighting by the Peace of Ryswyck in 1697. Strasbourg became the capital of Alsace.

Louis XIV was an ultra-Catholic monarch who revoked the Edict of Nantes by which Protestants had been given a measure of religious freedom in France. In Alsace the reality was rather different. For one thing, the Edict of Nantes had never applied there. Protestants had claimed and been granted their rights quite apart from royal decree. For another, even Louis XIV did not impose his own religion on his new subjects. Instead a curious and delightful religious arrangement which exists to this day was set up. Protestants and Catholics, the king decreed, should share the same churches, worshipping not at the same times but within the same devout walls. In addition Strasbourg University was allowed to preserve its Lutheran character and thus retained its part in the vastly impressive intellectual advances that European Protestants were making throughout the eighteenth century.

Even now new Protestant sects managed to infiltrate the region successfully without being persecuted, notably the Anabaptists, Christians who rejected infant baptism as contrary to the practice of the New Testament. These devout men and women found (and still find) a peaceful existence as farmers around Sainte-Marie-aux-Mines and in the valley of the Bruche. In its religions and in its dialects Sainte-Marie-aux-Mines in particular delightfully displays both the kiss of France and the lure of Germany, for it straddles the River Liepvrette, with for the most part French-speaking Catholics living on the left bank and Protestants speaking a dialect of German living on the right.

Strasbourg's Lutheranism even came to the rescue of Louis XV when that superb general and marshal of France, Maurice Saxe, having served France with distinction died at Chambord in 1750. The king's desire to have Saxe buried in Saint-Denis, Paris, was frustrated since the dead marshal was illegitimate, the bastard son of the king of Portugal, a foreigner and a Protestant. None of this disturbed the Lutherans of Strasbourg. Marshal Saxe's corpse was brought in triumph to the city. There it rested in a Lutheran chapel, while on the orders of Louis XV Jean-Baptiste Pigalle created in the 'Protestant cathedral' (the Alsatian Gothic church of Saint-Thomas) a magnificent tomb. It stands in the thirteenth-century apse, grandiosely decorated with the lion of England, the Austrian eagle, Hercules and a mourning Amour extinguishing a torch.

Strasbourg was becoming French, a republican city owing allegiance to a Bourbon king. On the south side of the cathedral square royalist France dominates in the architecture of the palais Rohan, built between 1732 and 1742 for Prince Armand-Gaston de Rohan-Soubise to plans by the royal architect Robert de Cotte. Four cardinals named Rohan were successively bishops of Strasbourg between 1701 and 1790, and this was their palace. Here in 1744 the cardinal sumptuously received Louis XV himself. Today the palais Rohan is the museum of fine art and you can visit its magnificent apartments every day of the week in summer between 10.00 and noon and between 14.00 and 18.00. (Visits to the museum between

October and March are slightly more restricted.)

Fascinatingly, although Armand-Gaston de Rohan-Soubise planned to outshine Versailles, German as well as French artists and architects were called on to embellish the palais Rohan, for the Berlin architect Johann August Nahl, decorator of the royal residences of Frederick II of Prussia, came here in 1741, commissioned to work on the interior decoration of the great entrance hall. Parisian tapestries were bought to adorn the room designed as the king's own chamber, and the king's salon (subsequently dubbed the *salon d'Assemblée*) has richly carved woodwork decorated with copies of works by Raphael. In the library are two more copies of royal portraits, both by the artist from Perpignan named Hyacinth Rigaud who brought a touch of genius to eighteenth-century royal portraiture.

Louis XV himself had grandiose ambitions for re-creating Strasbourg and commissioned the neo-classical urban architect Jacques-François Blondel to remodel the whole of the centre of the city, just as he had remodelled parts of Paris as a tribute to his royal master. Blondel's plans were approved by the Duke de Choiseul, Louis XV's chief minister responsible for the province, on 30 November 1764. Fortunately, the work was never finished, for its total completion would have involved destroying much of great charm and beauty.

That said, Louis XV's initiative bequeathed the city some splendid buildings, symbolic of royal power in a city that possessed the quaint distinction of remaining republican whilst living under Bourbon suzerainty. Altogether, of Strasbourg's 3,600 great houses, no fewer than 1,500 were either newly built or reconstructed under the direction of Blondel. Walk to them from the old city and you see here the old Alsatian German manner being transformed into the new taste for French.

Blondel's masterpiece at Strasbourg is the vast Aubette in the place Kléber, built in 1765 as the city garrison. (Its name derives from the French *aube*, meaning dawn, the time when the orders of the day were issued.) Badly damaged by bombardment on 24 August 1870, the Aubette was carefully restored at the command of those Germans who had harmed it.

In 1765 the place Kléber was known as the place des Armes, Blondel's royalist city planning intended to lead by monumental architectural stages from here to the place Royale. Today his scheme is neatly transformed by the fact that you leave place Kléber and walk east through the place Broglie past the town hall and the Opéra to cross the rampart and reach not the place Royale but the place de la République.

The eighteenth century was an age of prosperity for Alsace. Pottery and earthenware factories flourished, especially those founded by Charles Hannong at Strasbourg in 1720 and profitably run by his successors. Close by Niederbronn-les-Bains the Dietrich dynasty, who had become seigneurs of the town in 1764, built up the most powerful iron forges in France. They constructed sturdy decent homes for their workers, as you can still see at Niederbronn and even more at nearby Jaegerthal.

Independent as ever in spirit, many Alsatians subjected themselves with some reluctance to the Bourbon monarchs and were delighted when they were put down at the revolution. However, they had no desire to leave the new French republic and submit to other dictators. Mulhouse, a republican city already allied to Spain, now joined France. Alsatian Protestants rejoiced to recover their complete freedom of worship. With Strasbourg still as the seat of the Catholic bishop of all Alsace, the two *départements* that survive to this day, Haut-Rhin and Bas-Rhin, were created.

When the great powers of Europe turned against this new republic, they discovered in the opposing French army of the Rhine a goodly number of Alsatian volunteers. One of them was an officer and poet named Claude Joseph Rouget de Lisle. Stationed in Strasbourg, at the invitation of the mayor (whose name was Dietrich) he there composed a celebrated battle song, the 'Chant de la Guerre pour l'Armée du Rhin'. He sang it first in 1792 for Mayor Dietrich in Strasbourg town hall. It runs:

> *Allons enfants de la Patrie,*
> *Le jour de gloire est arrivé;*
> *Contre nous de la tyrannie,*
> *L'étendard sanglant est levé,*
> *L'étendard sanglant est levé.*
> *Entendez-vous, dans les campagnes,*
> *Mugir ces féroces soldats?*
> *Ils viennent, jusque dans nos bras,*
> *Engorger nos fils, nos campagnes.*
> *Aux armes, Citoyens!*
> *Formez vos bataillons!*
> *Marchons, marchons!*
> *Q'un sang impur abreuve nos sillons!*
>
> (Let us go, children of the Fatherland,
> The day of glory has come;
> Against us has been raised
> The bloody flag of tyranny,

The bloody flag of tyranny.
Can you hear in the countryside
The shouts of fierce soldiers?
They come into our hearths
To slay our sons and friends.
Arm yourselves, Citizens!
Form up your battalions!
Let us march, let us march!
Let an impure blood water our furrows!)

Ironically, neither Rouget de Lisle nor Strasbourg has properly been credited with this song. On their way to Paris republican volunteers from Marseille began to sing it, so this Alsatian song became known as the 'Marseillaise'. A citizen of this disputed territory had given France her national anthem, only to have applied to it the name of another city.

By 1806 around 24,000 men from Alsace were singing the 'Marseillaise' as part of the Grande Armée. Some of these men fought valiantly as Napoleon's generals. One of them, Jean-Baptiste Kléber, combined both the French and the German elements of the Alsatian character. 'He spoke German but fought like a Frenchman,' declared Bonaparte. Born in Strasbourg in 1753, Kléber had studied architecture in Paris before taking up the profession of a soldier, entering the military academy in Munich. He was brilliant in both fields. Reverting to architecture, he built the town hall of Thann, over whose entrance he placed the arms of the city: on the one side a golden pine tree on an azure ground, on the other side the arms of the house of Austria. He was inspector of public works at Belfort until 1792, when he volunteered for Napoleon's army. His courage at the siege of Mainz earned him the rank of brigadier-general. When the Vendée revolted, Kléber put down the insurgents. By 1794 he was commander of the Armée du Nord, before taking command of the Army of the Orient, to meet death by assassination in Cairo.

Almost as renowned were two other Napoleonic generals from Alsace: Lefebre and Kellermann. François-Joseph Lefebre was born in Rouffach (at No. 1, rue Poterne) in 1755. Orphaned, he was brought up by his uncle, the parish priest of Guémar. Enlisting in the Gardes françaises when he was eighteen, he had risen to brigadier-general by 1793 and was commanding his own division a year later. Soon he was military governor of Paris.

Lefebre fought for France at Fleurus and Jena. His distinctions included becoming a marshal of France in 1804 and then duke of

Danzig, the city he himself took by force in 1807. By 1812 he was commanding the imperial guard. After the restoration of the monarchy, Louis XVIII made him a peer of France. But Lefebre never forgot his own origins, and when he married his regiment's laundress, it was noted that she too came from Alsace.

By contrast with a boy who triumphed over ill-fortune in his youth, François-Christophe Kellermann came from a rich Strasbourg home and had become a marshal of the Bourbon army before the revolution, after valiant service in the Seven Years' War. Allying with the revolution, he was given command of the Army of the Moselle and, in 1795, of the Army of the Alps. Little wonder that, served by such men, Bonaparte said of the soldiers of Alsace, 'Let them speak German, so long as they use their sabres in French.' (*Laissez les parler allemand, pourvu qu'ils sabrent en français.*) Bonaparte made Kellermann marshal of the empire and duke of Valmy, only to see him in 1814 once again supporting the Bourbons.

Other Alsatians served Napoleon Bonaparte in different ways. Charles-Louis Schulmeister had the dubious distinction of serving as chief of his secret police. Euloge Schneider, sometime vicar-general at Strasbourg, was an even less savoury character, becoming a fanatical Jacobin and public prosecutor when the ardour of the French Revolutionaries turned murderous, thus consigning many decent men and women to death by the guillotine. Foolishly criticizing Saint-Just, he found himself arrested a few days before he was due to marry an Alsatian woman from Barr. His own execution prevented Euloge Schneider from reaching the altar.

By no means all the rest of the population had become republican. Alsatians had inherited a tradition of picking and choosing among those who had the gall to try to rule them. When Bonaparte rose to absolute power, many were ready to welcome him. His vigorous attempts to improve the economy and communications of his empire enhanced their prosperity. Napoleon also helped to foster a new system of education in Alsace (the first teachers' training college was founded at Strasbourg in 1810). In their eyes his victory at Austerlitz had pleasingly put down some of their former oppressors.

When the enemies of Bonaparte finally closed in on him, many in Alsace rallied to his cause. When that cause was lost, they set about surviving in the new world of the nineteenth-century bourgeoisie, while continuing to regard the place Kléber in Strasbourg as holy ground. Napoleon I's memory was still held dear. Only 5,000 Alsatians sided with the opposition to Napoleon III's *coup d'état* of 1852, against

205,000 who welcomed it. The plebiscite held to approve and ratify the Third Empire found only 6,000 Alsatians voting against.

Universal suffrage was introduced into Alsace as a result of the revolution of 1848. When Alsace was annexed to Germany in 1871 such advances were by no means lost, for the Germans endowed an intellectually sparkling new university at Strasbourg and set about creating a progressive system of education that soon involved some 4,000 elementary schools. As for communications, by 1903 Alsace-Lorraine boasted 1,998 kilometres of railway, the vast majority of them state-owned.

'The best that Germany possesses shall be offered in the service of Alsace-Lorraine,' wrote the German poet Theodor Fontane in 1871. As far as architecture was concerned, the victorious Germans were as good as Fontane's word. Since Strasbourg was decreed the capital of the Reichsland, the Germans invested in building here powerful expressions of their imperial dignity. Once despised for their 'historicism', today these monumental buildings are looked at with the considerable respect they deserve.

Architecturally no other town or city in Alsace benefited more from German largesse. The city actually tripled in size and saw the construction of forty majestic new public buildings, including the university, the central post-office, the main railway station, a new parliament building, several ministries and the new courts of justice. In this project the city architect Geoffroy Conrath was assisted by the distinguished Berlin city planner August Orth. Ironically, since so much of Berlin was destroyed in World War II, one of the most rewarding places to see what late-nineteenth-century German architects could achieve is Strasbourg.

The Berlin architect Edouard Jacobsthal built the railway station between 1878 and 1883 in the neo-classical style that his fellow-Berliner Karl Friedrich Schinkel had revived in the Prussian capital in the first half of the century. It was Strasbourg's first taste of what was to come. Imperial might would soon be displayed architecturally above all in the massive imperial palace (now the palais du Rhin), standing in the place de la République and built by Hermann Eggert between 1883 and 1889. Five years later on the other side of the square was completed the national and university library. The place de la République laid out by these megalomaniac German geniuses and Geoffroy Conrath is, inevitably, the largest in Strasbourg.

They had created the new university by fusing and re-endowing the old Lutheran university of 1621 and the Catholic university of 1702.

Though its chief architect, Otto Warth, was born in Karlsruhe, his plans for its new main building were based on those of the neo-Renaissance school of Berlin, and it stands today an imposing 125 metres long, fronted in the place de l'Université by a statue of Goethe as a student. Another Karlsruhe architect, Ludwig Levy, created for Strasbourg a neo-Romanesque synagogue in 1898 which the Nazis destroyed in 1940. A new 'synagogue of peace' was built on the same spot in 1955.

Since Strasbourg had been granted its own regional Diet of two chambers, the Germans decided to house it properly, in another mighty building standing in the place de la République. It is now the home of Strasbourg's national theatre and conservatoire of music. The architect was a native of Hamburg with a Danish name, Skjold Neckelmann, who had studied architecture not only in the city of his birth but also in Vienna. As well as this palace, he built the university library, the courts of justice and the Catholic church of Saint-Pierre-le-Jeune. The last two stand next to each other where the rue du Tribunal meets the rue Saint-Pierre-le-Jeune, and the contrast between them vividly displays the talented eclecticism of their architect, for the church is neo-Romanesque in style and the courts of justice neo-Renaissance. Neckelmann's arrogance here went too far, for he despoiled an already existing church of Saint-Pierre-le-Jeune which Pope Leo XI had consecrated in 1053 and which had been enriched throughout the centuries. Casualties of Neckelmann's restoration included medieval wall paintings and a late-medieval flamboyant chapel.

In spite of such deplorable insensitivity (which Strasbourg's twentieth-century restorers are trying to put right), in truth almost every conceivable historical style was used with panache by the architects who enhanced Strasbourg during the first German annexation of Alsace. Here you can find (in, for example, the former *ministère ouest*) the baroque style favoured by the Prussian court in the eighteenth century. And Hermann Eggert's imperial palace, though basically neo-Renaissance, deploys not just baroque elements but inside even rococo décor.

Everything was authorized at the highest level. Since Kaiser Wilhelm II himself favoured the neo-Romanesque style, his permission had to be sought before anyone dared construct the neo-Gothic façade of the post-office (alas, today much altered) in 1895. Soon Alsatian architects were themselves training in Berlin, returning to embellish their own capital in the Germanic fashion. The church of

Saint-Pierre-le-Vieux in the place Kléber, though originally founded in the late Middle Ages and filled with artistic treasures, was reconstructed by a group of such architects (who remained faithful to Louis XIV's injunction of 1683 that the Protestants should have the nave of the church for their worship and the Catholics the choir).

As late as 1912 German architects were still enriching Strasbourg with massive new buildings – witness the huge Magmod shopping centre in the boulevard du 22-Novembre, whose architects were called Berlinger and Krafft, and whose decorative statues are by a sculptor named Schulz.

Yet the citizens chafed. As pigs in the middle, they suffered in World War I even more than they had done in the Franco-Prussian War of 1870–1. The siege of Verdun in particular lasted some ten months in all and resulted in literally uncountable casualties, since most men who died were trampled, blasted and mutilated beyond recognition. Most authorities guess that the French suffered over 400,000 casualties and the Germans more than 300,000.

Verdun is in Lorraine, not Alsace, but its horrors can almost be matched by the sufferings endured by the two *départements* of Haut-Rhin and Bas-Rhin between August 1914 and November 1918. Immediately war broke out, the city of Mulhouse was perceived by both sides as the key to the Belfort gap, the natural route between the Jura and the Vosges, and thus an obvious target. For the same reason the town had been besieged and heroically defended in the Napoleonic Wars and in 1870. Between 8 and 19 August 1914 France painfully and costly liberated her from the Germans.

The Germans fought back to the end. Outside the city, soldiers of both sides bravely contested Altkirch, Thann, Cernay and Soultz. The Hardt forest provided cover for intrepid German troops. When they retreated into the towns, the French were obliged to drive them out of individual houses where many of them had taken shelter and were sniping at the advancing enemy. When they finally retreated across the Rhine, they left behind 3,000 prisoners. Such was the craziness of World War I that now most of the French troops were redeployed far away on the Somme. Germany reoccupied Mulhouse. The French took it back only on 17 November 1918. The memorial to the wasted lives of these campaigns was created by Maxime Real del Sarte and today dolefully stands in the rue de l'Arsenal, Mulhouse.

After millennia of suffering would peace finally prevail in Alsace?

In 1919 the Treaty of Versailles specifically insisted that the intention of the victorious powers was to 'redress the wrong done by Germany in 1871', both to the rights of France and to the wishes of the population of Alsace. Initially Alsatians seemed of one mind with their French compatriots over this intention. Their own friends had suffered and died in the previous four hideous years.

Germany was no longer universally loved in Alsace. Here just before World War I Hilaire Belloc spotted on the wall of an inn the French tricolour ('which,' he observed 'once brought a little hope to the oppressed') and at the head of it in broad black letters the words, 'Freedom, Brotherhood, and an Equal Law'.

One celebrated children's writer, Jean Jacques Waltz, who called himself Uncle Hansi and whose writings, beautifully illustrated with his own watercolours, charmingly describe the flowery villages and towns of the region as well as the customs and costumes of its inhabitants, published a new book in 1918 calling his land 'the paradise of the tricolour'. Apart from that nationalistic reference to the French flag, *Le Paradis tricolore* reveals only one other indication of the passions of those Alsatians who had survived World War I. Its dedication is:

> *A la mémoire de mon ami*
> *Jacques Preiss*
> *Député de Colmar*
> *emprisonné en Allemagne et mort en martyr*
> *le 8 Mars 1915, pour avoir trop aimer la France.*

Beneath Hansi's charming exterior seethed a cauldron of hatred for Germany and for Prussia in particular. Born at Colmar two years after the annexation of his beloved Alsace, he became famous for his caricatures of Prussian officers and outrageous German officials. Even the German children he portrayed were grotesque.

In spite of this understandably emotional response to the war years, the Alsatians none the less responded to the new French overtures with their traditional suspicion. Their written language was still predominantly Germanic. In the 1920s economic problems aggravated political suspicions. For their part, the French authorities were often utterly insensitive in their dealings with those whom Joffre had claimed to embrace for ever as his fellow-citizens.

Alsatians were particularly incensed in 1924 when the French ministry led by Edouard Herriot announced its intention to impose upon Alsace-Lorraine 'total republican legislation'. They recognized in this another threat to their own harmonious religious settlements and in particular to their concordat of 1801 with the Papacy. Assimilation was not yet a concept acceptable to Alsatians. The Alsace patriot Dr Eugen Ricklin responded by calling together a league dedicated to Home Rule (the *Heimatbund*). The response of the French premier Raymond Poincaré in 1926 was to ban all German newspapers in Alsace and in 1927 to arrest many so-called Alsatian subversives, ransacking their homes and properties. Two of those arrested were instantly elected by large majorities to the chamber of deputies. The French government denied them the right to sit.

In retrospect these squabbles appear as trivial squalls before an unprecedentedly savage storm. If the Treaty of Versailles planned to revenge France against German aggression, Adolf Hitler was determined to redress the wrongs which he believed that treaty had inflicted on Germany. Alsace inevitably suffered from his iron will. When he became chancellor of the German Reich in 1933, the French government gradually ceased to reinvest in Alsace, rightly perceiving that it was at risk from the German dictator's insatiable ambitions.

German planes bombed Alsace in 1939. German troops crossed the Rhine on 15 June 1940 and had taken Colmar, Mulhouse and Strasbourg within four days. No mention was made of Alsace in the subsequent armistice between France and Germany, but Hitler's own intention totally to annex this part of France was made clear to his associates and future collaborators when he visited Strasbourg on 28 June 1940. By 5 July, the customs frontier between his own country and France had been set not at the Rhine but on the western border of 'German-Lorraine', the border decreed when France capitulated to Germany in 1871. On 25 September Hitler implacably set out his true policy: 'The military authorities must treat Alsace and Lorraine not as occupied territories but as part of the German Fatherland itself.'

So when France capitulated before Hitler's onslaught, Alsace became once more annexed to Germany, part of it incorporated into the Westmark, another part into Baden. Family names and the names of towns and villages were transliterated into German. Some 18,000 of its men died fighting for Germany on the eastern front, many of them forcibly conscripted.

Hitler banned the French language throughout the province. Even people's names were changed – every Jean became a Hans. Nazi vandalism destroyed a unique work of art in the place Kléber,

Strasbourg. There the artists Hans and Sophie-Tauber Arp, along with Théo van Doesberg, had created a new décor for the building known as the Aubette. Geometric and colourful, it derived from the Arps's friendship and creative collaboration with Weimar avant-garde artists as well as with Kandinsky and members of the *Blaue Reiter* school. Hitler's disciples declared such art degenerate, and the décor was destroyed. It is said that the Alsatians sardonically renamed the 'street of the savage' (or rue du Sauvage) in Mulhouse Adolf-Hitler-Straße.

Even the French beret was proscribed. Hitler ordered his Gauleiter Robert Wagner to render Alsace totally Germanic within ten years. Whereas the rest of Vichy France was allowed considerable autonomy, steps were taken to bring Alsace increasingly under German hegemony. Absorbed into the region known as Oberrhein-gau, controlled exclusively by German and frequently petty officials, as the war dragged on the unhappy land was subject to the further misery of aerial bombardments by the allies.

In vain the puppet régime of Vichy, led by Marshal Pétain, protested – a hundred or so times between 1940 and 1944, that is throughout the whole of the German occupation of Alsace. No reply to their complaints ever came. Privately they were prepared to sacrifice Alsace and Lorraine for the sake of their own survival as collaborators. Alsace-Lorraine thus because the symbol of their weakness, persuading Hitler that whenever he wished to abrogate the terms of his armistice with France, he could do so with impunity.

In Alsace the Nazis even set up a concentration camp and gas chambers, at Struthof near Narzwiller in Bas-Rhin – the only concentration camp built in France. Today the camp is preserved as a grim memorial to the 40,000 deportees who passed through it and the 10,000 prisoners murdered there. Close by is the granite quarry where the prisoners were forced to work. When the allies liberated the camp on 23 November 1944 it was found to be empty. All the surviving prisoners had been transported to Dachau. At Struthof in 1976 neo-Nazis tried to burn down the deportation and resistance museum. The Deportation Memorial was erected here in 1960. You can visit the camp from April to August between 08.00 to 11.30 and 14.00 to 18.30. For the rest of the year it opens from 09.00 to 11.00 and from 14.00 to 16.30, closing on Christmas Day and New Year's Day.

Warmly after Hitler's defeat Alsace embraced the Fourth French Republic. Once again Alsace became two *départements* of France,

Haut-Rhin and Bas-Rhin. The Nazi occupation had seriously upset her economy, but slowly this recovered. The French authorities feared that alien occupation might also have affected her political stance. They vainly set about effacing every trace of the German legal mind and system.

The system might have been totally eradicated. But by 1949 Strasbourg was the seat of the Council of Europe; and soon Alsace would lie at the heart of the European Economic Community, of which both Germany and France were founder-members. At first these bodies possessed no permanent home in Strasbourg, but in 1972 in the new city the architect Henry Bernard began directing the building of the palais d'Europe, permanent seat of the Council of Europe and a main home of the European Parliament. The French president Valéry Giscard d'Estaing opened the finished building six years later.

Alsace remained that same land, designated part of the 'Middle Kingdom' after the dismemberment of Charlemagne's empire a thousand years previously, but its situation now gave it an enhanced importance. Alsace was French; but was it remotely likely that any governmental decree could efface the German elements in the spirit of her citizens?

In the end acute observers have made completely divergent judgments as to which elements predominate, German or French. You cross a great range of mountains and enter a level plain 'inhabited by a people totally distinct and different from France, with manners, language, ideas, prejudices, and habits all different', wrote Arthur Young in 1789. Seventy years later Matthew Arnold declared with equal dogmatism, 'the people here are among the Frenchest of the French, in spite of their German race and language'.

Is the language the clue to the Alsatian's real identity, or does it only confuse matters? On 14 February 842 two of Charlemagne's grandsons, Ludwig the German and Charles the Bald, met at Strasbourg with their followers and swore never again to plot with their brother Lothaire against each other. Their followers in turn swore that should either of their leaders break his oath, they would give him no support. A contemporary historian named Nithard watched the ceremony and wrote down what had happened (though our earliest surviving manuscript of his chronicle dates only from the late-tenth century). From this eye-witness account the incredible fact emerges that Charles and the supporters of Ludwig took their oaths in German (or what Nithard calls *teudisca lingua*). Ludwig and

Charles's supporters, on the other hand, took their oaths in what Nithard dubbed *romana lingua*. What was that tongue? Some say an early form of French. If so, in Nithard's *De Dissensionibus filiorum Ludovici Pii* the Alsatians have provided us with the first ever recorded text in French.

The question arises whether in those days everyone in cultivated circles could speak both languages, and maybe a third. Fourteen years after these Strasbourg oaths were taken a North Alsatian monk named Otrit dedicated a poem to Ludwig the German. It was called *Der Krist*, which is strictly speaking neither German nor French.

After all, no philologist can really tell you whence the very name of the country derives, whether from the Celts or the Teutons. The words *Alesacius*, referring to the country, and *Alesaciones*, referring to the people, appear in writing in the mid-seventh century. Some anodynely contend that the root word itself, Alsace, means simply 'the land of the [River] Ill'. Francophile philologists disagree, insisting that it is of Celtic origin, from *alis* meaning 'rock' and *atia* meaning 'in the region of', signifying a land at the foot of hills. Others (with equal plausibility) propose that the word truly derives from the Germanic *ali* or 'other' and *saz* or 'establishment', meaning 'the place where strangers have settled'. Ask Alsatians and they do not know. Ask them next if they are German or French and they will tell you that they are Alsatians.

Strasbourg, Mulhouse and Colmar

Strasbourg is dear to my memory not just because of the onion tart I ate there once in the place Gutenberg. I remember it also for spinach tarts, which I soon learned cost much less than the onion tart, provided I didn't buy them in the most expensive square in the city. Nowhere, however humble the restaurant, have I found that the chefs stint on the rich ingredients of *tarte aux épinards*. In Alsace a reasonably sized spinach tart is a concoction made from 125g (5oz) *pâté brisé*, 25g (1oz) butter, a finely chopped onion, two medium sized eggs, 125ml (5fl oz) single cream, 250g (9oz) finely chopped cooked spinach, some seasoning and 150g (5½oz) sliced Gruyère cheese.

If you would like the Alsatian method of cooking spinach tart, here it is. A 22-cm (8½-in) flan ring is lined with the pastry. The onions are gently cooked in butter or fat until they are soft but not brown. Then the eggs, beaten with the cream, are stirred into the onions and the spinach. Half of the cheese is placed on the bottom of the flan and the spinach mixture spooned over it, with the remaining slices of cheese placed on top. Finally the dish is baked in a moderate oven for about thirty minutes.

Thus fortified, one can set out on a satisfying tour of Strasbourg, a city inhabited long ago by Bronze Age men and women, conquered by the Romans in 12 BC and rebuilt by the Carolingians as one of the strategic towns of their empire, straddling the Rhine, waxing rich on trade, and taxing those who traded along the great river.

Paul Claudel called its cathedral the 'great pink angel of Strasbourg'. The warm sandstone of Notre-Dame de Strasbourg rises where once the Romans built a temple to the God of war. The first Christian church to stand here was constructed on the orders of Clovis in the first half of the sixth century and consecrated in 510. The Swedes burnt it down. In 1016 a second cathedral was built, a massive Romanesque church with a semi-circular apse. Nearly 200 years later Bishop Conrad of Hüneberg commissioned a complete rebuilding of the east end, at a moment when the Romanesque was about to give way to the Gothic style. Slowly the old Romanesque cathedral was to be transformed. The choir, the apse and the chapel of Saint-Andrew were finished around 1190. By 1220 the north crossing had been completed.

But new architectural ideas were in the air. Bishop Berthold de Teck, who ruled the Church in Strasbourg from 1223 to 1244, commissioned a French architect to build him a magnificent Gothic nave. Its slender pillars and delicate arches make it one of France's most beautiful religious interiors. The work took some forty years to accomplish. Then in 1277 masons began building the west façade. Seven years later the remarkable Erwin von Steinbach took charge, overseeing the astounding sculptures that were completed by the turn of the century, and succeeded as architect at his death in 1318 by his son Jean.

Now a succession of geniuses took charge of the great building. The magnificent rose window was completed by the mid-fourteenth century. In 1384 the architect Michael Parler of Freibourg built the bell-tower. Ulrich von Ensingen, who was architect of Ulm cathedral, began work on the octagon of the spire in 1399. Johannes Hütz of Cologne designed the spire itself in 1419, though it was not finished till 1439.

To walk along the narrow rue Mercière, a medieval street filled with lovely domestic buildings, and to emerge at the west end of the cathedral is a breathtaking experience.

> That hallow'd spire which rises to the skies,
> Fills ev'ry heart with rapture and surprise

as David Garrick wrote in 1764. The façade itself is sixty-five metres high and forty-four metres wide. The spire rises to 141 metres. Until the nineteenth century it remained the tallest spire in Christendom. Part of the stunning effect of the cathedral derives from the fact that it is asymmetrical. Secondly, the pierced octagon of the spire with its statues adds its own delicacy and lightness to the building. Thirdly, the rose window, with its sixteen petals, peers through slender tracery and is surmounted by a loggia containing statues of the twelve apostles. The third apostle is said to bear the features of Erwin von Steinbach himself. The statues of Carolingian and Merovingian kings, riding their horses on either side of the loggia, were redone in the nineteenth century.

The thirteenth-century statues on the west end of Strasbourg cathedral are magical. Though many of them were mutilated at the time of the revolution, all have been judiciously restored. The left porch is decorated with scenes from Jesus's childhood, along with carvings of virtues slaying vices. In the central doorway the Madonna is flanked by prophets. Jesus's passion and crucifixion are movingly portrayed. The enthroned statues of Solomon and the Virgin here are both modern. Twelve lions above the gable represent the twelve tribes of Israel. And the right doorway is embellished with statues of the wise and foolish virgins, the wise beckoned by Jesus, the foolish tempted by Satan, as well as with a Last Judgment. A secular note is provided by carvings of the signs of the zodiac and the traditional labours of each month.

Strasbourg cathedral is powerfully supported by flying buttresses. On the north side Jacques de Landshut between 1495 and 1505 added the chapel of Saint-Lawrence, whose doorway is a superb example of the French flamboyant style, topped with pinnacles, sheltered by a garlanded baldachin, sculpted with the martyrdom of St Lawrence along with statues of the three Wise Men, Lawrence again, a Madonna and Saints Gregory, James, Maurice and Vincent. The sculptor was named Jean and he came from Aix-la-Chapelle.

Yet more exquisite Gothic statues decorate the Romanesque doorway of the south transept. One represents the Jewish synagogue and, with the Christian triumphalism of the time, she is shown blindfold, deluded. By contrast the powerful allegorical figure of the Church triumphant gazes confidently to the future. (These statues are in fact copies; the originals are in the cathedral museum.) In the lunettes of the doorway are two reliefs depicting the death and coronation of the Virgin Mary, masterpieces of 1230, while two more statues (this time nineteenth-century) represent Solomon and, again, the Virgin.

Above this doorway is the external face of Strasbourg cathedral's celebrated astronomical clock. Its colourful face in no way prepares you for the magnificent Renaissance clock inside the cathedral. It was begun in 1547 (replacing one built in the mid-fourteenth century), abandoned and then completed in the early 1570s. Many hands – those of clockmakers, mathematicians, architects and painters – contributed to its design. The astronomical part indicates not only eclipses, the phases of the moon and the movement of the planets, but also the feasts of the Christian year. Every quarter of an hour wooden figures appear: Christ pursues Death on the hour; the four ages of man ring the quarters; at half-past noon the apostles appear for the Master's blessing, he blesses those who have come to watch the scene, and a crowing cock spreads its wings.

In the south transept there is another masterpiece, the so-called Angel pillar. Whereas the vault of the north transept is supported by a massive column, here is a cluster of eight slender pillars. Carved on these are first, the four evangelists, and then above them four angels with trumpets, and above them the enthroned Jesus, surrounded by more angels who carry the symbols of his passion. An unknown sculptor created this pillar in the early thirteenth century.

Strasbourg cathedral's nave is so uncluttered that you might almost miss the masterpieces inside. Half-way along it stands a marvellous pulpit, carved in the 1480s for one of the city's most famous preachers, Geiler von Kaysersberg. Look out for the carving of a dog asleep. Popular legend has it that this was Geiler's dog, enjoying its customary doze while its master harangued the faithful. To the left you see the organ case, dating from 1385 though enlarged by an organ and case which were built by Friedrich Krebs in 1489. The organ was rebuilt by Andreas Silbermann in 1741. The case is ornamented by curious carvings: a bearded Samson sitting on a lion; a guardsman playing a trumpet; and a marionette which in medieval times would open its mouth and mock the preacher and congregation.

Veit Wagner sculpted a scene of Jesus in the Garden of Gethsemane in 1498. He was commissioned by the church of Saint-Thomas, Strasbourg, but it was brought to the cathedral in 1667. From elsewhere too come two fine sixteenth-century gilded and painted triptychs, which today flank the stairs to the choir. The apse itself is beautiful in proportion, but I find it spoiled by a painted nineteenth-century ceiling which imitates a Byzantine mosaic and by the 1956 stained glass by Max Ingrand. This, however, is the only poor glass in Strasbourg cathedral, for all the rest, in the transepts, the chapels and the Romanesque crypt, date from the thirteenth and fourteenth centuries. Here are Old and New Testament scenes, along with saints, martyrs and emperors. The glass in the rose window was restored in the nineteenth century, but restored so well that you would never guess. The glass in the two rose windows high up in the south wall is thirteenth-century.

That delightfully opinionated American traveller Charles Hitchcock Sherrill described the cathedral's astronomical clock as ridiculous. The stained glass, dating from the twelfth to the fifteenth century, thrilled him. 'Perhaps we ought to examine the windows in due chronological order,' he wrote, 'but if you have any red blood in your veins, any susceptibility to beauty, you simply cannot be so systematic. You will doubtless enter by the south portal in the western front. Almost everybody does except those who come only to see the famous clock, and they do not count! I defy you to resist the immediate spell of this vast cavern of deep glowing colour opening before and above you.' Charles Sherrill's advice was 'plunge headlong into the deep pool of its beauties, and cast chronological sequence to the winds'. I agree.

The intimate, pedestrianized cathedral square offers a delightful contrast to the mighty cathedral. Here is the Kammerzell house, whose stone lower storey was built in the fifteenth century, to be topped with the elaborately carved upper storeys at the request of Martin Braun, who bought it as a warehouse in 1571. Though today the Kammerzell is a restaurant, the winch for hauling up goods still survives. Nearby is one of the oldest dispensing chemists in Europe, the Pharmacy of the Deer (la pharmacie du cerf), again with a stone-built ground floor topped this time by half-timbered upper storeys. To the south of the cathedral stands the château de Rohan, which Robert de Cotte designed for the bishops of Strasbourg in an attempt to outdo Versailles. Its main façade looks out not into the square but over the River Ill. The façade overlooking the place du Château boasts allegorical statues by Robert de Lorraine. Today the château de Rohan houses the museums of fine art, archaeology and decorative art. The porcelain collection of the last of the three is almost unrivalled.

West of the château are yet more picturesque houses, in the place Marché aux Cochons de Lait, where once pigs were bought and sold. No. 1 used to be a bootmakers, and its sign derives from the occasion in 1415 when the Emperor Sigismund reached here when the snow was so thick on the ground that his boots were ruined. The ladies of Strasbourg generously kitted him out with a new pair. Nearby the former customs house, first built on the riverside in 1385 and enlarged in the sixteenth and eighteenth centuries, is now Strasbourg's museum of modern art. Here are displayed not only masterpieces by those you might expect: Picasso, Dufy, Degas, Braque and the like, but also a work that seems to have strayed from *fin-de-siècle* Vienna, 'The Kiss' by Gustav Klimt. Above all, the museum celebrates the two geniuses of twentieth-century Strasbourg painting, Sophie-Tauber Arp and her husband Hans.

Walk west past the bridge of Saint-Nicolas and along the quayside to reach the church and square of Saint-Thomas. This stern Gothic church dates chiefly from the thirteenth and fourteenth centuries, and inside lies the magnificent tomb of the bastard and Protestant marshal of France, Maurice Saxe, a tomb which Jean-Baptiste Pigalle and his apprentices laboured over between 1756 and 1777. This is by no means the only great tomb in the church of Saint-Thomas. Bishop Adeloch, who died in the early twelfth century, lies in a fine sculpted sarcophagus. As for the grisly early-sixteenth-century monument to Nicolas Roeder de Diersbourg, its sculpted half-skeleton/half-corpse makes my stomach turn. Speedily turn away and look at the rose window or the Silbermann organ (on which Albert Schweitzer used to play).

Between the church of Saint-Thomas and what are still called the 'Covered Bridges' (though long ago they ceased to be covered) lies 'La Petite France', a quaint neighbourhood of Strasbourg so named because it once housed a hospital for treating soldiers with syphilis (i.e. the 'little French disease'). Today it has been exquisitely restored, its corbelled, half-timbered houses washed by the River Ill, its restaurants still surprisingly cheap. Here I once ate chicken that had been poached in white wine and flavoured with herbs and vegetables – carrots, an onion, some leeks and celery stalks. I ate it with rice and liked it so much that I went back the next day to try the house *rognons de veau aux raisins* – tender kidneys cooked in oil and dry white wine, and then simmered in a casserole with white grapes for a few minutes.

Make your way back along rue du Fossé-des-Tanneurs to the place Kléber, named after Strasbourg's most celebrated general. Philippe Gras, a sculptor of the city, set up Kléber's statue in 1840, but the square itself is basically the creation of Louis XV's architect Jacques-François Blondel. Kléber's mortal remains lay buried underneath the statue until the Nazis removed them and buried his urn in the cemetery at Kronenbourg. They also removed the statue, but after

World War II the people of Strasbourg moved it back.

From here rue des Grandes-Arcades leads south-east to place Gutenberg. Here in 1840 the sculptor David d'Angers created a monumental bronze statue of the inventor of printing. He leans on his press, holding a page with the inscription 'And there was light.' Gutenberg's invention is compared to God's creation of the universe. Four panels in bas-relief depict the enormous benefits said to have flowed from printing (including even the freeing of black slaves). Since until 1781 this square was known as Strasbourg's vegetable market, it is flanked by a remarkable Renaissance building of 1585, the Chamber of Commerce. The bust over the doorway is that of Hermes, patron of commerce and markets.

There is much more to be seen in Strasbourg, and I have written about some if it elsewhere in this book. But we must hurry to Mulhouse, partly to visit its extraordinary collection of museums, but chiefly to see the magnificent stained glass of its Protestant parish church.

'We found a very beautiful big plain, flanked on the left hand by hillsides covered with vineyards of the most beautiful and best cultivated sort and of such an extent that the Gascons who were there said they had never seen so many in succession.' So Michel de Montaigne dictated to his secretary as they approached Mulhouse on 29 September 1580. The vintage was in progress, and they dined at the Sign of the Grapes.

Their host was a Mulhouse councillor, indeed the president of the city council, yet on his return from the council meeting ('held,' Montaigne observed, 'in a very magnificent gilded palace') he found it no shame to serve his guests at table. Montaigne, warming to him, 'took infinite pleasure in seeing the freedom and good government of this nation'.

Michel de Montaigne was an eirenic, ecumenical man if ever there was one, and the French visitors were delighted at the way in which Catholicism and Protestantism, so divisive elsewhere, seemed to have found a *modus vivendi* at Mulhouse. 'A man without retinue or authority who served them with drink,' Montaigne's secretary recorded, 'had led four companies of foot into France against the king.' Yet he also told them that, though a Protestant, he had no scruples about serving the king against the Huguenots. As for mixed marriages, 'They indiscriminately marry women of our religion before the priest,' the scribe noted, 'and do not force them to change.'

'Monsieur de Montaigne went to see the church,' his secretary recalled, 'for they are not Catholics here. He found it, like the churches throughout the country, in good condition; for there is almost nothing changed, except for the altars and images, whose absence was not found disfiguring.'

The town hall of Mulhouse, built in 1551, remains much as it was in Montaigne's day. In 1858 the Protestants, for some reason, decided to dismantle their fourteenth-century church of Saint-Étienne and replace it with the present neo-Gothic building. They had the excellent sense to take out the stained-glass windows from the old church and put them in the new one. Nowhere else in the world have I found precious glass that you can examine so closely, without any supervision and with a fascination that comes from seeing at first hand colours at once warm and surviving through the centuries. The green of the sea and the scales of the whale that clasps a pink-clad Jonah in its jaws remain as clear as they must have appeared when they first emerged from the kiln.

Mulhouse also astonishes the visitor by its number of celebrated, sometimes quaint museums. The most important – not necessarily the most intriguing – is that in the town hall (place de la Réunion), the Musée historique. Apart from a large section appropriately devoted to Mulhouse itself, the museum includes much regional history, comprising archaeological finds, beginning with those made in 1858 in the tumulus of the Rixheim forest, and extremely rich neolithic finds made since 1962. To these have been added Bronze Age and Iron Age treasures. Masterpieces from churches throughout the region have been brought here. Games, dolls, glass, furniture, faience stoves, ceramics, the works of local writers, caricaturists, artists, metal-workers and sculptors are on display. The Musée historique opens except for Tuesdays from 10.00 to 12.00 and from 14.00 to 17.00 (closing one hour later from 15 June to the end of September). It also closes on New Year's Day, Mayday, Easter Monday and Whit Monday.

The Musée des Beaux-Arts is the eighteenth-century maison Steinbach at No. 4, place Guillaume-Tell. The most celebrated local artist whose works are displayed here is Jean-Jacques Henner (1826–1905), followed by Léon Lehmann (1873–1953), a friend of Matisse, Dufy and Rouault.

Artists of international renown whose works are on display here include Courbet, Rigaud and Cranach the Younger. A 'Venus and Cupid' is attributed to Cranach. Pieter Bruegel the Younger contributes a skating scene. From Boucher's hand is a 'Judgment of Paris'. This museum's opening times coincide with those of the Musée historique.

The Musée de l'Impression sur Étoffes at No. 3, rue des Bonnes-Gens is unique in the world. Printed textiles prove extraordinarily rich, the museum drawing on all five continents for magnificent examples of the genre, bringing together an archive of eight million patterns and designs, displaying textile machinery and including the achievements of the celebrated Mulhouse textile factories from 1746 to the present day.

Mulhouse's textile museum is open every day, except Friday mornings, from 10.00 to 12.00 and from 14.00 to 17.00 (closing an hour later from May to September). From May to September fascinating demonstrations of textile printing are given on Mondays and Wednesdays at 14.30. You can get in free on Sunday mornings.

Almost as unique is the French railway museum (Musée français du Chemin de fer) in rue Alfred de Glehm (in the western suburb of Dombach). The word 'French' conceals the fact that this collection ranges the length and breadth of Europe, beginning in the 1840s. The oldest locomotive on display dates from 1844, is called 'Saint-Pierre' and would steam from Paris to Rouen at sixty kilometres an hour. In one huge hall are twenty-four steam locomotives, two electric trains, five driven by other ingenious methods and other rolling stock, all standing on some 860 metres of track. Here are the great European trains of yesteryear, including the lamented Golden Arrow. Some of the locos occasionally burst into life, startling visitors to the museum, which opens every single day from 10.00 to 17.00, except for Mayday, Christmas Day and Boxing Day. Since it does not close for lunch, you can eat here at its cafeteria. Next to it is an entertaining fireman's museum (Musée des Sapeurs-Pompiers).

Equally remarkable is Mulhouse's automobile museum, the Musée Schlumpf, at No. 192, avénue de Colmar. The name refers to the Swiss brothers Schlumpf (Hans and Fritz), who founded it as a private museum. Only when their industrial empire collapsed in 1976 did this virtually secret museum become a national trust. Its pride is the Bugatti collection, including two of the great 'Royal Bugattis' of which only three other examples survive in the world. Naturally the firm of Rolls-Royce is given due honour, as are Hispano-Suiza, Mercedes, Porsche, Alfa-Romeo and the rest. The museum is said to be open every day except Fridays from 10.00 to 17.00, though I advise enquiring at the Mulhouse tourist office before setting out on a visit.

In the suburb of Rixheim, five kilometres along the main road to Basel, is a wallpaper museum (Musée du Papier peint, at No. 28, rue Zuber). Here in 1796 the Zuber family founded a wallpaper factory and developed brilliant techniques and equipment, all on display along with letters, patterns, dyes and above all examples of the art. The museum has the additional delight of being housed in a wing of the former commandery of the Teutonic knights, which Jean Zuber had bought and turned into his family factory. It opens daily except Tuesdays from 10.00 to 12.00 and from 14.00 to 18.00.

Finally the former chapel of the knights of Malta (opposite the library in the Grand'Rue at Mulhouse), built in 1351, now houses the Musée lapidaire. The Reformation interrupted plans to decorate this chapel with wall-paintings created by the workshop of Hans Herbster of Basel, which at this time included both Hans Holbein the Younger and his wife, and the work remains alas incomplete. The museum's chief contents are medieval tombstones and stone sculptures, as well as some fragmentary sculptures from the abbey of Lucelle. Here are given regular concerts, and the museum is open daily save Tuesdays from 10.00 to 12.00 and from 14.00 to 17.00. (It also closes on Whit Monday and 14 July).

Mulhouse means the house of the mill. Colmar's derivation is far less peaceable, unless one accepts that it comes from the Roman *colombaria* (i.e. place of the doves). More likely is the derivation *colles Martis*, the hills of Mars. Its citizens have fought bravely in wartime, for Napoleon at the revolution, and against the Nazis in 1944. One famous military response was made by a Colmar soldier to General Rapp in Napoleonic times. Rapp asked him where he came from. 'I am from Colmar, *mon général*,' replied the soldier, 'and if I wasn't from Colmar, I'd be ashamed.'

If legend is true, Colmar has also seen some warlike women as well. In 1235 the Emperor Frederick II fell out with his Alsace governor, the ambitious Wölfelin, and confiscated his goods. Wölfelin's wife promptly murdered her husband in case her goods were also seized.

Little survives in Colmar from before the thirteenth century, save for its ecclesiastical buildings, yet today it has the appearance of a sleepy medieval town. The parish church of Saint-Martin was begun in 1263; and its little south porch dedicated to Saint-Nicolas is a thirteenth-century treat, with its merry grotesque masks. The church of the Dominicans began to be built in 1283, and the Franciscan church was started in 1292. Saint-Martin is still called Colmar's cathedral, though the city has no bishop. After a fire in 1572, a belfry was added to the south tower. Its octagonal choir, built in 1366 by Guillaume de Marbourg, boasts intricate stalls which reveal the unsung skills of nineteenth-century woodcarvers. The remaining fifteenth-century stained glass is worth an hour of anyone's scrutiny. As our enthusiast Charles Sherrill noted in 1927, the middle panel shows St Martin arrayed as the Bishop of Tours engaged in the cheery task of leading a skeleton by the hand. 'Perhaps the saint's gruesome companion depicts someone he raised from the dead,' Sherrill guessed, adding, 'in any event it is a unique picture on ancient glass.'

The Dominican church stands on the corner of the rue des Boulangers and the place des Dominicains. In 1283 Emperor Rudolph of Habsburg laid the first stone of this simple and utterly satisfying building, but the whole church was not completed until the fourteenth century. The nave dates from around 1320. The fourteenth-century stained-glass windows are outrageously beautiful. The choir stalls were made in the eighteenth century by Gabriel Ignaz Ritter of Guebwiller. All these masterpieces pale beside the painting of the Blessed Virgin amidst roses, done by Martin Schongauer in the fourteenth century, a superb picture in a superb church. In 1972 it was stolen, only to be recovered a year later at Lyons.

Martin Schongauer is also well represented in the nearby Unterlinden Museum, housed in the former Dominican convent. He was born here at Colmar sometime between 1445 and 1450, the son of a goldsmith named Casper. Casper Schongauer had moved to Colmar from Bavaria, and his son too led a peripatetic life, studying at the University of Leipzig, living for some time in Flanders and buying property not only in the town of his birth but also in Breisach. This pattern of life enriched his skills, as a painter and master engraver. In Flanders, for instance, he grew to admire the work of Roger van der Weyden, developing Weyden's skills at giving depth and delicately varied tones to his work.

Soon Schongauer was known throughout Europe by the nickname 'Beautiful Martin', a play on his name (Schön Martin), which became 'Beau Martin' in French and 'Bel Martino' in Italy. At Colmar he set up an important school of engravers. Its pupils spread as far as Nuremberg and deeply influenced later German art – including that of Dürer's assistant Hans Baldung Grien, who later migrated to Strasbourg and became a member of the city council there.

But the acknowledged masterpiece in the Unterlinden Museum at Colmar, in spite of Schongauer's superb Orlier altarpiece, is the polyptych which Mathias Grünewald painted in 1515 for the Hospital of St Anthony at Isenheim. Grünewald was born in Würzburg in the second half of the fifteenth century. By the time of his death in 1528 he was, like Hans Baldung Grien, sympathizing with the Protestant Reformation. Unlike Grien he kept these sympathies to himself, probably because most of his commissions came from Catholics. What appears in his paintings is neither specifically Catholic nor Protestant, but a unique Christian vision, mystical and at the same time sometimes grimly realistic.

The nine panels of the Isenheim polyptych display his astonishingly varied skills. They depict the annunciation and birth of Jesus, his crucifixion, the lamentation of his mother and followers, his resurrection and finally scenes from the life of St Anthony. The crucifixion is horrifying. Jesus hangs pock-marked and rotting, his blood-spattered body green and corrupt. Yet the painting was not designed simply to shock. The Antonites at Isenheim ran their hospital to nurse the epileptic, the gangrenous and the syphilitic. Grünewald's altarpiece depicts the dying Jesus as identified with them, especially the latter two groups. In another panel their hope is radiantly displayed in an exquisite, etherealized resurrected Christ.

Only eleven other paintings by Grünewald survive, and crowds flock to see this Isenheim altarpiece. See it of course, but also find time to wander round the rest of the impressive art collection housed in what must be one of the loveliest art galleries in France.

Colmar is littered with fine old houses: in the rue Mercière stands the maison Pfister of 1537; close by in the rue des Marchands is the Haus zum Kragen, which the sculptor Adam Keller decorated in 1609 with a bearded effigy of himself; and countless others. In their dialect the citizens call their former customs house the Koifhus, its eighteenth-century roof blazoned with coloured tiles, its balconies bespeaking the rich past of this city. Outside the customs house the sculptor Bartholdi in 1897 created a statue of the imperial general Lazarus von Schwendi. He brandishes not a sword but a bunch of Tokay grapes.

Just as Strasbourg has its watery 'Petite France', so Colmar has its own 'little Venice', some say yet more charming, washed by the River Lauch which reflects begonias and half-timbered houses in its waters. In 'little Venice' I often wonder how the tetchy Voltaire could have described Colmar as 'half-German, half-French and completely Iroquois' (by which he meant savage). Georges Duhamel's alternative judgment is worth repeating: Colmar, he wrote, 'is the most beautiful city in the world'. For once Voltaire was wrong. Duhamel was closer to the mark.

Gems of Alsace

Altkirch

The hill-top town of Altkirch, peering down at the River Ill, once belonged to the counts of Ferrette, who gave it as a dowry to the house of Austria in 1324. Occupied by the Swedes in 1633, it was ceded to France by the Peace of Westphalia in 1648.

From the high Middle Ages dates the church of Saint-Christophe. Above it the village developed around the château of the counts. Of its fortifications survives the fourteenth-century main gate. Napoleon's General Kléber designed the eighteenth-century town hall, with a French façade and a Germanic tiled roof. There are numerous twelfth-century houses, and where once was situated the château now stands the neo-Romanesque church of Saint-Morand, which retains not only the saint's tomb and twelfth-century statues but also a twelfth-century tympanum with Christ between Saints Peter and Paul. Altkirch lies in fine hunting, riding and fishing country. The neo-Gothic fountain in the place de la République, set up in 1853 to bear a sixteenth-century statue of the Virgin Mary, fits in well with the ambience of old Altkirch.

To the right of the town hall the former baillif's house, built in the sixteenth century, now houses a museum of Sundgau art and local history, with works by the local artists Jean-Jacques Henner and his disciple Léon Lehmann, the friend of Rouault. For more on Altkirch see the index to this book.

Ammerschwihr

Along with the remains of its square keep, the former thirteenth-century château, the wine village of Ammerschwihr has preserved of its fortifications three impressive gates: the sixteenth-century 'thiefs' gate' (so named because it also served as a prison); the sixteenth-century gate of the burghers, giving on to ancient streets; and the thirteenth-century Obertor. In the place du Marché stands a fountain dedicated to a wild man (la fontaine de l'homme sauvage), set here in 1569. The former town hall dates from 1552 and was much damaged at the end of World War II. The church of Saint-Martin was built two years later than the town hall and shelters a Christ riding on a donkey on the way to Jerusalem sculpted in the sixteenth century – to be found in the side chapel on the south – as well as a huge Christ crucified of 1606, hanging at the entrance to the choir and flanked by gilded carvings of the Virgin and St John; a pretty sixteenth-century staircase leading up to the organ loft; a neo-Gothic bell-tower constructed in 1910; and a massive statue of Jesus displaying his sacred heart, dating from 1930.

This is one of the towns of Alsace whose citizens love to decorate their windows with flowers. It is hard to accept that much of the village (including its church) is a restoration, after the destruction of December 1944. Its wine fair takes place during the first fortnight of April. See the index to this book.

Andlau

The ruins of the thirteenth/fourteenth-century château of Haut-Andlau are magnificent. Its treasures include two circular keeps, round towers and Gothic gateways and windows. To the north on the Kastelberg is another ruined château, also dating from the thirteenth and fourteenth centuries, with a polygonal wall and a square keep.

The town itself is crammed with half-timbered houses, ornamented with carved corners and pointed gables, notable among them the Renaissance house at No. 15, Grand'Rue (once the town hall) with its balustrade and two oriel windows; the house known as the barracks (la Caserne) at No. 17, rue du Docteur Stoltz, whose courtyard doorway is dated 1573; and the eighteenth-century canons' houses, one of which boasts Romanesque arcades.

Andlau grew up around an abbey founded by St Richarde (Charlemagne's wife) in the ninth century. The abbey-church of

Sainte-Richarde, though its Gothic nave was restructured in the seventeenth century, is a Romanesque treasure, with a superb twelfth-century east end, with a sculpted frieze no less than thirty metres long, depicting magical imaginary beasts (with an occasional real one), carved in the third decade of the twelfth century, and a carved tympanum which depicts Jesus blessing the founder of the abbey, flanked by David and Goliath and Samson and the lion he so easily killed. The abbey's square tower is topped by an eighteenth-century dome. Its choir dates from the same century, its Gothic nave from 1698 to 1702. Inside, you can find St Richarde's reliquary (*c.*1400); fine stalls and a statue of the Virgin, both dating from the fifteenth century; fifteenth-century flamboyant balustrades, and a baroque pulpit made around 1700 which Samson himself is carrying. The eleventh-century crypt, which you reach by steps in the north crossing, is filled with more saints' bones in their reliquaries.

If you have time to visit the eighteenth-century church of Saint-André which stands at the eastern exit of the town, you will discover that it incorporates a fifteenth-century bell-tower and frescos painted early in the same century (if not a little earlier). The town hall square has a nineteenth-century fountain embellished with St Richarde accompanied by a bear. It is also flanked by a Renaissance house of 1552, notable for its tower and gable. From here the street that leads to the church has a fifteenth-century well, also decorated with St Richarde and her bear.

Aubure

Surrounded by pine forests, Aubure is the highest inhabited village in Alsace, 800 metres above sea-level and situated between the crest of the Vosges mountains and the Alsace plain. Tourists come for its bracing climate, and the hiking which reaches its apôgée at the 1,041-metre-high signal d'Aubure and the 1,229-metre-high summit of the Brézouard. Marauding troops destroyed the village during the Thirty Years' War, but it recovered its prosperity by weaving, farming and setting itself up as a health resort.

Take the D11 for seven kilometres to reach Fréland, a village made up of isolated hamlets and out-of-the-way houses and farms. The name of this village means 'free land', and derives from the fact that the charcoal burners who established themselves here in the fourteenth century were exempted from taxes. It boasts an eighteenth-century church and a neo-Gothic chapel at the other side of the river.

Avolsheim

Devotees of thirteenth-century frescos should make their way to Avolsheim in Bas-Rhin, situated where the River Mossig meets the canal de la Bruche (which Louis XIV's renowned engineer Vauban constructed). Here is one of the oldest sanctuaries of the province, the tiny chapel of Saint-Ulrich which was built just before the year 1000 and stands next to the parish church of 1911. The dome of the chapel is decorated with thirteenth-century paintings depicting in a simple, gracious fashion evangelists and angels. In 1160 the chapel was embellished with an octagonal bell-tower. The Alsatian Pope Leo IX gave this chapel a reliquary containing a part of St Ulrich.

Look out for the cemetery to the south of Avolsheim. Locals claim that the massive lime tree of Avolsheim sheltering the cemetery chapel is over a thousand years old, and they dub the chapel Dompeter (or Domus Petri, i.e. 'house of the apostle Peter'). In this unlikely spot Christianity was first established in Alsace. Dompeter is a typical Merovingian word, and excavations carried out in 1914 established that the foundation of this chapel dates from the fifth century. Its bell-tower over the doorway is much younger, added in 1767; the apse was rebuilt in 1829; but the nave remains that consecrated by Leo IX in 1049. Go inside to admire the polychrome wood statues of the sixteenth, seventeenth and eighteenth centuries, as well as an eighteenth-century reliquary containing the head of St Petronilla, given by Leo IX to the church when he consecrated the nave.

Barr

This exquisite old town, seventeen kilometres' drive from Sélestat, is situated among vineyards at the foot of the Vosges mountains and where the valley of the River Kirbeck opens up. Some of the finest vintners' houses can be found at the heart of the town. Untouched by the fighting here between American and German troops in November 1944, Barr has preserved twisting streets and ancient houses with projected upper storeys and courtyards and gables. Light industries, such as shoemaking and tanneries, have failed to spoil its ambience.

The paved town hall square (place de l'Hôtel de Ville) stands on the site of the former château and is a seventeenth-century building entirely in keeping with the other half-timbered houses of the square and the fountain. Go inside to see the double staircase in the Louis-XV style and the colonaded pavilion. In the square itself a grille marks the spot where formerly began an underground passageway leading from the château of Barr to the château of Landsberg, seven kilometres away.

Barr celebrates in one way or another each Sunday in summer, celebrations that swell the town with tourists sampling its various fine wines. The two major wine festivals occur in mid-July, when the town hosts a celebrated wine fair, and at the wine harvest, whose festival is held on the second Sunday in October.

Just as you leave Barr to the north, at No. 10, rue du Docteur Sultzer, is an eighteenth-century folly. Built in 1763 by the baillif of Barr, Louis-Félix Marco (who died penniless), it is now known as the museum of la Folie Marco. Dedicated mostly to displaying French and Alsatian furniture of the eighteenth and nineteenth centuries, it is well worth a visit simply to enjoy the careful re-creation of the interior of a house of yesteryear, to relish its ceramics, its eighteenth-century mahogany furniture and to climb its intricate twisting staircase. Its main room is decorated to display man's three vital drinks: water, beer and wine.

Don't forget a visit to its so-called 'English' garden (on the left of the house) and above all to its cellar, purveying the wines of Barr, which you naturally taste before buying. Both house and cellar are closed on Tuesdays. Otherwise you can visit the house from June to September from 10.00 to 12.30 and from 14.30 to 18.00. As for the cellar, except for the Tuesday day of rest, it is open all the year round from 10.00 to 18.00.

Close by Barr is Mittelbergheim, an ancient village one and a half kilometres to the south, boasting an ancient town hall, winding streets and fine Renaissance houses. Either at Mittelbergheim or at Barr, sample the snails.

Benfeld

In 1331 a traitor named Stubenhansel betrayed Benfeld to its enemies, the house of Wurttemberg. When the citizens rebuilt their town hall in 1530, they added to it a clock tower with three working models, one of whom represents the dastardly Stubenhansel, the other two a knight who strikes the hours and Death, turning over and over his hour-glass. In one hand the traitor holds the bag of gold which bought him, in the other he carries a baton, which he waves every hour while his mouth opens and closes soundlessly.

The bishops of Strasbourg who were lords of Benfeld as early as

765 found the village a handy retreat, since it lies no more than twenty-eight kilometres from their cathedral. In 1306 Bishop Jean de Dirpheim fortified his retreat. During the Thirty Years' War the Swedes demolished the fortifications. The bishops' castle lasted longer – it was demolished only in 1855. On its site now stands a huge building known as a Régie, the depot for tobacco, a major industry here since the poisonous weed was introduced to Alsace by a misanthropist named Benjamin Maucier in 1618.

Benfeld's neo-classical church of Saint-Laurent dates from the early 1840s, but it retains its fourteenth-century Gothic choir and houses a fifteenth-century font and stone tombs. The town is blessed with delightful half-timbered houses.

Two kilometres north-east on the E1 is the site of the Roman town of Heelvetum (or Ellelum), where archaeologists have uncovered a treasure-trove of Roman remains.

Bennwihr

Half-way between Colmar and Riquewihr, the wine village of Bennwihr was almost entirely destroyed during World War II and is an example of what can be done when a community decides to restore its lost architectural treasures. The citizens are also proud of their modern parish church of Saint-Pierre (designed by the architects Pouradier and Pillon and completed in 1960; a man named Martineau is responsible for its stained glass), which I cannot say I like. The wine festival is very pleasant, on the first Sunday in August, and makes palatable even a visit to this modern church. Twinned with Bennwihr is nearby Mittelwihr, whose vine-covered slopes are said to be the sunniest in Alsace. The village is guarded by the Mittelberg, a hill whose name has been given to one of their classic vintages. Alas, Mittelwihr too was virtually obliterated at the end of World War II, and its Protestant church dates from 1959. The bell-tower of the former church stands forlornly.

Bergheim

Still fortified and lying some three kilometres from Ribeauvillé, Bergheim's ramparts, fourteenth-century gate and nine towers enfold enchanting narrow streets and courtyards. A village has stood here, under the name 'home' *(Heim)* on the 'mountain' *(Berg)* since the eighth century, but excavations have revealed that its origins go back as far as the Stone Age. Its double ring of walls dates from the early fourteenth century. The château de Reichenberg is a late-nineteenth-century version of the medieval style. By contrast many vintners' houses are genuinely Gothic and Renaissance. This is a village devoted to Gewürztraminer. The town hall dates from 1776; the church of Notre-Dame boasts a Gothic doorway/bell-tower with an adoration of the Magi carved on its tympanum, fifteenth-century wall-paintings, a fourteenth-century apse and choir and a nave built in 1718; the market square retains its old fountain; and next to the church you can find a grisly ossuary of 1550 and a former hospital of the same date. Presumably the first served the second.

Just outside Bergheim is a German military cemetery, with the graves, among others, of parachutists killed in January 1945. Their graves face Rhinewards, towards the homes they will never reach.

Betschdorf

The clays of Betschdorf proved ideal for firing pottery, and still today the ancient tradition of creating blue and grey ceramics is continued here, in a town that lies seventeen kilometres from Haguenau. You can buy them from the potters themselves, in whose kilns the pots and jugs and bowls are baked for up to two whole days at a heat of 1,250 degrees Centigrade. Naturally, there is a museum of pottery.

Betschdorf's long high street is embellished with sixteenth- and seventeenth-century half-timbered houses. In three of its component suburbs the churches are remarkable. That of Niederbetschdorf boasts fifteenth-century frescos contemporary with its polygonal choir and a seventeenth-century name. The frescos depict a busy Last Judgment, the Eucharist and the Lamb of God with the four Evangelists. The church of Oberbetschdorf has a baroque nave and an eighteenth-century bell-tower. The church in the northern suburb of Kuhlendorf, though built in the nineteenth century, is the only half-timbered church in Alsace.

Bischoffsheim

Tradition has it that King Clovis gave this village to St Remi, the saint who converted and baptized him – hence the imposing fountain with a statue of Remi. Later, as the name of Bischoffsheim implies, it became a country seat of the bishops of Strasbourg. Here Franciscans founded a convent. The nearby Bischenberg rises to a height of 381 metres above sea-level. Today the church of the convent of Bischenberg displays both Gothic and baroque features, since it was built from the sixteenth to the eighteenth century. Inside is a Lamentation sculpted in wood around 1500. In the convent cemetery stands a Way of the Cross created in 1732.

Bischwiller

In the twelfth century the bishops of Strasbourg owned a farm here, around which the little town grew, hence its name (town of the bishop or *Bischofswiller*). These religious connotations dropped away, but between 1686 and 1789 new ones were added, especially the annual festival of the minstrels, held on the Feast of the Assumption (15 August) when the minstrel brethren gathered at Bischwiller to celebrate and sing. Although their confederation was then dissolved, Bischwiller on the Sunday after the Feast of the Assumption and on the second Sunday in October still celebrates its Pfifferdag or Minstrels' Day, when the place becomes packed with tourists.

Here the preferred drink is locally brewed beer. Le Laub, the former town hall, is a half-timbered building of 1665. The church of Hanhoffen dates from the twelfth century and painted inside are sixteenth-century frescos.

Boersch

Lying four kilometres from Obernai, Boersch delights the visitor first of all by its total ensemble, especially as displayed in the place de l'Hôtel de Ville, with half-timbered houses, a Renaissance town hall of 1578 and a well of 1617 with no fewer than six buckets. Some of the fortifications built in the mid-fourteenth century at the expense of Bishop Berthold II of Strasbourg remain (especially three gates) to add a further charm. Every turn brings fresh delights, especially from seeing the houses along rue Sainte-Odile. Although the church of Saint-Médard dates mostly from the eighteenth century and boasts a fine altar of 1772, its bell-tower is Romanesque and inside are twelfth-century frescos. Go behind the church to see Christ and his disciples on the Mount of Olives, sculpted in the seventeenth century.

Close by at Saint-Léonard a genius named Charles Spindler (who lived from 1865 to 1958) set up a marquetry works that has become deservedly world-famous. The Kirsch of Boersch is excellent.

Bouxwiller

There are two Bouxwillers in Alsace, the finest lying in the
département of Bas-Rhin some fifteen kilometres from Saverne and
at the entrance to the Vosges natural park. At the foot of the slopes of
the Bastberg, this Bouxwiller boasts in its narrow streets lovely
wooden-faced houses, with gables as well as oriel windows giving on
to balconies. (Look for them especially in the Grand'Rue, the rue des
Seigneurs, around the Protestant church and in the market square,
but in many other streets too.) Numerous old buildings, now used,
for example, as a baker's shop and a drapers, were formerly part of
the château, escaping its general destruction at the time of the
Revolution, as was the Renaissance town hall with its seventeenth-
century reception rooms, façade and roof. It houses a museum of
local history and stands in the enormous place du Château. The Corn
Hall at Bouxwiller was built in 1614. As for the churches, the
Protestant parish church, though in its present form basically a
seventeenth- and eighteenth-century building, incorporates a fourteenth-century bell-tower (topped in the eighteenth-century), a
carved seventeenth-century pulpit and an organ by Silbermann (see
p. 176). The Catholic parish church with its square Gothic tower has
an eighteenth-century baroque nave. In Bouxwiller too there is a
fifteenth-century chapel of Saint-George of Lichtenberg.

Bouxwiller was once the capital of Hanau-Lichtenberg, and its
counts founded the hospital whose grounds (with a fountain and
statues) are still lovely. They became Protestant and set up here a
Latin school in 1612 (the oldest Protestant school in Alsace). In the
mid-eighteenth century landgrave Caroline further embellished the
hospital gardens in the French style.

If you find yourself in the Bouxwiller of Haut-Rhin, which
contains fewer than 350 inhabitants, relish the seventeenth-century
woodwork in the church of Saint-Jacques, which comes from the
former Cistercian monastery at Luppach (suppressed in 1790 and
demolished ten years later), the side altars from the abbey of Lucelle,
and the baroque high altar.

Brumath

The little town of Brumath was long ago the capital city of the
Gaulish Triboci. It developed into a Roman camp (Roman baths
were excavated here in 1968) and then in the thirteenth century

became the capital of the landgraviate of lower Alsace. The Protestant church was formerly the chapel of the eighteenth-century château of Princess Christian of Saxony, redone in the first decade of the nineteenth century in the neo-classical style.

You eat well in Brumath, and if you are there on 24 September you can enjoy the curious experience of attending the great onion fair.

Cernay

Although Cernay was grievously destroyed both in World War I and in World War II, the town retains some of its fortifications of 1268, in particular the Thann gate with its tower (now used as a museum of local history). Here, as well as some industrialization, there are French and German military cemeteries. An old steam train takes one and three-quarter hours to run the fourteen kilometres from Cernay to Sentheim, calling *en route* at Aspach, Burnhaupt and Gewenheim. It runs daily from July to the end of September, and sometimes on Sundays in other months.

Châtenais

Situated on the old Roman route along the Vosges, Châtenais was fortified by the bishops of Strasbourg, which did not prevent first the citizens of Sélestat and then the Armagnacs from taking it. Impressive parts of the thirteenth-century château still remain, in particular the tour des Sorcières where storks have made their nests. The eighteenth-century church of Saint-Georges incorporates a fine Romanesque belfry, a carved stone crucifixion of 1612 and a Silbermann organ. Châtenais also boasts a town hall of 1493 and other Gothic and Renaissance houses. Its citizens happily make and sell wine, standing as Châtenais does where the Alsatian wine route crosses the road from Saint-Dié to Sélestat.

Cleebourg

This delightful village in Bas-Rhin with its narrow streets and old half-timbered houses also preserves parts of two châteaux and a moated defence made of stone and earth, which is scarcely datable but must have been constructed in the early Middle Ages at least.

Dambach-la-Ville

If you want to explore a quintessential Alsatian village try Dambach-la-Ville in Bas-Rhin: decorated everywhere with flowers; still surrounded by the ramparts of 1340 with three impressive gates, all topped with towers; its romantic ruined château retaining intact a pentagonal keep, a chapel in the tower, and its well; old half-timbered houses; the thirteenth-century chapel of Saint-Sébastian with its Romanesque belfry, fourteenth-century Gothic polygonal choir, an early sixteenth-century Madonna, sixteenth-century charnel house, a Calvary dating from 1687 and seventeenth-century high altar with a baroque retable dated 1697, made from oak, pear-wood and lime; the Romanesque-Gothic chapel of Saint-Jean-Baptiste; shoemakers' shops; the fountain of the bear in the place Centrale; a sixteenth-century town hall; a wine-festival on the first Sunday in August; and wrought-iron signs outside shops and workshops.

Dambach is a corruption of Tannenbach, which means 'stream of pine trees', hence the pine in the town's coat of arms.

Dambach-Niederbronn

Although the troops of Louis XIV demolished most of the château of Schoeneck near here in 1680, its towers and bastions, its wall and its Romanesque dwellings are still very much worth visiting, as are two other ruins: château Wineck, again walled, with a square keep built in the twelfth century, and château de Wittschloessel, which stands on a 440-metre-high rock.

Dettwiller

On the banks of the Zorn and the canal de la Marne-au-Rhin, Dettwiller's château, though set on fire in 1879, was not entirely destroyed and two romantic towers remain. Both the churches are eighteenth-century, the Protestant church of Saint-Jacques housing fine funeral monuments of the counts of Rosen (bearing their motif of three roses). Dettwiller is enhanced by a water mill and several half-timbered houses, mostly dating from the seventeenth and eighteenth centuries.

Duppigheim-Kolbsheim

Duppigheim-Kolbsheim on the banks of the River Bruche and the canal de la Bruche is worth visiting for its half-timbered houses, its classical château of 1700 (with lovely terraces, its 'English' park and garden, and a couple of gazebos). The church which both Catholics and Protestants share was built in 1768, with a bell-tower added in 1870. Inside, the furniture is eighteenth-century, and there is a box-pew to set apart the Protestant lords of the manor from the groundlings.

Ebersmunster

Set beside the River Ill, Ebersmunster's former abbey church is a magnificent baroque building of 1727 by the Austrian Peter Thumb, the three arcades of its doorway matched by its three double-onion domes. Thumb was commissioned to replace buildings ruined in the Thirty Years' War. Inside are unusual eighteenth-century wall paintings, those of the Assumption in the dome and the paintings in the choir by Joseph Mages of Tyrol. Roof paintings represent the life of St Benedict (as well as that of St Maurice). The stucco is breathtaking, as are the baroque furnishings (with nineteenth-century statues on the stalls), especially the high altar of 1728 and the two side altars created three years later. The Andreas Silbermann organ, still retaining its original pipes, dates from 1732, and above it is fittingly painted St Cecilia, patron saint of music, and her angel choir. The chandeliers and the ironwork of the gallery match the other fittings of Ebersmunster church.

The monastery here dates back to the mid-seventh century, when it was founded for the Benedictines by Adalric (sometimes called Eticho), duke of Alsace and father of St Odile. Some of the former monastic buildings still remain, as well as beautifully preserved Alsatian houses. The monastic gateway of 1772 is decorated with a carving of St Arbogast, his son Dagobert and a wild boar. The boar had wounded Dagobert, whom Argobast then miraculously healed. The Latin for wild boar is *aper*, hence the name Ebersmunster – 'monastery of the wild boar'.

Every Sunday in May Ebersmunster deploys its Silbermann organ for unmissable 'musical hours'.

Éguisheim

Six kilometres away, in the Unterlinden Museum at Colmar is the oldest excavated skull of Alsace, discovered at the hamlet of Bühl just outside this entrancing wine village. Although Éguisheim means the home of Egino, a German who lived here in the tenth century, its origins can be traced back into prehistory, certainly to palaeolithic times. Stone Age man occupied the site of the three ruined châteaux whose three grey-red keeps dominate the village. (Three châteaux were needed because Egino's successors, the counts of Éguisheim, though pious and charitable, were also quarrelsome, and in the twelfth century some way of separating the three branches of the family was called for.) Here is a prehistoric burial mound. At the entrance to the village once stood a Roman fort; and archaeologists have found around Éguisheim numerous Merovingian and Carolingian sarcophagi.

The family of the counts of Éguisheim has the distinction of providing the Christian Church with a celebrated Alsatian pope and saint, Leo IX. Born here in 1002 to Count Hugo IV of Éguisheim by his wife Countess Heildewige of Dagsburg, he was consecrated bishop of Toul in 1026 and after his election as pope in 1048 insisted until his death in 1054 on the essential unity of the whole Christian Church. Alas, his reign saw the final division between the Catholic Church of the west and the Orthodox Church of the east.

Most tourists will soon forget these ancient discoveries and stories as they wander by way of the remains of no fewer than three concentric sets of fortifications, the first constructed by the bishops of Strasbourg in 1295 (they are but remains because the Armagnacs bashed them down in 1466). Then walk along the old, flower-bedecked streets with their stone-built or half-timbered vintners' houses as far as the still extensive ruins of an octagonal château at the centre of it all, said to have been founded in the eighth century, though its present buildings date essentially from the thirteenth. Its original owner was Count Eberhard, the father of St Odile. Look out for the statue of Leo IX, standing on a fountain in front of the château; also for the interior courtyards of many sixteenth- and seventeenth-century houses.

The streets are circular because so were the ramparts of Éguisheim. On the way watch out too for the fountain of Our Lady, set up in 1542, as well as a couple of other fountains and the White Horse Inn (dated 1613: many of the houses are inscribed with the date of their construction). Here too you can find the old tithe houses and courtyards of the abbeys of Murbach and Ebersmunster. After these riches, find time to visit the church of Saints-Pierre-et-Paul, up the street to the left of the central château. Although the present church was built only in 1807, its belfry is Gothic and has preserved an even older Romanesque portal from the former church. Architectural historians date it around 1235, and the tympanum depicts not only Jesus between the two patron saints of the church but also his parable of the wise and foolish virgins. These carvings are in remarkably good condition, their folding robes looking as if put on only this morning, Jesus holding the Gospels on his knee and blessing us at the same time. I do not like the modern glass inside the church, depicting the life of Leo IX.

In one street an ancient metal plaque depicts the divine blessing of wine when Jesus created it out of water at the wedding at Cana. Éguisheim vintners buy and sell their *vin nouveau* here each year on the last weekend of March.

Ensisheim

Seat of the Habsburgs' regents from 1523 to 1632, the city became known as the abattoir of Alsace because of the brutal way in which the leaders and followers of the Peasants' War were executed here. Colbert de Croissy, Louis XIV's administrator of Alsace from 1648, here set up his government. Ensisheim has preserved intact the regent's palace, built between 1533 and 1547 and now its town hall. Its Renaissance decoration is delightful, and its octagonal tower encloses a staircase leading up to the council chamber, with its fine wood carvings and Renaissance ceiling. Opposite the town hall stands an eighteenth-century baroque church, dating from 1614 to 1764, once belonging to the Jesuits and at present used by the Protestants of the village. Its school is now a borstal. To the left of the borstal stands the Renaissance hôtel de la Couronne, with its magical double oriel window and two gables. Ensisheim also possesses a neo-Gothic church of 1863.

The town suffered much damage at the end of World War II, remaining in German hands until 8 February 1945. It had suffered a similar catastrophe once before, in 1492 when a meteorite fell on its town hall. Bits of it can be seen in the local museum, where also you can see neolithic remains. To the south of Ensisheim you can find the neolithic excavations from which they came.

Ergersheim

This village in Bas-Rhin beside the River Bruche is surrounded by

Merovingian tombs, enhanced by numerous eighteenth-century half-timbered farms, and blessed by an early eighteenth-century chapel of Our Lady (containing fourteenth-, fifteenth- and sixteenth-century statues) as well as by a richly endowed eighteenth-century baroque church with an organ dated 1818.

Erstein

Today the village of Erstein prospers from tobacco, witness the courtyards where the weed is dried and processed. Half-timbered houses lead to a nineteenth-century church in which General de Gaulle at Christmas 1944 was present for the first Midnight Mass celebrated by the liberated Alsatians. Drive four kilometres south-west to reach the Renaissance château at Osthouse, guarded by two medieval towers. The church here houses a fourteenth-century tomb and is decorated with a doorway and tower built in 1716 by Jacques Tarade to designs of the celebrated baroque architect Peter Thumb. With hunting, sailing and canoeing facilities, swimming and horse-back riding, tourism bids fair to replace tobacco as the village's staple income.

Eschau

Close to Strasbourg, washed by the Rhine and the Ill, Eschau became famous for its abbey, founded in the seventh century and proud of possessing the relics of St Sophie. During the Thirty Years' War the Swedes pillaged the abbey and threw away her saintly bones. But much remains of the Gothicized convent church (well restored in 1955), which has preserved what is basically the sole remaining major piece of Ottonian Romanesque architecture in Alsace. Look among the fifteenth-century carvings in the nave for the statue of St Christopher. Then relish the town's half-timbered houses.

Archaeologists have excavated the rest of the convent (to the north of the church), but you must visit the Musée de l'Oeuvre de Notre-Dame at Strasbourg to see most of the Romanesque treasures they have discovered. I have eaten well here at the hôtel au Cygne.

Feldbach

This lake-surrounded village in the Sundgau was once the home of Benedictine monks from Cluny, who left behind their Romanesque church of Saint-James (built in 1145) and their Renaissance priory (with a tower housing a spiral staircase) when the peasants revolted in 1525. The count of Ferrette founded the abbey on his return from a pilgrimage to Santiago de Compostela.

Some architects have suggested that the columns incorporated in this superb church derive from an even older building. The whole complex was well restored in 1977.

Ferrette

Close by the Swiss frontier, this former capital of the Sundgau took its name from the counts of Ferrette around 1100. For its ruins and their history see Ferrette in the index to the book. The neo-Gothic church of Saint-Bernard-de-Menthon (to the left of the place Centrale) dates from 1914, but it incorporates an earlier Gothic belfry and a fifteenth-century Gothic choir. Inside the sixteenth-century town hall is a museum with prehistoric, Gallo-Roman and medieval objects on display, as well as much relating to the history of Ferrette itself.

Thirteen kilometres to the south you reach the heart of the Jura mountains and the tiny commune of Lucelle, which boasts the remains of a twelfth-century Cistercian abbey dissolved at the revolution and partly demolished in 1800. What remains is used today as a charming family hostelry. Lucelle is the highest commune in the Sundgau, and its twentieth-century church actually lies in Switzerland.

Fleckenstein

The ruined château of Fleckenstein perches perilously on its rocky height (370 metres) and lies seven kilometres north-west of Lembach. Built in the thirteenth century, it constitutes the most important feudal castle in the upper Vosges. Take an hour to visit it (guided tours daily between mid-March and the end of October, starting from 08.00 and ending at 18.00). You climb twisting steps to reach a platform with a panorama of northern Alsace, as well as visiting subterranean cellars cut out of the rock and admiring the château's twin towers and the stone tombs of the lords of Fleckenstein.

Froeschwiller

At Froeschwiller on 6 August 1870 took place a celebrated battle between the Germans and the French, during which the village's church was destroyed. Two years later the victorious Germans restored it in the neo-Romanesque style, carefully preserving some fine seventeenth-century tombstones.

The Nazis were less magnanimous towards Froeschwiller. In the park adjoining the fine nineteenth-century château had been set up ancient statues, and some new ones commemorating both sides in the 1870 combat. The Nazis destroyed the French ones.

Geispolsheim

The town has wisely kept its industries outside its ancient quarter, whose half-timbered houses possess large doorways leading to interior courtyards. The church of 1771 preserves its thirteenth-century belfry as well as baroque furnishings and a late-fourteenth-century *pietà*.

Do not miss the Corpus Christi procession, when the citizens dress in traditional costumes. The town's annual *Sauerkraut* festival takes place at the beginning of September and its nut festival in mid-October.

Grandfontaine

Grandfontaine is close by the 1,009-metre-high summit of Donon, known to the Romans, whose ancient roads lead to the top for a panorama of the Vosges. Here, a monument tells you, Victor Hugo was conceived. The village church dates from the eighteenth century. In 1869 someone built an extraordinary pseudo-Greek temple. The flora and fauna of the region are rare enough for it to be an offence to pick some of them.

Griesbach-au-Val

Griesbach-au-Val, given over to tourism, is a commune that has the rare distinction of possessing no church. Its thirteenth-century château Schwarzenburg was partly ruined in the seventeenth century and bombed in World War I, when it served as a look-out point. Amongst its remains are not only parts of the surrounding wall with its semi-demolished towers but also a 1914 bunker.

Gueberschwihr

This village, sheltered by the Heidenhöhle rock, fortified in the thirteenth century and besieged both in 1338 and 1445, retains fine fortifications, three gates, two former châteaux and several vintners' houses in both stone and half-timber. Of its Romanesque church only the bell-tower survives, now ringing worshippers to a building of 1878.

Guebwiller

Owing its early importance to the nearby abbey of Murbach, Guebwiller in consequence is blessed with superb churches of its own, pre-eminent of which is the magnificent Romanesque Saint-Léger. Begun in the twelfth century, its superb sandstone façade dating from 1230, the church possesses a tympanum whose naive sculptures represent Jesus between his mother and St Léger. The vaulted nave is massive. The fourteenth-century choir (with a five-sided apse) houses magnificently carved eighteenth-century stalls. Here too are preserved ladders left behind by the Armagnacs after they besieged the town in 1445. Beside this church a statue of St Léger stands on a fountain set up in 1735.

Next in time comes the former Dominican church, a Gothic building begun in 1312, with a rood-loft and rare fourteenth- and fifteenth-century frescos. These had been whitewashed, to be rediscovered in the eighteenth century. They include scenes of Jesus crucified, legends of the life of St Dominic, a Last Judgment, the vision of St Catherine of Sienna, St Martin cutting his cloak in two to give one half to a beggar, and a portrait of St Christopher. Today this church serves as a concert hall, especially during the classical musical festivals held annually at Guebwiller on the first Saturdays of June, July and August.

Finally visit the baroque church of Notre-Dame, built between 1760 and 1785. The statues around the dome represent the four doctors of the church, Saints Ambrose, Gregory, Jerome and Augustine. Its square is graced by a contemporary fountain supported on dolphins, by the neo-classical former abbot's palace (to the left), as well as by several canons' houses and by an hôtel which now houses treasures of religious art (including a Virgin from the church of the Dominicans, carved in the thirteenth century, and a Christ on a donkey from the abbey of Murbach) as well as traditional Alsatian costumes. Splendours inside the church of Notre-Dame include the organ case, the carved stalls and, behind the high altar, an Assumption carved by Fidèle Sporrer. He also began carving the stalls, and the work was finished by his daughter Hélène. Guebwiller owes this church to the last prince-abbot of Murbach, Casimir de Rathsamhausen, who came here when the abbey was secularized in 1759.

Between the church of Saint-Léger and the church of Notre-Dame you pass the flamboyant town hall, with its five-sided oriel window, its mullions and its staircase, built by a rich draper in 1514.

Lying on the River Lauch, Guebwiller is a busy wine town and also the sub-prefecture of Haut-Rhin and the third largest town in the *département*. The textile and chemical industries have enriched without spoiling the place, leaving intact the masterpieces and treats along the rue de la République. The latter include not only (at No. 45) a house of 1611 with a statue of the Virgin Mary, but also a modern house built in 1903 (No. 104).

Ascension Day at Guebwiller is also the annual wine festival.

Guémar

Still guarded by a fourteenth-century gateway (the Porte-Haute or Obertor) and some sixteenth-century fortifications as well as the remains of its château, the village of Guémar stands on the River Fecht. Its eighteenth-century church is topped by a Gothic belfry.

In origin Guémar derives from a Gallo-Roman town, known as 'Herbarium' to the Romans and 'Ghermari' by the mid-eighth century. It passed into the possessions of the seigneurs of Ribeaupierre 500 years later. In 1260 Ulrich von Ribeaupierre built here a chapel which remained a place of pilgrimage till 1797, when the revolutionaries destroyed it. One of its treasures, a fifteenth-century statue in wood of St Maximin, is now housed among other fine works of art and baroque furnishings in the main church. In Guémar you can find stone and half-timbered houses, buy wine and set off for a day's fishing or swimming.

Gunsbach

Gunsbach is famous not for its beauty, though it does lie amid gentle hills and in the valley of the River Fecht, but first because when Albert Schweitzer was six months old his father moved to the village as Protestant pastor, and second, because here with the money of the Goethe prize which Schweitzer won in 1928 he built himself a home. Today this house is the Schweitzer museum. Here you find his organ and his piano with organ pedals, his papers, portraits, the cot in which he was born, his annotated music, his library and his own works – in short, a unique memorial to the great missionary doctor, organist and Christian.

In the parish church, built in 1828, was an organ on which Albert Schweitzer first learned to play. When this organ was severely damaged by bombs in World War I, Schweitzer himself raised the cash to restore it to his own specifications. World War II damaged this organ in its turn. Again Schweitzer raised money for rebuilding, commissioning Alfred Kern of Strasbourg to complete the work. Each year on 4 September (the anniversary of Schweitzer's death in 1965) a leading organist performs a concert in the church.

Schweitzer used to climb the rock that overhangs Gunsbach on the road to Munster. As his fame increased, admirers decided to commission a sandstone monument to the philanthropist, to be sculpted in sandstone by Rodin's Alsatian disciple F. Behn. Schweitzer refused to allow the monument to be erected before his death, but he was pleased, and wrote:

It is there where I was absorbed in thought. It is there I should like to remain in stone, so that my friends can pay me a visit, devote a thought to me, and listen to the murmur of the river – the music that accompanied the movement of my own thoughts. On this rock my book *Civilization and Ethics* was conceived, and there my understanding of the historical Jesus emerged. In this creative solitude let me be preserved in stone . . .

See Gunsbach also in the index to this book.

Haguenau

Lying on the edge of the vast forest of Haguenau (once called the sacred forest and now mapped out with walks), the city today has a population of nearly 30,000. Its historical importance (see the index to this book) is revealed as you penetrate to the centre, encountering an increasing number of old houses (many with fine ironwork and tiled roofs), fountains and – in the pedestrianized heart of Haguenau – the church of Saint-Georges, its nave dating from the twelfth century, its choir and transept from the next, its pulpit sixteenth-century Gothic (sculpted by Veit Wagner), its bell-tower octagonal and basically Romanesque. Two of the bells of Saint-Georges date from 1268 and are the oldest in Alsace. Its retables are superb, especially that of the Last Judgment over the high altar (painted in 1497) and the delicate Virgin of the Annunciation in the left transept.

Close by the same square are two museums, one (in a *belle-époque* château of 1905, at No. 9, rue du Maréchal-Foch) devoted to the history of Haguenau, the other (in the former chancellery of 1486, place Thierry) containing a rich collection devoted to the history of the whole of Alsace.

To the north of the city (near the Wissembourg gate) the church of Saint-Nicolas, Haguenau, was built between the thirteenth and the fifteenth centuries. The fifteenth-century Saint-Sépulcre is finer still, with its contemporary wall paintings, its statues, a bas-relief of Jesus crushed in a wine-press and its eighteenth-century furniture. If your taste is for the baroque and rococo, look out for the decoration on the chapel of the civic hospital. Look too for the hôtels in the place d'Armes (where the civic hospital stands) and in the Grand'Rue.

Haguenau has an ancient Jewish cemetery and a neo-classical synagogue built in 1820. Since the city was set on fire by the French in 1677, little remains of the old Haguenau fortifications, except for three gates. Vauban demolished the walls and took the stone away to fortify French strongholds elsewhere.

The bakers of the city are rightly proud of their *tartes flambées*, and the brewers of Haguenau celebrate a festival of hops on the first Sunday in September. The last week of August sees a gastronomic festival and entertaining processions here.

Hattstatt

This tiny village in the valley of the Lauch prospered from the sixteenth-century wine trade and has preserved a town hall with a double, external staircase built at the beginning of that century as well as some Renaissance houses. The church dates back even further, its porch and nave to the twelfth century (maybe the eleventh), its choir fifteenth-century Gothic, its furnishings eighteenth-century. Although the walls and château of Hattstatt have long disappeared, outside the village, 820 metres above sea-level, stand the remains of château Hoh-Hattstatt.

Haut-Koenigsbourg

For the celebrated château of Haut-Koenigsbourg and its history see the index to this book. Visits can be made from 1 April to the end of September between 08.00 and 12.00 and between 13.00 and 18.00. During March and October the château closes one hour earlier. For the rest of the year it is open only till 16.00.

In 1937 the film director Jean Renoir utilized the château to the full and (some would say) far beyond in *La Grande Illusion*.

Heiligenstein

This village on the slopes of the Vosges profits from wine, has a church (shared by Protestants and Catholics) with a Romanesque belfry and romantic remains of the medieval château de Landsberg.

Hoffen

A village filled with flowers, especially when the geraniums are in bloom, Hoffen also boasts half-timbered houses with white plastered walls, an eighteenth-century church with a Gothic choir, and a covered well beside which grows a lime tree planted at the time of the French Revolution.

Hunawihr

The village derives its name from the grandparents of St Odile, apparently named Huno and Huna, who lived here in the seventh century. Huna was a particularly charitable woman, given to washing the linen of sick poor people. The Renaissance fountain named after her here is reputed to have flowed with wine during a year when the vintage was bad.

Hunawihr is still noted for its wines, and also for its church of Saint-Jacques, built in the fifteenth century, decorated in 1492 with wall paintings depicting the life of St Nicolas, shared by Protestants and Catholics since 1687, and enriched with a fine eighteenth-century organ. The town hall was built in 1517, and you should not miss the curious fortified cemetery, whose hexagonal wall has six bastions dating from the sixteenth century.

The hotel named Cigogne is a reminder that Hunawihr has pioneered the reintroduction of storks into Alsace, incubating them artificially and hand-rearing the young birds.

Hunspach

The region known as Outre-Forêt or Unterland lies at the north end of Alsace and borders on the Palatinate. Amongst its more picturesque villages is the tourist centre of Hunspach, with its numerous half-timbered, red-tiled houses, many of them built by Swiss settlers after the Thirty Years' War. Few other Alsatian villages have quite such an ensemble of magnificent houses, the white *crépi* (or cob) of their walls gleaming in the sun. Here there are ancient wells, wine casks and cellars in abundance, and occasionally a couple of old ladies walking together in antique Alsatian costumes.

Ingersheim

The town lies in wine country in the valley of the Fecht and has preserved numerous old vintners' houses, built in the Renaissance style, as well as the eighteenth-century town hall and a baroque church (beautifully furnished) with a Romanesque tower.

Ingwiller

Surrounded by remains of its old fortifications (built by Ludwig the Bavarian in 1340), Ingwiller lies in the north Vosges natural park and has preserved several half-timbered houses. Today it prospers from manufacturing glass, thermometers, shoes, cookers and stoves. A nineteenth-century synagogue occupies the site of the former château. The town hall was built in 1824, and the Lutheran church has a Romanesque choir and belfry.

Itterswiller

If you pass through Itterswiller, with its superb view of the wooded valley known as the Bout du Monde, don't miss the Romanesque frescos in the church belfry. Just outside the little village is a farm which was once the monks' lodgings belonging to the Cistercian abbey of Baumgarten, which was founded in 1125 and ruined at the Peasants' War of 1525.

Jebsheim

Although its ancient Romanesque church was very badly damaged during World War II, what remained has been well incorporated in a new church. Remains of the old church include the Romanesque façade, its Gothic apse adjoining an eleventh-century chapel, tombs of the lords of Bergheim (dating from the fourteenth to the sixteenth centuries) and sixteenth-century stained glass.

Kaysersberg

The birthplace of Albert Schweitzer (and twinned with Lambaréné in Gabon where he founded his jungle hospital), Kaysersberg stands on the River Weiss. The Romans called the place Caesar's Mount *(Caesaris Mons)*, hence the name Kaysersberg. Here were planted the first Tokay vines of Alsace, and you can taste and buy excellent wines in some of the numerous sixteenth-century Renaissance houses, many of them with spacious courtyards. The ruined château dominating the town belonged in the thirteenth century to Heinrich VII, king of the Romans.

The finest ensemble of buildings centres on Kaysersberg's fortified bridge, thrown across the Weiss in 1511 and carrying a small oratory. Pause on the bridge for a view of the ruins of the château. The remains of Kaysersberg's other fortifications include four towers, known as the Spitalturm, the Hexenturm (or witches' tower), the Oberturm and the Kesslerturm, all built in the fifteenth century. Across the bridge, on the left bank of the Weiss, stands a Renaissance house of 1592, decorated with wood-carvings, and the hôtellerie du Pont of 1600. On the right bank (on the corner of rue du Général de Gaulle and rue des Potiers) is an even more richly sculpted house of 1594. To the north on this bank of the river stands the chapel de l'Oberhof, built in 1391.

Follow rue du Général de Gaulle with its Renaissance houses to find Schweitzer's birthplace, part of which is a museum devoted to his life and achievements. At No. 62, rue du Général de Gaulle a Gothic house built in 1521 serves as another museum, filled with religious art and local history (Stone Age axes, old-fashioned plough-shares, clogs and so on) and opens between June and September from 10.00 to 12.00 and from 14.00 to 18.00.

From here retrace your steps to the left bank of the river and turn right at the hôtellerie du Pont to reach the church of Sainte-Croix. The church square is surrounded by old corbelled houses and ornamented by a Renaissance fountain topped by a statue of Constantine, the first Christian emperor. Although the tower of Sainte-Croix was not added until 1830, the bay supporting it dates from the second half of the twelfth century and the nave was built in the next. The side aisles were added 200 years later. The most fascinating part of the church, to my mind, is its tympanum, topping a thirteenth-century doorway and decorated in the first quarter of that century not only with carvings of the coronation of the Virgin Mary, who sits between the archangels Michael and Gabriel, but also with a portrait of its builder, Maître Canradus. Go inside to discover riches of church art: superb and huge fifteenth-century carvings of Jesus on the cross, flanked by his mother and St John; a holy sepulchre carved by Jacques Wirt in 1514; a seventeenth-century pulpit; an organ case built in 1730, and much more – especially a gilded and painted triptych behind the high altar, sculpted in wood by the Colmar master Jean Bongartz in 1518 and depicting Jesus's passion.

Next to the church is the cemetery where lie the dead of 1944 and where stands a plague cross of 1511. North of this, the fifteenth-century chapel of Saint-Michel holds both an ossuary of 1463 and a fine collection of medieval and Renaissance religious paintings and sculptures. And to the east of the church of Saint-Croix you find Kaysersberg town hall, first built in 1521 in the Renaissance style, and extended in 1604: an oriel window on its façade, its interior courtyard ornamented with a wooden gallery, its tower climbed by a stone spiral staircase.

An easy walk from the town hall leads up to the château, where you can then climb the thirteenth-century keep for magnificent views. Though sacked by the peasants in 1525 and mostly pulled down by the Swedes in 1632, the ruins remain romantically impressive.

Kaysersberg also boasts a 1519 chapel of Saint-Wolfgang which once ministered to a leper colony, and the remains of the former abbey of Alspach. The façade of the former abbey church is twelfth-century, and behind the building stands a stone crucifix carved in 1511.

For Kaysersberg see also the index to this book.

Kientzheim

In the sixteenth century Lazarus von Schwendi not only fought for the emperor against the French and the Turks but also brought the Tokay grape to Alsace after his campaigns in Hungary. His château is now owned by the wine fraternity of Saint-Étienne (see the index to this book) and is the premier museum of Alsatian viticulture (open every day from June to September, from 10.00 to 12.00 and from 14.00 to 18.00). It stands near the lower gate of the town. Some of the old ramparts still remain, and this lower gate (porte Basse) is ornamented with the sculpted head of a man putting out his tongue at the town's enemies. Though the ancient chapel of Saints-Felix-et-Regula was much destroyed in the battle for Colmar in 1944–5, it has been restored; and the church of Notre-Dame, rebuilt in 1772 and containing baroque altars, has a fifteenth-century Gothic belfry and choir. Here too are the tombs of Lazarus von Schwendi, who died in 1594, and of his son Jean-Guillaume, who died in 1609.

Kientzheim has several fine old houses, wells and decorated squares.

Kintzheim

This village has devoted itself to bird life. Eagles, condors and vultures are bred, tamed and shown off by gloved dressers in the half-ruined twelfth-century château, which has preserved its walls, bastions and keep, as well as a fifteenth-century chapel of Saint-Jacques. Demonstration flights take place most days around 14.00 from April to September, unless the weather is bad. Storks are also bred here, and nearby 300 monkeys live in considerable freedom on the so-called montagne des singes. Brought from North Africa and accustomed to snow, they breed happily in Alsace, and can be visited daily in summer from 10.00 to 12.00 and from 14.00 to 18.00. (From October to March the zoo is closed on Mondays, Wednesdays, Thursdays and Fridays.) To find them, leave the château car park and take the forest road. After two kilometres a road to the right takes you shortly to the monkeys' ranges.

Lautenbach

The Carolingians founded a Benedictine abbey here on the left bank of the River Lauch, an abbey whose sandstone church and cloister alone remain. A wing of the cloister now houses the town hall and post-office. The church was built around 1080 and rebuilt towards the end of the fifteenth century. The reconstructed church retains the older Romanesque doorway, whose frieze depicts in cartoon form the sin and punishment of an adulteress. Equally delightful are the carvings of fantastic animals and the misericords under the seat of the fifteenth-century choir stalls. The stained glass in the choir also dates from the fifteenth century. A belfry was added in 1862. The rest of the church has preserved its Romanesque character, with fine pillars, though the pulpit is an eighteenth-century baroque master-piece. The four evangelists and the Virgin Mary are carved on its sides and, above, St Michael rescues a soul from the devil. Outside to the left of the church is the Gothic cloister built in the sixteenth century.

The cemetery chapel of the town has a Gothic choir and an eighteenth-century reredos. The cross in the cemetery was carved in 1693. The finest houses in Lautenbach were formerly inhabited by the canons of its church. Just outside the village is an artificial lake covering over eleven hectares and filled with fish.

Lauterbourg

Lauterbourg, situated where the Romans built a fort, suffered greatly during the wars of the seventeenth and eighteenth centuries, as well as in 1870 and during World War II. Yet parts of its medieval fortifications are still there (reconstructed by Vauban, with a gateway embellished with the sign of his master, the Sun King, Louis XIV), as are eighteenth-century Renaissance houses, the former episcopal château of the same date, and the church of the Trinity, whose polygonal choir and sacristy are Gothic, whose nave was rebuilt in the eighteenth century, and whose high altar is baroque. The Jews had their own cemetery at Lauterbourg which you can still visit, and their partly ruined synagogue also remains. Outside the town you can discern parts of the twenty-kilometre-long fortified line created during the War of the Spanish Succession.

Lembach

The charm of Lembach derives from its half-timbered houses, from its situation on both sides of the River Sauer and from the extensive ruins not just of the château Fleckenstein, which was built on its rocky prominence in the twelfth and thirteenth centuries, but also of the thirteenth-century château Froensbourg, likewise on a rock though partly a troglodyte château as well.

From château Fleckenstein one has the best panorama. In the neighbourhood men have mined silver and iron. The wild flora and fauna are precious and unusual. Camping is encouraged, as are fishing and hunting. And the position of this town in the north Vosges natural park and close to the lake of Fleckenstein, as well as to the Alsace plain, makes it an ideal location for the nature-lover and explorer.

Lichtenberg

A thirteenth-century keep dominates the château at Lichtenberg, its twin semi-circular towers connected by machicolated walls. The ruins of the later buildings impress, and the fifteenth-century chapel houses a splendid Renaissance tomb. Vauban fortified the village and the château, but even his work was hardly equal to the bombardments of 1870. An orientation table in the castle keep points as far as the spire of Strasbourg cathedral, fifty-three kilometres away.

Lièpvre

The locals pronounce the name of this town as if it were a hare — *lièvre*. Though the town, lying on the River Lièpvrette, is now partly industrialized, its church of Notre-Dame, rebuilt in 1752, preserves the old Romanesque bell-tower, and in the cemetery chapel is a Romanesque ossuary. If you drive one kilometre west of Lièpvre, you reach the hamlet of Rombach-le-Franc, where clogs are made and cloth is woven in the old-fashioned way.

Marckolsheim

Marckolsheim was on the Maginot Line and in consequence was bitterly fought over in World War II. A small war museum recalls the struggle.

Marlenheim

This picturesque wine village, with its 1716 church of Sainte-Richarde boasting a Romanesque doorway, its nineteenth-century château and its Renaissance houses, has dedicated itself to folklore. This devotion reaches its apôgée in mid-August when the citizens deck themselves in traditional costumes to re-enact the marriage of Fritz Kobus and his bride Süzel — a festival loosely based on the novel written in 1864 by Émile Eckermann and Alexandre Chatrian.

The favourite wine here is Pinot noir which in this town is called *rouge de Marlenheim*.

Marmoutier

A sixth-century abbey was here reformed in 724 by St Maur and took the name *Mauri-Monasterium*, hence the present name of the town. Marmoutier's abbey-church is superb, designed in Ottonian times to represent what was conceived of as the pattern of the heavenly Jerusalem, and enriched subsequently with twelfth-century capitals, with a lovely choir and a five-sided apse, with sumptuous furnishings and a Silbermann organ (installed in 1710, restored in 1965). Note the two stylized lions carved at the entrance. The ancient cemetery chapel (basically twelfth-century) and the church of Saint-Blaise at Sindelsberg (two kilometres north, on a vine-covered hill and built basically in the sixteenth century) add to the ecclesiastical riches of the town.

Some of the convent buildings remain at Marmoutier, which does not lack fine houses. Here on the first Sunday in September an annual onion market is held. Five kilometres south-west you reach the Renaissance château of Birkenwald.

Masevaux

Here, before joining the army, Napoleon's General Kléber designed some canons' houses. Little remains of a convent for noble ladies founded in the eighth century, but its fourteenth-century church has been put to secular use and can be recognized by its south chapel with an Adoration of the Magi carved on its typanum around 1400. The classical church of Saint-Martin, built between 1787 and 1842, possesses two fine organs both created by Gallimet in 1892, and a fifteenth-century *pietà*.

Masevaux is surrounded by lakes, some of them artificial. On the way to Niederbruck on a promontory near the lake of Lachtelweiher stands the 'Virgin of Alsace', sculpted by Bourdelle in 1923.

Merkwiller-Pechelbronn

A flowery village in Bas-Rhin with fine half-timbered Alsatian houses, Merkwiller-Pechelbronn is singular as the former centre of Alsace's now defunct petrol industry. Long before the invention of the internal combustion engine, petrol had been discovered and exploited in this region, and at Merkwiller-Pechelbronn a curious museum (partly in the former town hall, partly in the open air) celebrates the fact and records its history. The museum seems almost always to be closed, but you can visit it by appointment (telephone 88 80 52 75).

In the fifteenth century, it seems, crude oil was not only used as grease for wagon-wheels and the like, but was also sold to hapless peasants by quacks who promised it as a cure-all and then speedily moved on to the next village. Prospecting and drilling flourished towards the end of the nineteenth century and in the early twentieth, helping to make Alsace prosper. Then the oil ran out, after supplying an average of 50,000 tonnes a year up to 1960. Happily, drillers in 1910 discovered not an oil well but the thermal spring of the Hélions, which now, the citizens of Merkwiller-Pechelbronn claim, scores notable successes at curing rheumatism, sciatica and arthritis. At sixty-five degrees Fahrenheit (eighteen degrees Centigrade), the thermal waters are among the hottest in Europe.

Around this have developed numerous tourist attractions – rural *gîtes* and fishing, tanneries and traditional woodcrafts, hunting, walking in the north Vosges natural park, along the banks of the Seltzbach and in the communal forests.

Mittelbergheim

This wine village in Bas-Rhin, usually decked with flowers, once belonged to the abbey of Andlau, and its tithe barn bears witness to the dues the villagers paid to their spiritual masters. Although much of the church is today of nineteenth-century origin, its belfry is Romanesque, its nave is Gothic and it preserves fifteenth-century frescos. Look out in the restaurants for *pâté vigneron;* and as for wine, try AOC Zotzenberg.

Modern

Till 1973 Modern was two villages – Zutzendorf and Obermodern – which joined together and took a new name. This is where the French revolutionary army first began to turn the tide against Austria. Both parts of the new village have retained fine Alsatian half-timbered houses, with galleries. The old tithe house dates from 1520, and the former presbytery houses a stork's nest. Zutzendorf Lutheran church has an eighteenth-century nave and a thirteenth-century Gothic tower.

Mollkirch

Though partly ruined, the twelfth- to fifteenth-century feudal château de Guirbaden, perched on its 565-metre-high peak, still retains its keep, seigneurial dwellings, towers and five fortified gateways in its successive encircling walls.

Molsheim

Still surrounded by most of its fortifications (including the fine fourteenth-century gateway to the south known as the tour des Forgerons), Molsheim boasts the remarkable Metzig, an imposing Renaissance hall built by the butchers' company in 1525, its double façade, double staircase, gargoyles and mechanical clock all testifying to the importance of this company in the Middle Ages and sixteenth century. As a museum of local history it is fortunately open to the public. And you can take wine in its cellars.

On the way to the Metzig from the south gate you will have passed at No. 15, rue de Strasbourg a fine house dated 1618. The town hall square in which the Metzig stands contains other such houses, both sixteenth- and seventeenth-century, as well as a sixteenth-century fountain. (The lion on top of its column holds the town's coat of arms.) Take the rue de l'Église west of the square and then turn left into the rue Notre-Dame. On the way to the church you can see the tribunal, built after the Franco-Prussian War but in the style of the Metzig. Everywhere there are typical old houses.

Although Molsheim was the birthplace of the celebrated Erasmus Guerber, executed for his part in the Peasants' War of 1525, it became the chief centre in Alsace of the Counter-Reformation. Here in 1580 Bishop Jean de Manderscheid founded for this purpose a Jesuit college, which became so famous that in 1617 Pope Paul V elevated its status to that of a university and in 1702 Louis XIV had it transferred to Strasbourg. On the right of rue Notre-Dame can be seen the former Jesuit college. Its church is remarkable, built by the architect Christopher Wamser between 1615 and 1617. The interior is a highly successful mixture of Gothic, Renaissance and flamboyant architecture, filled with statues and an air of religious triumphalism.

Take the rue de la Monnaie north of the church to find the former mint (1573) and to reach the place de la Liberté and shortly afterwards the church of Saint-Georges (1530–1806), to the south of which in Molsheim's market square rises the *cité administrative* in a high-roofed building (once the granary of the counts and built in the seventeenth century). To the south of the market square the rue de l'Hôpital reaches the late-sixteenth-century hôtel de l'abbaye d'Altorf. To the north of the square the rue de la Chartreuse leads to the house of the prior of the former charterhouse of Molsheim.

A distinguished citizen of Molsheim was General Westermann, who perished on the scaffold in 1794 aged only forty-three. The Bugatti factories have brought their own special fame to the town. Riesling is favoured here, and reputed local wines include two named after the Vosges hills on which they are grown: the Finkenberger and the Hahnenberger. Two kilometres to the north of Molsheim (at Avolsheim) is Alsace's oldest church, the Dompeter (*Domus Petri*), an eleventh-century building based on a seventh-century foundation.

Munster

Deriving its name from the Benedictine monastery founded here by St Oswald, Munster is now devoted to cheesemaking and tourism (see the index to this book). The monastery was dedicated to St Gregory, and here the Munster valley is still known as Val-Saint-Grégoire. Becoming an imperial city in the thirteenth century, the town which had developed around the abbey was fortified in 1311. Citizens and monks quarrelled over each other's rights. The citizens welcomed the Peasants' War and opted for the Reformation. Everyone suffered during the Thirty Years' War, after which France tried to impose Catholicism and the Munster Protestants stubbornly resisted. Not surprisingly, the citizens took up the cause of the revolution, and the abbey was secularized – its buildings demolished or sold, their stones carted away for other uses, its church pulled down.

The textile industry helped to restore Munster's fortunes, though scarcely its architectural heritage. Today the Catholic church is 1860s' Gothic, the impressively huge Lutheran church 1867 Romanesque. The finest building is the former town hall of 1552 (now a museum), with its wall paintings created 150 years later by Gabriel de Mulhouse. Inside the museum is the Munster *Klapperstein*, which was hung round miscreants' necks before they were paraded through the streets proclaiming their wicked ways. The town fountain dates from 1506, and a house named le Laub from 1503.

What gives the town its true flavour and its role in tourism is its position in the Vosges mountains, where the little River Fecht joins the main Fecht and winter sports have been carefully developed. The Albert Schweitzer park near the Catholic church houses the health cure centre of the Munster valley. A yet more charming park is that dedicated to André Hartmann, to the west of the rue de la Gare.

Murbach

The splendid abbey founded here by St Pirmin in 728 (with the finances and support of Count Eberhard) flourished until the thirteenth century, when its abbot became a prince of the Holy Roman Empire. But financial problems overtook it in the next century, and religious conflicts never ceased for another 200 years, with the result that in 1739 the monks left their home and moved to Guebwiller.

They left behind a chapter for noblemen which the revolution suppressed. What remains today is their marvellous Romanesque church, Lombardic in spirit, from whose contemporary choir and transept rise two twelfth-century square towers, pierced with simple, delicate openings. Notice the oriental influence of a couple of lions and palms carved over the tympanum. Inside is stillness; the sarcophagus of the monks massacred by the Hungarians in 929, and the splendid fourteenth-century Gothic tomb in which lies the seventh-century benefactor, Count Eberhard. Four busts inserted in the sarcophagus of the massacred monks are the earliest tenth-century sculptures of humans in Alsace. The remaining monastic buildings date from the seventeenth century. Higher up stands the chapel of Notre-Dame-de-Lorette, built in 1693 to house an exact reproduction of the Holy House of Loretto.

Mutzig

Five kilometres west of Molsheim lies Mutzig, one of the great beer-brewing towns of Alsace. The Wagner brewery was founded here in 1812. Yet the town remains charming, preserving its fourteenth-century fortified gateway and a château rebuilt by the prince-bishops of Strasbourg in the seventeenth century. It houses a museum of history, partly of the city but chiefly of armaments which were once made here in the château. (Antoine-Alphonse Chassepot, inventor of the deadly rifle named after him, was born here in 1833 and worked at Mutzig.) The town fountain was built in the seventeenth century.

A melancholy carved head peers at you from above the town clock. As well as its nineteenth-century parish church, Mutzig possesses two earlier chapels: that of St James the Less, and the former Franciscan chapel, both built in the seventeenth century, the latter baroque.

A forty-minute walk in the direction of Schirmeck takes you up the Feldsberg, which dominates the town, to reach the sixteenth-century chapel of Saint-Wendelin. Continue through the woods to reach a splendid panorama of the surrounding countryside and gain a thirst for some genuine Mutzig beer.

Neuf-Brisach

To appreciate that Louis XIV's military engineer was also a considerable architect, a visit to Neuf-Brisach is enlightening. By the Treaty of Ryswick in 1697 Louis XIV of France had ceded Vieux-Brisach to Austria. This part of his territory now had no defensive fortress. The monarch offered unusual privileges to those who would agree to live in a new town he intended to build – they were given free building land, the right to hold fairs and markets, and exemption from taxes. Then he ordered Vauban to build here, where once late Stone Age man had lived, where the Romans had established a strategic camp, and where the Merovingians had left a cemetery.

Vauban had finished the work in 1708. Today the octagonal ramparts remain in a quite remarkable state of preservation. The streets are straight, meeting at right-angles and enabling defending citizens speedily to reach any corner of their town. The gates stand formidably. The Belfort gate today fittingly contains a small museum dedicated to the military genius who never fought a battle. Inside, the houses are charming and the least militant would take pleasure in living in them. The church at Neuf-Brisach was not built until 1750, though architecturally it fits in well with everything else, especially in being dedicated to St Louis, an almost blasphemous reference to the Sun King rather than to the Christian saint. Its architect was François Chevalier. Vauban, it need hardly be said, had planned something much more formidable, a mini-citadel capable of being defended should enemies ever break through his walls with their twenty-four defensive towers.

Neuwiller-lès-Saverne

This ancient village sitting at the feet of the Vosges once boasted one of the most sumptuous abbeys in Alsace. Founded by the Benedictine bishop of Metz in 725, just over a hundred years later the monks were presented by another bishop of Metz with the 400-year-old relics of St Adelphe, then able to work powerful miracles and in consequence attract innumerable pilgrims. The town became rich, and though today it houses little more than 1,000 citizens, it boasts two remarkable churches as well as splendid half-timbered houses and others with fine façades and remarkable tiled roofs.

The former abbey-church of Saints-Pierre-et-Paul was restored in the mid-nineteenth century by the intelligent and sensitive architect Jacques-Émile Boeswillwald and boasts a huge transept and a smaller chapter house, both dating from the twelfth century and later embellished with ogival arches. The tower is Romanesque, although its upper storeys were added in the nineteenth century. Statues of St Peter and St Paul guard a thirteenth-century doorway into the church. The tympanum of another doorway, which is almost certainly earlier, shows them joining the angels and a couple of monks in flanking Jesus, who is blessing the world. The façade of the church, built five centuries later, is ornamented with colossal statues and topped by a square eighteenth-century bell-tower.

Inside, the bones of St Adelphe lie in a columned fourteenth-century tomb, designed to enable the devout to prostrate themselves beneath it. The pillars of the church are decorated with capitals; the two chapels are Romanesque, as is the font on which are depicted a lion and the heads of a monk and a woman; fifteenth-century statues of the Virgin Mary sit at peace; Lambert Laer, provost of the abbey of Neuwiller-lès-Saverne and vicar-general of Strasbourg, donated the stone pulpit in 1683. The organ case dates from 1772.

The eighteenth-century choir stalls came from the abbey of Sturzelbronn, and underneath them you find the crypt-chapel which long ago housed Adelphe's relics. Dedicated to St Catherine, its *martyrium* where Adelphe's bones once lay is Carolingian. Find the doorway to yet another chapel, this one dedicated to St Sebastian, where hang exquisite tapestries depicting twenty-one scenes from the life of Adelphe. Woven at the very end of the fifteenth century, they were presented to the church by Philippe III of Hanau-Lichtenberg.

St Adelphe is also commemorated at Neuwiller-lès-Saverne in the dedication of the Lutheran church. Standing on the site of a chapel built by the monks to receive the gift of Adelphe's bones, it was rebuilt around 1220, long before Luther was born, and pleasingly combines Romanesque and early Gothic elements. The thirteenth-century chapter house is intact, as are parts of the cloister. The west façade boast two remarkable slender towers.

Fine secular buildings here frequently derive from former ecclesiastical ones, such as what was once the eighteenth-century house (hôtel) of the provost of the monastery chapter, with its splendid façades and tiled roof. Neuwiller-lès-Saverne boasts fountains and old wells, ancient stone and half-timbered houses, and two châteaux: the ruined château de Herrenstein, retaining some of its defensive walls, a thirteenth-century tower and sixteenth-century bastions, and parts of its fourteenth-century chapel; and another château built in the eighteenth century. The citizens are proud of their cemetery, where rest many of Napoleon's soldiers, including his war minister Marshal Clark in his own mausoleum. The marshal had found and married a bride here, and died in 1818.

Niederbronn-les-Bains

The Romans and the Celts discovered and relished the two thermal springs that give the spa of Niederbronn-les-Bains part of its name, and today you are invited to use them to cure liver ailments, arteriosclerosis, rheumatism, kidney trouble, neuralgia, gout, digestive problems, difficulty at urinating, hypertension and arthritis. (Actually, it does require two separate springs to achieve all this.) After one of them had cured Philippe of Hanau of gout in the sixteenth century, he built a hospital here, and the spa began to grow again in repute. The commune acquired both springs in 1806, and soon Niederbronn-les-Bains was adding to its own resources the celebrated health techniques invented by the Bavarian priest Sebastien Kneipp.

While you are being cured, whether by the thermal waters or by the Kneipp method, don't miss visiting the ruined fourteenth-century château de Wasenbourg or the casino (set up in 1824 and rebuilt in the place des Thermes after World War II, when much of the town was badly damaged). This is the only casino in Alsace, and open-air popular concerts with folk-dancing are held in its park at 14.30 every Sunday and festivals from May to September. If you are looking for the Celtic spring, it is not here but in its own park farther north-west along the rue de la République, just beyond the railway station.

The half-timbered houses of the town are entirely typical of the Hanau region. The eighteenth-century Protestant church has an organ contemporary with its building. Roman and Celtic remains abound in the town museum. You can fish in the neighbourhood and, if sufficiently cured of your ailments, hire bicycles. Some forty minutes' walk along the path leading north-west from the town you reach a Celtic camp whose megaliths were erected around 500 BC.

See also Niederbronn-les-Bains in the index to this book.

Niederhaslach

Niederhaslach lies at the foot of the Vosges mountains where the River Bruche meets the River Hasel. Here Gerlach de Steinbach, whose father Erwin was a principal architect of Strasbourg cathedral, was responsible for building most of the impressive thirteenth- and fourteenth-century church of Saint-Florent. (Building had begun in 1274 but was mostly destroyed by fire thirteen years later.) But for the splendour of its sculpted façade and the church's forty-two-metre-high tower, the whole enhanced by a rose window and recalling the masterpieces of Gerlach's father, one ought to rush inside to admire first the fourteenth- and fifteenth-century stained glass and then the architect's own tomb, for he died at Niederhaslach in 1329.

The statues on the west façade depict God the Father presiding over prophets, angels, the Virgin Mary and the Archangel Gabriel. The tympanum is carved with the coronation of the Virgin and the legend of St Florent. St Florent and the Virgin (this time with her son) also appear in the stained-glass windows, as do St John and St Arbogast. The octagonal font dates from the thirteenth century, as does the choir, the oldest part of the church, which houses stalls of 1691. In a niche in the choir wall a copper reliquary of 1716 holds the bones and dust of St Florent, patron saint of the church and the town. Some of the former canons of the church are buried in the garden outside.

Niedermohrschwihr

Since the Middle Ages the little wine village of Niedermohrschwihr has been blessed with fine harvests, and you can find good wine here and several Renaissance vintners' houses, some built of stone, others half-timbered, as well as a house with an oriel window in the main street. The eighteenth-century church of Saint-Gall has retained the thirteenth-century Gothic belfry of its predecessor. Inside is a Silbermann organ built in 1726.

Nearby is the health resort of Les Trois-Épis, a bracing 658 metres above sea-level. The hamlet derives its name from a vision of the Blessed Virgin granted here in 1491. She carried in one hand three ears of corn (symbol of munificence) and in the other a hailstone (symbol of ill-fortune). The spot became a place of pilgrimage and, despite damage in World War II, retains its pilgrimage chapel. The Gothic choir dates from 1493 and its Holy Sepulchre and terracotta *pietà* are contemporary with it. For a rewarding hour's walk (there and back) climb the path to le Gatz, a rocky promontory with a view of Haut-Koenigsbourg, the Alsace plain, the Rhine, Germany and the Vosges mountains. Here a monumental statue of Jesus has been erected with steps inside, so you can climb to the top for an even better view.

Niedersteinbach/Obersteinbach

The ruins of the double château of Wasigenstein remain impressive and turn out to be partly troglodyte. A second ruin on a rocky perch is the fourteenth-century château of the Romanies' rock (rocher des Tziganes). On the nearby Maimont height is a so-called Druidic stone circle.

A little farther west along the D3 is Obersteinbach with two other partly troglodyte castles: the thirteenth-century château de Lutzelhardt, in ruins but retaining its keep, halls without roofs, walls, staircases; and the fourteenth-century château du Petit-Arnsberg, with a couple of towers still standing, corridors tunnelled through the rocks, staircases, a fifteenth-century doorway and a moat.

Oberbronn-Zinswiller

Gaullish remains and Merovingian tombs have been found near this ancient spot. Today Oberbronn-Zinswiller boasts Renaissance houses, a Gothic Lutheran church dating from the fifteenth century with a font dated 1505, a colonnaded classical town hall (1846), a Jewish cemetery and a Renaissance château (the convent of the sisters of Niederbronn). Hunting and fishing are among the delights offered to the tourist.

Oberhaslach

Oberhaslach is situated on a spot where St Florent set up a hermitage in the sixth century. Here are no fewer than three ruined châteaux.

Small wonder legend has it that once on this site lived giants, since the people of Alsace equate ancient ruined châteaux with them. The remains of the thirteenth-century château de Nideck include a fine square keep and partly ruined domestic quarters. On the way in you notice a medallion of the poet Adalbert de Chamisso, who wrote a poem about the daughter of one of the giants. A path leads from the château to one of the finest water cascades in Alsace. Château du Grand Ringelstein is even earlier in origin than château de Nideck, and parts of its towers and polygonal defences date from the twelfth century. Château de Hohenstein, contemporary with château de Nideck, has retained its keep, walls, another tower and its lower courtyard.

The eighteenth-century church at Oberhaslach has a fine statue of St Florent.

Obernai

Situated on the wine route of Alsace (see the index to this book), this favoured tourist spot at the foot of Mont Sainte-Odile has preserved almost its entire ramparts and many medieval houses in its picturesque twisting streets. Some are half-timbered, some stone-built, many corbelled, others with oriels and balconies. The nineteenth-century château d'Oberkirch incorporates some of the towers of its fifteenth-century predecessor, as well as the remains of a Romanesque chapel.

At Obernai there are actually three sets of ramparts with fifteen towers, and you can walk round them. Two surround the city, and another the cemetery. The interior and oldest rampart was erected in 1250 (though its towers are sixteenth-century); the external rampart was built in 1298; the third finished in the seventeenth century.

St Odile was born here, and her statue adorns the 1904 fountain in the market square. The town hall in the same square was built before 1525 but enlarged then and later enlarged again. Its seventy-two-metre-high belfry (the Kapellturm) was built in 1285 as the belfry for a chapel of the Virgin Mary. The upper storey was added in 1597. Opposite the town hall is the sixteenth-century former corn hall.

The place de l'Église has a monument to Monsignor Freppel, bishop of Nantes (see index). His heart lies inside the church, a building of 1867 replacing the former fifteenth-century church, but preserving inside some of the original glass and an altar and reredos of 1504 in the flamboyant style. The modern wall paintings are by

Martin Feuerstein, who died in 1931. In the graveyard is a Calvary chapel, with sculptures of Jesus and his disciples on the Mount of Olives, the chapel and sculptures dating from 1517. Obernai also boasts a Jewish cemetery and a nineteenth-century synagogue. The choir of the former Kapellkirch is fifteenth-century, the former Capuchin church seventeenth-century.

Obernai's annual wine fair takes place on the second Sunday in October, and its patronal festival on 29 June. There are splendid camp sites and tourist attractions (horseback riding, cycling, fishing, walking).

Obersteinbach see Niedersteinbach/Obersteinbach above.

Orschwihr

This village which once belonged to the abbey of Murbach has sixteenth- and seventeenth-century vintners' houses, an eighteenth-century presbytery with a door dated 1561 and a well dated 1766, and the remains of its fifteenth-century château. The tower of the 1782 church of Saint-Nicolas dates from 1576.

Today the vintners of Orschwihr grow wine over some 200 hectares and you can taste and buy it (among other outlets) in the château cellars. The annual wine festival at Orschwihr takes place on the first weekend of October.

Orschwiller

As well as its late-eighteenth-century baroque sandstone church of Saint-Maurice, its fifteenth-century houses and the thirteenth-century ruins of château d'Oedenbourg, Orschwiller is famed above all for the château of Haut-Koenigsbourg (see the index to this book).

The Orschwiller wine festival (known as *cave ouverte*) takes place annually on 15–16 August, otherwise known as the Feast of the Assumption.

Ortenbourg

High on its vine-covered hill in Haut-Rhin and dominating the Rhine valley, the château d'Ortenbourg is one of the chief masterpieces of feudal military architecture in Alsace. Defended by two encircling walls, the second higher up than the first, its polygonal keep towers above the rest. Built for Rudolph of Habsburg, reinforced around 1300 and strengthened in the fifteenth century, this mighty bastion was not impregnable. Otto of Ochsenstein took it in 1293 during the struggle over Rudolph's succession. The duke of Lorraine damaged the château in 1374. The Burgundians took it in 1470. The Swedes set it on fire in 1632. It remains imposing, and from its walls you can see for miles around.

Ottmarsheim

This 1,000-year-old Habsburg village possesses a superb octagonal church built around 1030, modelled on Charlemagne's palatine chapel at Aix-la-Chapelle. It is flanked by a chapel of 1582 whose frescos date from the fourteenth and sixteenth centuries and whose organ was built in 1726. (See Ottmarsheim in the index to this book.)

Ottrott

The wine village of Ottrott is in fact composed of two villages, a lower one (Ottrott-le-Bas) and upper Ottrott (Ottrott-le-Haut). The church of Saint-Nicolas in the lower part was built in the eleventh century, though subsequently much renovated. In the lower village too is the square keep of the former thirteenth-century château d'Altkeller, in the park of the eighteenth-century château de Witt-Guizot.

Around Ottrott are no fewer than eight other ruined châteaux: Lutzelbourg (thirteenth- to fifteenth-century), with its keep, central hall and moat; Rathsamhausen, larger and of the same date, retaining its keep, barbican and other buildings; the contemporary Birkenfels, with a pentagonal keep; the thirteenth-century Kegenfels, whose two walls retain towers and bastions; two châteaux named Dreistein, one thirteenth-century, the other fourteenth; château Koepfel, with its Romanesque walls; and the fourteenth-century Hagelschloss.

The main parish church of Ottrott is a building of 1771 with baroque furnishings and a Silbermann organ. See Mont Sainte-Odile in the index to this book.

On Sundays and holidays a train built in 1906 runs along a track laid in 1902 from Ottrott to Rosheim and back.

La Petite-Pierre

Towards the end of the eleventh century the counts of Lutzelstein built a château in the Vosges forest which was rebuilt between 1566 and 1588, attacked by Turenne in 1674 and in the next century transformed by Vauban into a citadel. Its garrison chapel, dedicated as usual in Vauban towns to St Louis (for his master was King Louis XIV), was built in 1684 and now houses a museum of old Alsatian family, ecclesiastical and municipal seals. La Petite-Pierre boasts a sixteenth-century guard house and several delightful seventeenth- and eighteenth-century houses. The church of the Assumption (1884), serving both Catholics and Protestants, houses fifteenth-century wall tombs and incorporates from its predecessor a flamboyant Gothic choir of 1417, with some well-restored wall paintings. Nearby is a swan reserve and an animal park, with deer, roe and boar. The citizens have given picturesque names (the frog, the crow, Cupid, etc.) to several bizarrely shaped rocks outside the village.

Pfaffenheim

Close by the church of Saint-Martin at Pfaffenheim is a Merovingian tomb. The church itself boasts a Romanesque choir, a nave of 1894 and a bell-tower of 1976. In the fifteenth century Pfaffenheim became a place of pilgrimage, and the pilgrimage church of Notre-Dame de Schauenberg has a Gothic choir and a late-sixteenth-century nave. The village has a good number of vintners' houses.

Pfaffenhofen

Pfaffenhofen was ravaged during the Thirty Years' War and retains only vestiges of its former fortifications, but a good number of sixteenth-century half-timbered houses were spared and more were built afterwards. The synagogue is dated (in Hebrew and Arabic letters) 1791. The nineteenth-century town hall has a small museum dedicated to Albert Schweitzer, and at No. 37, rue Albert-Schweitzer is a museum of popular Alsatian painting (including the earliest paintings on glass in France). It opens on Wednesdays and at weekends from 14.00 to 17.00.

Reinhardsmunster

Founded only in 1616 on the site of a village that had died, Reinhardsmunster is dominated by the thirteenth-century ruins of château d'Ochsenstein, whose chapel was Gothic and whose steps are carved into the rock itself. A Renaissance hunting lodge of 1621 in the village was once the presbytery of the church. The cemetery chapel, rebuilt in the seventeenth century, retains its Romanesque font.

Ribeauvillé

Since neolithic times men and women have lived on this site. Its modern name (or nearly so: Ratbaldo) first appears in a manuscript of 759. Known in German as Rappolstein, it passed into the possession of a family who took the name and built the eleventh-century château of Saint-Ulrich, whose keep, twelfth-century knights' hall and other buildings still survive. They also built what today is another noble ruin at Ribeauvillé, the thirteenth-century château de Hohrappolstein. By order of the emperor the Rappolsteins became 'kings of the minstrels', who still perform at Ribeauvillé on Pfiffertag at the beginning of September (see the index to this book).

In the late-thirteenth century they fortified the town, and continued to add to these fortifications (most of which survived World War II) until the fourteenth century. The south gate has towers surmounted with storks' nests. Formerly four branches of the Rappolstein family, to keep peace with each other, added to these fortifications by dividing walls which split the town into quarters, but today all that survives of these is the wide, square tour des Bouchers (1536) at the heart of the town.

Ribeauvillé boasts a monastic church (formerly Augustinian) of the mid-fifteenth century; the Gothic church of Saint-Grégoire-le-Grand built between 1282 and 1473 (restored in 1876; note the fourteenth-century ironwork of its great door, and inside a lovely gilded fifteenth-century Madonna); the fifteenth-century pilgrimage chapels of Dusenbach just outside the town; and an eighteenth-century town hall. Inside the town hall is a museum rich in furniture and above all magnificent goblets, dating from the fifteenth to the eighteenth centuries.

The villagers produce and sell white wine, and the most famous

Winstub is known as the maison de l'Ave Maria because of a carving of the Virgin Mary on its oriel. Everywhere fine old houses abound, with fountains, *Winstube* and wells. The Gothic corn market is arcaded. The citizens make renowned pottery, and on the second Sunday in June they celebrate the feast of the *Kougelhopf* (see *Kougelhopf* in the index). Ribeauvillé's annual wine festival takes place at the end of July.

Riquewihr

Nearly three-quarters of the houses in Riquewihr were built before the Thirty Years' War began. The town came into the possession of the counts of Wurttemberg in 1324 (when they bought it from the Horbourg family instead of fighting for it), and until Riquewihr became French in 1793 it remained in their hands – not always peacefully, for the counts were rapacious and tyrannical and the citizens of Riquewihr were frequently at odds with them, even joining the Peasants' War of 1525 and turning Protestant (both Lutheran and Calvinist) partly to spite their masters. Nevertheless, Riquewihr prospered, especially from its vines in the sixteenth and seventeenth centuries. The present-day town, everywhere emblazoned with the Wurttemberg coat of arms, crammed with rich vintners' houses and resplendent in summer with geraniums, is an architectural testimony to those times.

The predecessors of the counts (the seigneurs of Horbourg) had fortified Riquewihr in 1291, and from that era remain not only the walls but also the so-called tour des Voleurs. The Obertor (also known as the tour Dolder) is partly thirteenth-, partly sixteenth-century in construction. The outside is fierce; the side facing the town is charmingly half-timbered. Also from the thirteenth century derive the ruins of the château de Bilstein, built at the very beginning of that century and destroyed in 1636, apart from its square tower and a few other stones. Bilstein is not the only château of Riquewihr. The present delightful museum of postal history is housed in a Renaissance château of 1540, and the thirteenth-century château de Reichenstein, though ruined, preserves one of its five-sided defensive towers.

Invidious though it may be to single out one street in Riquewihr as especially fine, the Grand'Rue is marvellous. One need not guess at the age of most of the buildings, since they have it inscribed over their doors and on their walls (sometimes along with a sign illustrating the profession of the persons who built them). Some boast wells, others oriel windows and gables, others little towers and entrancing doorways, many with courtyards, staircase towers and balconies decked with flowers.

Strike off into the other streets to fine houses equally attractive, to discover ancient wine-presses and Renaissance fountains. A fountain of 1560 to the right of the Dolder gate bears the arms both of the Horbourg family and of the town itself. A house dated 1574 in rue Saint-Nicolas sports a carving depicting Death carrying off its builder. The inscription defiantly observes, 'Death, you have no power over me; I have demonstrated my splendour by building this dwelling.' Death replies, 'My good friend, forget your splendour; you built this dwelling for someone else to live in.' Inside is a courtyard with a staircase tower, a well dated 1576 and an old wine-press.

In the place des Trois-Églises stands the former house of the midwife (la maison de la Sage-Femme), once the home of the vintners' company of Riquewihr. Today the vintners grow 300 hectares of vines, vines which today grow up to the town walls. A passage at No. 14, rue du Général de Gaulle leads to the 'courtyard of the vintners', where the inscription in German reads:

> This house rests in the hand of God
> I am called the courtyard of the vintners
> God guard me from fire and conflagration.

Almost opposite, at No. 52, is the tithe house where the counts of Wurttemberg collected their dues, no doubt many of them barrels of wine. Frost was, and remains, a far deadlier hazard to the vines than fire. Maison Behrel, at No. 5 in the Grand'Rue, is dated 1514 below and, above, 1709. The date above refers to the dreadful year when ice killed off virtually every grape. To study the history of wine here, visit the Musée historique du Dolder (in the tower of the gateway), a museum both of local history and of wine-making.

I should add that the Protestant parish church of 1846 shelters an organ case of 1781 and that the chapel of the hospital of Saint-Erhard was built between 1441 and 1536.

Riquewihr is justly packed in the tourist season, and its citizens have wisely pedestrianized it and offered car parking outside its double walls. The post-office museum opens every day in July and August from 10.00 to 12.00 and from 15.00 to 19.00. It closes on Fridays and one hour earlier each day during the other months of the year, and completely from December to the end of March.

Rosenwiller

Lying two kilometres north-west of Rosheim, the thirteenth- and fourteenth-century church of this little village has a bell-tower and a polygonal choir both from the fourteenth century, fourteenth-century stained glass and wall paintings, a flamboyant doorway and eighteenth-century baroque altars. The nave is nineteenth-century Gothic. Rosenwiller's Jewish cemetery is probably the oldest in Alsace, with several 300-year-old gravestones. Rosenwiller has preserved its old mill.

Rosheim

On the Alsace wine route, Rosheim boasts the oldest house in Alsace, known as the house of the pagans and built around 1170, maybe even a decade earlier. Four gates survive from the fourteenth-century ramparts. The city wells date from 1527, 1592 and 1605, the last equipped with six buckets. Everywhere are begonia-decked houses, most of them Renaissance, many of them half-timbered and embellished with the trade signs of those who lived in them long ago.

The twelfth-century church of Saints-Pierre-et-Paul is a Romanesque masterpiece, with an octagonal tower that you can see is just turning Gothic in its upper windows. Walk round the exterior to enjoy the carvings and spot the man sitting on a roof with a goblet in his hand. Inside are Romanesque and Gothic capitals, and the eighteenth-century organ is from the workshop of Andreas Silbermann. When the troops of the count of Mansfeld were pillaging Rosheim in 1622, legend has it that angels with flaming torches drove them from the church.

The eighteenth-century church of Saint-Étienne, Rosheim, is by Salins de Montfort and retains its late-twelfth-century Romanesque belfry. See also Ottrott for a picturesque train journey.

Rothbach

A village of half-timbered houses dating from the seventeenth to the eighteenth century, Rothbach also has a twentieth-century Lutheran church with a thirteenth-century ogival choir and an ancient well. People would come on pilgrimage here to pray for their sick pets, and some fifteenth-century ruins remain from the pilgrimage chapel. Outside the village archaeologists have discovered neolithic remains.

Rouffach

Until the thirteenth century Rouffach, a town founded in neolithic times if not earlier and then inhabited by the Romans, was the only fortified city in the upper Rhine. Today it offers a splendid collection of medieval and Renaissance buildings, dominated by the towers of the church of Notre-Dame. The church was begun in the last quarter of the twelfth century, and a transept and some chapels survive from that era. The west façade is basically fourteenth-century. Thirteenth-century doorways, a rose window, buttresses and an octagonal tower rising to fifty-six metres above the crossing create an immediate impression of sumptuousness (though some of the sculptures of the west front, modelled on those of Strasbourg cathedral, were mutilated at the revolution). The font is a marvel of stone-carving, dating from 1492. Don't miss the gilded fifteenth-century Madonna in her Gothic niche.

Rouffach's Renaissance former town hall (1575) has a double gable. In the same place de la République rise the corn market of 1569 and the thirteenth-century tour des Sorcières, with a stork's nest. Rouffach is full of picturesque old houses, wells and statues of the Virgin Mary. Once it also contained convents and monasteries, but of these all that remains is the former Franciscan church, built between 1280 and 1300, reordered in the fifteenth century and equipped with an open-air pulpit. Château d'Isenbourg, Rouffach, was built in the nineteenth century on the site of a Merovingian palace, and retains the old fourteenth-century cellars.

See also the index to this book.

Saint-Amarin

Although St Amarin founded a monastery here in the mid-seventh century, the town is now more a relic of the failing Alsace textile industry. Well worth a visit is the Serret museum, named after a World War I general who died of his wounds in 1916 and full of souvenirs from the Vosges front of 1914–18. It opens each day except Tuesday from May to September, from 14.00 to 18.00. The eighteenth-century church houses a Gothic Madonna. The French cockerel perches on a fountain of 1830 in the Grand'Rue.

Saint-Hippolyte

Dedicated to a saint and martyr who met his death by being dragged by wild horses, and some of whose ravaged bones were placed in the parish church by the abbot of Saint-Denis, Saint-Hippolyte has a fourteenth-century church, with an ogive-vaulted choir, eighteenth-century furnishings and an eighteenth-century reliquary. The paintings on its wooden ceiling represent the Fathers of the Church set around Christ in majesty. Outside is a Renaissance fountain dated 1555. The château built by the dukes of Lorraine was destroyed in the Thirty Years' War and the present one dates from 1718. Saint-Hippolyte possesses a Renaissance fountain, a good number of Renaissance half-timbered houses and remains of its old defences. The town hall was built in 1792.

The town stands surrounded by vineyards at the foot of Haut-Koenigsbourg, and its wine festival takes place at the end of September.

Saint-Jean-Saverne

The massive church once belonged to a Benedictine monastery founded by Count Pierre de Lutzelbourg and suppressed at the revolution. Its bulbous tower is eighteenth-century; the rest dates from around 1150. The ogival vaulting of the nave is the oldest in Alsace. The organ case dates from 1725. Happily, the sixteenth-century monastery tapestries were not sold at the revolution and hang now in the church.

Take the path from the cemetery to reach the 393-metre-high Mont Saint-Michel, with its magnificent panorama and a seventeenth-century hermits' chapel on the rocky peak. Count Pierre de Lutzelbourg's wife Ita was not so pious as he, indeed was reputedly a witch. The cavern just beyond the chapel is known as the Witches' School *(Hexenschule)* and here Ita is said to have led a coven celebrating the black mass on the feasts of the church. Still higher up is the so-called fairy cave, with a sepulchre cut out of the rock.

Sainte-Marie-aux-Mines

In the old days snow would often block the way through this Alsace frontier town. Today a toll-tunnel enables you to pass easily into the Lièpvrette plain as far as Sélestat and beyond. The mines in question are former silver mines, first opened in 1522, which you may visit in July and August. Here too is a mineralogical and mining museum, at No. 70, rue Wilson, open from 10.00 to 12.00 and from 14.00 to

18.00 during the same two months. Sainte-Marie-aux-Mines has a few half-timbered houses and churches dating from the sixteenth century to the present day (the church of Saint-Pierre-le-Haut is entirely sixteenth-century), and it makes up for its relatively poor architectural heritage by concentrating on winter sports and leisure activities.

See also the index to this book.

Sainte-Odile

Mont Saint-Odile is Alsace's sacred and wooded mountain, from which a huge monastery on the edge of the line of the Vosges dominates the plain. The view is astounding. You can see as far as Strasbourg, Obernai and the Black Forest, as well as countless villages in between (there is a useful orientation table). Surrounding the height are eleven kilometres of the so-called Pagan Wall, reaching in parts over 3.5 metres in height and 1.7 metres in width and incorporating three separate fortified camps.

St Odile (see the index to this book) founded not only the convent on top of the Hohenbourg but also a more accessible religious house, the Niedermunster, farther down the mountainside. The bones of the saint made her foundation a place of pilgrimage, and so revered were her relics that Charles VI opened her tomb in 1354 to take a bit of her forearm away with him to Prague. Pilgrims still gather at the saint's shrine on Easter and Whit Monday, and several other times in the Christian year.

St Odile's religious houses reached a new peak of religious inspiration in the twelfth century under the Abbess Herrade, author of the celebrated *Hortus Deliciarum* or *Garden of Delights* (see again the index). Several times pillaged and attacked after Herrade's death, the convent was repeatedly rebuilt and restored until a terrible fire on the Feast of the Annunciation in 1546 brought about such a conflagration that the nuns left, never to return. (In the preceding decades several of them had taken to Protestantism and others to sexual licence.) Premonstratensian monks took possession of the buildings, their efforts at restoration hampered by the Thirty Years' War but rewarded afterwards with over a century of peaceful scholarship and contemplation. Then the revolution forced them out. The monastery passed into secular hands and was several times bought and sold until in 1853 the diocese of Strasbourg acquired the sacred buildings and set about a massive restoration.

Today you can drive and park there, taking a drink from the hôteliers who have also established themselves. The convent church of 1687 is a hall church with a triple nave, supported by twelfth-century buttresses, housing eighteenth-century furnishings and a Madonna of the same era. Older is the chapel of the Cross, built in two stages in the twelfth century – here in their ninth-century sarcophagus lie Odile's parents, Adalric and his wife Bereswinde, and the walls are frescoed with illustrations from Abbess Herràde's *Hortus Deliciarum*. The chapel of St Odile herself may well be a century older than the chapel of the Cross, though its vaulting and choir are Gothic and its furnishings eighteenth-century. Odile's own sarcophagus is a century older than that of her parents, though Charles VI had it embellished after he had taken a piece of her away. Bas-reliefs done at the turn of the eighteenth century show Odile's baptism and her prayers redeeming her father from purgatory. In the cloister, adorned with carvings depicting the history of the foundation, stands a Romanesque stele, depicting (among much that is virtually indecipherable) Adalric offering the monastery to his daughter.

Two other small twelfth-century chapels have been beautifully restored on the great terrace of Mont Sainte-Odile (which boasts an eighteenth-century sundial): the chapel of the tears (its name, according to the 1930s' mosaics inside, referring to the tears of Odile as she prayed for her father, but almost certainly deriving from the fact that this was the nuns' cemetery chapel); and the chapel of the angels, decorated with mosaics of 1948 depicting the birth and ascension of Jesus and the archangel Michael fighting the dragon.

Amongst the miracles said to have been performed by St Odile during her lifetime were restoring the sight of a blind child and the healing of a sick old man, in both cases by washing them with water from her still extant spring, which to this day is said to have curative powers. You reach it after a fifteen-minute walk through the pine trees, and twentieth-century pilgrims still wash their eyes in the water. Nearby is a series of stations of the cross portrayed in ceramics by L. Eichinger in 1935. Follow a path from the spring down to the abbey of Niedermunster, which was abandoned after a fire in the sixteenth century a few years before the nuns quitted the upper convent. Most is in ruins, though the chapel of Saint-Nicolas was restored in 1845 on the site of the eleventh-century original.

Sarre-Union

At the heart of this industrial town on the bank of the River Sarre are numerous sixteenth- to eighteenth-century typical Alsatian houses, many with fine doorways and oriel windows, some with splendid roofs. The churches, like the town, display features from several centuries, all with eighteenth-century furniture. Sarre-Union has a Jewish cemetery and a synagogue restored after World War II.

Sarrewerden

The fifteenth-century church of Saint-Blaise at Sarrewerden is worth a visit, for a sight of its polygonal choir, its Renaissance tomb and its sixteenth-century statue of the Virgin. Towers still stand from its former château and defensive walls.

Saverne

This Gallo-Roman town on the banks of the River Zorn and the Rhine-Marne canal, close to the Saverne forest and the 410-metre-high Saverne peak, has become a winter health resort. It always was a resort, on the road from Lorraine to Strasbourg, and its very name derives from the French for three taverns. As Louis XIV descended the Saverne peak on his way into Alsace he is said to have exclaimed, 'What a beautiful garden!' Saverne's history has included treachery: the peasants took it in 1525 and were persuaded on promise of pardon to cede the town to Duke Antoine de Lorraine, who proceeded to massacre them all, 18,000 of them, including their leader Erasmus Guerber.

Today it has been discreetly industrialized. Here Nicolas Salins de Montfort built the immense eighteenth-century classical château de Rohan known as the Versailles of Alsace. The bishops of Strasbourg had it built as their escape world, prompting Goethe to observe that these princes of the Church lived like monarchs. They had taken refuge at Saverne from 1561 to 1681, driven out of Strasbourg by the Protestant Reformers, and Cardinal Louis-René de Rohan commissioned the new château in 1779 when a fire burned down their old one. The façade of this château looking out on to the garden, with its pilasters and Corinthian columns, justifies the comparison with Versailles. Today it houses a museum of fine arts and an archaeological museum, both opening from 14.30 to 18.00 except Tuesdays from mid-June to mid-September. (On Sundays it opens also from 10.00 to 12.00.) In the tourist season *son et lumière* performances are given here.

Saverne boasts two other noble ruined châteaux (Haut-Barr, south-west of the town, and Greifenstein, west of the town), both first built in the twelfth century, both retaining towers, chapels and other buildings that are immensely picturesque. The under-prefecture of Saverne is also a château, though a mini-one built in the late-seventeenth century.

The town also has many fine houses, mostly Renaissance, some earlier; many are half-timbered and some, such as the 1605 maison Katz, are embellished with carvings of grotesques. As for its churches, the main one (Notre-Dame) has a belfry and doorway built in the twelfth century, along with a Gothic nave and choir, a fifteenth-century Christ in the sepulchre, a pulpit of 1495 by Hans Hammer who created the one in Strasbourg cathedral, a sixteenth-century *pietà,* some stone tombs of the bishops of Strasbourg from that and the previous century, a Renaissance font of 1616, lovely eighteenth-century ironwork protecting a chapel of 1496 and an organ case of 1717. During World War I an airman dropped a bomb on the church. Belatedly, but in time, the citizens removed the fifteenth-century stained glass, putting it back after cleaning in 1927. Some of the scenes are said to have been designed by Kaspar Eisenmann of Colmar. Look out for the fifteenth-century painting on wood of Jesus carrying his cross to Golgotha: the man carrying a hammer and three nails in order to nail Jesus to his cross is represented as utterly grotesque, and every other face is a study in itself.

As if that were not enough for one town, Saverne's church of the Récollets was begun in the fourteenth century and boasts wall paintings of the same era, fine tombs and eighteenth-century furnishings; the Romanesque chapel of Haut-Barr has a Lombardic frieze; and not far from Haut-Barr is a ruined Gothic chapel of Saint-Vite, once a centre of pilgrimage for those seeking a cure for St Vitus's dance. The synagogue has been restored, the Jewish cemetery is intact. And in the rose park at Saverne are 1,300 varieties of roses which you can see blooming from June to September from 09.00 to 12.00 and from 14.00 to 19.00. You can sail in a barge along the Rhine-Marne canal past this rose garden and view the château de Rohan.

Three and a half kilometres along the N4 to the west of the town is a botanical garden with another 2,000 different plants. It was created in 1931 and opens from June until the autumn from 09.00 to 18.00.

Sélestat

Sélestat was pre-eminently the city of the humanists, the birthplace of such late-fifteenth- and early sixteenth-century luminaries as Martin Bucer, Beatus Rhenanus and Jacques Wimpheling (see Sélestat and these names in the index to this book). Beatus Rhenanus's library, now in the nineteenth-century corn market which also houses a museum (with Gallo-Roman remains, stained glass, and a head of Jesus in polychromatic wood sculpted in 1464) opens from 09.00 to 12.00 and 14.00 to 17.00 on weekdays and on Saturday mornings.

The Swedes took Sélestat in 1632 and abandoned it to Louis XIII of France two years later. When Louis XIV took control of most of Alsace, he ordered Vauban to fortify the city. He took care not to spoil what remained of the medieval fortifications. You can walk round the ramparts and view the Vosges, the River Ill and Haut-Koenigsbourg. The nearby Illwald forest is a nature reserve with deer, wild boars and protected birds. The Bavarians bombarded Sélestat in 1815, the Germans annexed it in 1870 (when it assumed its old name, Schlettstadt) and the French took the town back in 1918.

Of the fourteenth-century ramparts the clock-tower gateway had a gallery, little towers and a dome added in the eighteenth century. Its charm is enhanced by an old painting of the crucifixion, first done in 1614 and many times redone. The sorcerers' tower has a base dating from 1300. Nearby is Vauban's classical Strasbourg gate. Renaissance buildings abound, and some Gothic ones too. The arsenal Sainte-Barbe in the place de la Victoire dates from the fourteenth century, the hôtel d'Ebersmunster at No. 8, rue de l'Église from the sixteenth.

But Sélestat's masterpiece is the church of Sainte-Foy. In 1087 Frederick of Hohenstaufen's widow Hildegarde built for the town a small chapel. Her three sons, on a pilgrimage to Santiago de Compostela in Spain, came across the church of Sainte-Foy at Conques, far away in the Rouerque. On their return they persuaded their mother to present her chapel in Sélestat to the monks of Conques. They took it over and later replaced it with this sandstone and granite masterpiece, built in the second half of the twelfth century. It has been many times restored, sometimes badly, but its towers and spire and the austerity of its lines have never been obliterated. Inside, its capitals are sternly carved; and the crypt, fancifully modelled on the Holy Sepulchre in Jerusalem, retains the sole vestiges of Hildegarde's modest chapel. Four winged symbols of the Evangelists uphold its gilded classical pulpit. To the right of the church stands the granary of the former priory, built in 1601.

Between the thirteenth and the fifteenth centuries another church was being built in Sélestat, on a Romanesque foundation. Saint-Georges, which stands just along rue du Babel a few steps from Sainte-Foy, is frequently called the cathedral of the town. Its tower rises sixty metres and was finished in the fourteenth century. Meanwhile frescos were being painted inside, to be finished a hundred years later. The rose window above the south doorway dates from 1400; the stained glass of the church from between 1435 and 1460. A local glazier named Hans Tieffenthal created these magical blues and reds and greens. A kneeling stone Samson holds up its pulpit of 1552. The choir stalls were also chiselled in the sixteenth century.

Sélestat is a town enriched with flowers and every year on the second Sunday in August holds its *corso fleuri,* with countless decorated floats and tourists crowding its streets. On the evening of 5 December takes place the Feast of St Nicolas, with everyone gobbling spicy breads.

Sessenheim

While a student at Strasbourg in 1770 and 1771 the young Goethe fell in love with a girl from Sessenheim called Frédérique Brion, whose father was pastor here. When he left Strasbourg, Goethe broke off their relationship, though he did see her once again in 1779. She never married. A former guard house, dated 1820, is now the Goethe memorial, with his bust and a small exhibition. (It opens in the mornings between 09.00 and 12.00 and in the afternoons between 14.00 and 18.00.) The presbytery where Frédérique lived was rebuilt in the mid-nineteenth century. Her parents' tombstones are on the outside wall of the parish church, which was enlarged in 1912, retaining from the older building the Gothic nave and choir. Goethe buffs meet in the restaurant Au Boeuf, where there is another, private museum in his honour.

Soufflenheim

This industrial town has been making superb pottery for centuries, indeed for millennia if you count archaeological discoveries. Its modern renown for the craft dates from the twelfth century, its first potters' guild from 1622. You can visit the potters' workshops as well as buying direct from their shops.

Soultz-Haut-Rhin

Renaissance houses, a seventeenth-century corn house (now the town hall), the château d'Helckeren-Anthès (built from the seventeenth to the nineteenth century), the former town hall of 1547 and the superb fourteenth- and fifteenth-century church of Saint-Maurice make Soultz-Haut-Rhin a little-known treat. St Maurice himself is sculpted on horseback over the church doorway. Soultz-Haut-Rhin also boasts a former chapel of the knights of Malta, dated 1774.

Thann

'Our first town in Germany,' Montaigne laconically dictated to his secretary on their journey to Italy in 1580, 'subject to the Emperor, very beautiful.' It remains beautiful, in spite of prospering as a result of the industrial revolution. Louis XIV ordered the demolition of its thirteenth-century château d'Engelsbourg, but part of its round tower still stands and is now known as the witch's eye. The remains of Thann's fortifications include the fourteenth-century storks' tower (tour des Cigognes) and another known as the witches' tower, built two centuries later. (There is a romantic view of it from the bridge over the River Thur.) Contemporary with it is the corn market of 1519 (now a museum) and the town hall built by the future General Kléber (see Thann and Kléber in the index to this book).

The name Thann derives from the German for pine trees, and legend tells that St Thiébaut's servant, after his master's death in 1160, kept one of the saint's thumbs as a relic. Lying down to sleep amidst three pines, he was startled by three heavenly lights appearing above them, attracted by the saint's thumb. The lord of the château d'Engelsbourg spotted the lights and raised a pilgrimage chapel on the spot. Thann still celebrates the burning of the pine trees *(la crémation des sapins)* annually on 30 June. The coat of arms on the façade of Thann town hall naturally includes a pine tree.

The sandstone church of Saint-Thiébault is an impressive replacement of the first chapel, begun in the fourteenth century and finished in the seventeenth. Its celebrated square tower topped by a spire was completed by Remigius Faesch in 1516 and stands 76.3 metres high. Equally celebrated are its fifteenth-century vaulting and its triple tympanum of 1420 over the west doorway. The sculptures illustrate the life of the Virgin Mary and the birth and death of Jesus. Even finer, I think, is the north doorway of 1456 depicting the Virgin, St John and St Thiébaut. The interior of the church has fifteenth-century wall paintings and stained glass, as well as many contemporary statues and lovely fifteenth-century Gothic stalls. The suburb of Vieux-Thann, alas, lost most of its splendid stained glass when the parish church was bombed in World War II.

Here in 1727 was born Jean-Baptiste Gobel, who became bishop of Paris and was guillotined in 1794. The museum of the Friends of Thann attached to the former corn market hosts statuary and objects of local history. It opens daily from 10.00 to 12.00 and from 14.30 to 18.30 between 15 May and the end of September.

Thierenbach

Three hundred thousand pilgrims are said to pay an annual visit to the church in the little village of Thierenbach in Haut-Rhin at the foot of the Grand Ballon, for this is Alsace's premier pilgrimage site. Here Peter the Venerable, abbot of Cluny, founded a Benedictine priory, which was burned down in the eighteenth century. Today's church, simple outside with an onion-topped tower, has riotous baroque furniture inside and a lovely painted ceiling.

Turckheim

Waters of the River Fecht, diverted down gulleys, wash clean the Grand'Rue of Turckheim, a village set among the vineyards of the Vosges and boasting narrow alleyways, a Renaissance town hall of 1595 and fine vintners' houses. Three fourteenth-century gates defend it, the painted porte de France (which carries a stork's nest on top), the porte de Brand (named after one of the local wines) and the porte de Munster, through which would pass those condemned to death (including in the past countless deemed to be witches). Near it is a memorial to Henri de la Tour d'Auvergne, Viscount Turenne, who took Turckheim from the imperial soldiers in 1675, after which he won a celebrated battle which cost him 1,800 soldiers, two generals and his own horse, shot from under him. The place Turenne has an eighteenth-century fountain. See also Turckheim in the index to this book.

Vosges Natural Park

The northern Vosges mountains, for the most part forested, though interspersed with meadows, now constitute a remarkable regional national park, set up in February 1976 and officially known as the *Parc naturel régional des Vosges du Nord*. Covering some 120,000 hectares and stretching to the border with Germany, the park embraces ninety-four communes between Bas-Rhin and the Moselle. Across the border its German counterpart is the Natural Park of the Palatinate.

The rich and diverse heritage of this park includes the regions known as the Hanau, Arrière-Kochersberg, the pays de Bitche and the Outre-Forêt. Since this is frontier country, some thirty mountain châteaux and fortresses sprinkle the summits of the park, and here too was set up the ill-fated Maginot Line. Deep valleys, forests of pine and beech, rare flora, lakes and some carefully ordered agriculture (though the park houses scarcely 80,000 people) have been combined with well-marked paths for ramblers and nature watchers, and the animal park at Schwarzbach, where deer and roe roam in their natural state. The Club des Vosges has developed campsites, rural *gîtes* and chalets.

Traditional activities in this region have been iron- and glass-making as well as forestry and farming. At Meisenthal there is a glass museum; at Offwiller a museum of popular art; at Volmunster a nature museum and a museum of clog-making. The main administrative seat of the park, as well as its information centre, is in the château of La Petite-Pierre, 69720 Wingen-sur-Moder (telephone 88 70 46 55). See also La Petite-Pierre in the index to this book.

Walbourg

This long village (scarcely more than a street) retains a former Benedictine abbey-church, founded by Count Thierry I of Mont-béliard in 1170 and mostly rebuilt in the fifteenth century. Its massive tower, its fifteenth-century frescos, its baroque altars and above all its fifteenth-century stained glass by Pierre d'Andlau are all over-whelming in their diverse fashions. So is the exquisite forest site of the church. Where the rest of the abbey once stood now stands a château of 1912.

Wangenbourg-Engenthal

This attractive village, perched some 500 metres above sea-level, is protected by the important ruins of the fourteenth-century château de Wangenbourg (its pentagonal keep, its vast polygonal defences, its Renaissance dwellings) and of the earlier château de Freudeneck, with its circular keep and polygonal walls. The chapelle d'Ober-steigen has preserved nearly all its Romanesque-Gothic features. Wangenbourg-Engenthal calls itself the Switzerland of Alsace and is a winter health and sports resort, with much hunting in season.

Wasselonne

The town of Wasselonne on the left bank of the River Mossig has a baroque Lutheran church with a Silbermann organ dated 1749, a synagogue rebuilt after 1945 and the remains of its fifteenth-century château. On the town hall a medallion celebrates the liberation of Wasselonne by General Leclerc in 1944. The village prospers on tourism.

Westhoffen

At Westhoffen four towers and some walls remain from the fourteenth-century fortifications. Stone and half-timbered houses, some with oriel windows and fine doorways, make this a typically picturesque Alsatian village. The town hall was built in 1753, and the much restored Lutheran hall church in the thirteenth and fourteenth centuries. Its stained glass is fourteenth-century, its organ case dates from 1768. The fourteenth-century château de Rosenbourg has two medieval towers.

In mid-June Westhoffen celebrates a cherry festival. Two kilometres north-east lies the partly fortified wine village of Wangen, where on the Sunday after 3 July a wine festival includes free drinks (not water) at the fountain in front of the church.

Wissembourg

The town of Wissembourg on the River Lauter boasts the largest Gothic church in Alsace after Strasbourg cathedral. The sandstone

Saints-Pierre-et-Paul was consecrated in 1284, and its Romanesque square west tower survives from that date. The rest is mainly fourteenth-century, with a modern spire on its octagonal tower. Statues, an eighteenth-century organ case and medieval frescos (including one of St Christopher said to be the biggest in France and discovered only in 1967) embellish the interior.

The administrative building of the sub-prefecture, opposite the church, dates from 1784. But the old quarters are best explored along the quai Anselmann and the quai du Bruche. Also worth seeing are the Romanesque and Gothic church of Saint-Jean; the Romanesque church of Altenstadt; the former church of the Dominicans (thirteenth-century); and the eighteenth-century church of Mary of the Seven Sorrows. When King Stanislas Leszczynski was exiled from Poland in 1720 he took refuge at Wissembourg, and his daughter used to worship in the church. At Wissembourg also lived the monk who wrote *Der Krist* (see index). The local history museum (Musée Westercamp) is in a sixteenth-century building. It opens from 10.00 to 12.00 and from 14.00 to 17.00, except on Tuesdays, Sunday afternoons and during the month of January.

Some Wissembourg streets seem cooler because of the water at their centre. The remains of the town's medieval fortifications are picturesque, with several towers still proudly standing (especially the 1420 tour des Husgenossen). Here too are a Jewish cemetery and a synagogue restored after 1945. Fishing, hunting, horseback riding, a race-track, the nearby Vosges natural park and numerous festivals attract many tourists.

The spiritual legacy

But for a remarkable medieval German poet named Gottfried who lived in Strasbourg in the early years of the thirteenth century we should know hardly anything of the greatest hero of knightly romance, the north British prince Tristan. Great lover, accomplished liar, musician, chess master, huntsman, Tristan as a youth was kidnapped by North Sea pirates, who set him down in Cornwall where he found his way to Tintagel and the court of his uncle King Mark. Tristan charmed the whole court. When it was revealed that his mother Blancheflor was sister to Mark, everyone was delighted. Even more pleasing to the hapless king (and galling to the useless knights of Tintagel) was the way Tristan responded to the three-yearly demands of King Gormond of Ireland that Cornwall pay him a toll of thirty young men and maidens. When Gormond's champion, the giant Morôlt, brother of Gormond's wife Isolde, arrived to claim the toll, Tristan challenged him to battle and killed him, leaving a tiny splinter of his sword in Morôlt's skull.

Unfortunately, in the combat he himself was wounded by a poisoned weapon. Only Queen Isolde possessed the antidote. Tristan was laid in a vessel, along with his harp and sword, and the waves carried him to Ireland. Passing for a minstrel, he was cared for and healed by the queen and her daughter, also called Isolde. Once recovered, Tristan feigned that he already had a wife in Cornwall and returned home. The jealous knights, knowing Gormond's rage at

Morôlt's death and his consequent intense hatred of Cornish knights, persuaded King Mark that he should wed Princess Isolde and that Tristan should be despatched to seek her hand. Tristan insisted that twenty of them go with him. Among Tristan's adventures on this mission he slew a dragon terrorizing the Irish, though the dragon's evil breath plunged him into a coma, from which once again Queen Isolde and her daughter rescued him.

Exposed by the splinter in Morôlt's skull as the slayer of Gormond's champion, Tristan once again found himself in mortal danger, but when his valiant fight against the dragon was revealed he was pardoned. He returned to Cornwall with King Mark's destined bride, and also with a fatal love potion made up by Queen Isolde. On their way he and Isolde drank the potion and fell passionately in love.

The poem then unfolds their remarkable skills at cuckolding the king, as they devised increasingly clever ways of allaying his suspicions. In one famous scene they are sleeping together in a cavern, but Tristan, knowing that King Mark is hunting nearby, places a sword between himself and his mistress. Once again Mark presumes their innocence.

Such ruses cannot work for ever. Tristan eventually flees for his life to Brittany, there to marry yet another Isolde. Still in love with Isolde of Ireland, he returns in disguise to Cornwall and meets her again. Here in a quarrel with a knight he is fatally wounded, again with a poisoned arrow. Only Queen Isolde of Ireland has the magical arts to save him. Will she come? A ship is despatched for her. If she is aboard when it returns, it shall bear a white sail; if she refuses to come, the sail shall be black. Queen Isolde agrees to save Tristan, but his jealous wife treacherously tells her sick husband that the sail is black. He turns away in despair and dies. Queen Isolde, grief-smitten, flings herself on his bier, passionately embraces Tristan and dies herself.

In the twelfth century an Anglo-Norman poet, Thomas of Brittany, set all this out in verse, much of which was lost. Happily, Gottfried von Strasbourg translated it into German. Other poets had by this time enriched medieval German literature. A contemporary of such masters as Walther von der Vogelweide and Wolfram von Eschenbach, in his *Tristan und Isolde* Gottfried surpassed them all – stylistically brilliant, subtle and refined, exquisitely skilled at wringing the pathos and the courtly love out of the whole tale. He did not live to finish this work, but by good fortune his 19,552 lines break off just where the surviving Anglo-Norman fragments begin.

Gottfried von Strasbourg wrote much else. This is his masterpiece. His preface states that he aims to present his readers with the ideal of courtly love. Spontaneous love, even though prompted by a love potion, demands complete devotion and will ennoble those who suffer such passion by their inevitable suffering. Gottfried's readers, he himself says, are noble souls filled with both bliss and grief.

His *Tristan und Isolde* shares with other Alsatian literature a remarkable ability to inspire others. Two other poets, Ulrich von Türheim and Heinrich von Freiberg, wrote a finale to his work. Above all, Gottfried's poem served as the inspiration for Richard Wagner's 1859 opera on the theme of the tragic lovers.

A hundred years later a Dominican mystic known to us as Meister Eckhart became professor of theology at Strasbourg. His inspired teachings were not well-loved by the inquisition. As he preached, enemies took down suspect sentences and laid them before the agents of Archbishop Heinrich of Cologne. Two Cologne inquisitors tried Meister Eckhart. He vigorously defended himself, writing a powerful vindication of his views and appealing to the Pope at Avignon. Setting off for Avignon in a bid to clear his name, he died before the case was decided. Had he lived he would have seen himself only partly vindicated by Pope John XXII.

What disturbed his critics? First, they were profoundly troubled by his insistence that God was utterly unknowable, transcendent and beyond the reach of human intellect. Secondly, he insisted that anyone who wished to have revealed to him God's reality must be totally detached from the world. Thirdly, he wrote in German. Historians have perceived that his enemies rarely sought his precise views when he set them out in Latin, and the mystical language of his German sermons bamboozled them.

Yet this quasi-heretic had great influence on the late-medieval world. One successor and disciple was another inhabitant of Alsace, the Dominican preacher Johannes Tauler. Tauler was born at Strasbourg around 1300. Learning from Meister Eckhart, he refused to accept the adverse judgments of John XXII on his master. 'He talked about eternity,' Tauler would say, 'but you took him to refer to time.' Tauler was a pithy preacher, and the nuns to whom he mostly preached took down his sermons. He followed Meister Eckhart in insisting on the unknowable nature of God. Any exposition of the doctrine of the Trinity, he asserted, was bound to be more a lie than the truth. The subtlest scholars, he averred, can only 'stammer' insights about the nature of the divine.

Tauler died in Strasbourg in 1361, after he had taken the teaching of his master to Cologne, where he influenced another Dominican mystic, the Blessed Henry Suso. Henry Suso's *Little Book of Eternal Wisdom* published in 1328 became the most widely used manual of meditation in the fourteenth and fifteenth centuries. The followers of these mystics came to be known as the 'Friends of God', a group of fourteenth-century Christians who spread throughout the Rhineland and into Switzerland. Condemned in his own time, Meister Eckhart thus lived on in the writings and lives of countless disciples.

Another Alsatian writer, far less profound than Gottfried von Strasbourg, Meister Eckhart, Johannes Tauler or Henry Suso, was paradoxically even more fecund in inspiring imitators. Whereas Gottfried's *Tristan und Isolde* daringly seems to sanction licentiousness, adultery and deceit, the *Ship of Fools* of his fellow-countryman Sebastian Brant is a satire unsparingly berating the vices of his time.

Brant was a humanist, born at Strasbourg in 1457. Studying at Basel, he became a doctor of laws and was made professor there. He returned to Strasbourg and, through the influence of his friend Geiler von Kaysersberg, became clerk to the city. Sebastian Brant died there on 10 May 1521.

He first attracted literary attention because of his Latin poetry. He edited legal and religious tomes, translating Virgil, Latin hymns, Cato and the Fathers of the Church, as well as all the works of Petrarch. Then in 1494 his famous *Das Narrenschiff* appeared, an allegory in which fools steer a ship laden with other fools by way of Utopia of Schlaraffenland to the fools' paradise of Naragonia. This poem became the most famous German literary production of the sixteenth century, even though Brant wrote it in what is much closer to Alsatian than to anything like High German.

In it every sort of idiot is castigated: drunks, criminals, corrupt judges, sex-crazed clerics, sensuous women, the improvident, those who borrow too much, those who lie in court, people who cannot take a joke. No one reaches the fools' paradise, for the *Narrenschiff* is wrecked and everyone drowns.

The 112 fools on board the *Narrenschiff* include some entertaining oddities, such as a learned numbskull who has collected a library of useless books. He keeps the flies off their pages, but hardly ever reads them. His Latin is in fact limited to such words as *vinum*, meaning wine, and *gucklus*, a cuckold. A woodcut depicts him with his fly-whisk, wearing huge spectacles. Brant also mocks 'old fools' in a character who, though aged a hundred, is still a naughty boy. In the accompanying woodcut he already has one foot in the grave. A third idiot is a peasant who has become a priest in the hope of adulation and has lived to regret it. Here the satire deepens into a dangerous attack on the pre-Reformation church. Brant blamed the bishops for ordaining such illiterate and uncommitted priests in the first place.

Undoubtedly what contributed to the book's popularity was Brant's nose, on the eve of the Reformation, for the moral lapses of monks and priests. His rough, homely language helped too. Most of all, the *Ship of Fools* was prized for its woodcuts, one for every chapter and all of them almost certainly by Albrecht Dürer.

Brant's book spawned a prolific school of fools' literature. Jacobus Locher produced a Latin translation (*Stultifera navis*) scarcely three years after it first appeared. In Britain Alexander Barclay in 1509 adapted this version as *The Shyp of the Folys of the World*. The following year Wynkyn de Worde printed another imitation of *Das Narrenschiff* called *Cock Lovell's Bote*, in which a crooked currier fills a ship with other rascal tradesmen. Others translated Brant's work into Latin, Dutch, Low German and French. Under Brant's inspiration Erasmus produced his satire *In Praise of Folly (Encomium moriae)* in 1509. A Swiss Franciscan named Thomas Murner wrote a savage *Exorcism of Fools (Narrenbeschwörung)*, modelled on Brant's satire, in 1512. Geiler von Kaysersberg preached over a hundred sermons drawing on the fools his friend had depicted. The genre is not yet exhausted, as Katharine Anne Porter's novel *Ship of Fools* showed in 1962.

A key to the immense success of such works was the invention of the printing-press. Again, as the place Gutenberg in Strasbourg indicates, Alsace – on the borders of France, Germany and Switzerland – was centrally important in the development of the new skill and in its utilization of humanists and Reformers. The man who was primarily responsible for the new invention, Johann Gutenberg, is said to have been born at Mainz in Germany at the end of the fourteenth century to a family frequently in debt. Soon he and his family fled to Strasbourg to avoid their creditors, arriving there around 1430. Not long after their arrival they were in trouble again. This time Gutenberg himself, claiming that the town of Mainz owed him 310 Rhenish guilders, seized the town clerk of that city and kept him prisoner until the councillors of Strasbourg persuaded him to release the unhappy man and give up his claims to the cash.

Gutenberg's experiments always led him into financial difficulties. In the late 1430s he was begging cash from friends in order to keep up his schemes for manufacturing looking-glasses and polishing stones. In 1438 he borrowed money from two friends to pursue what was to be his immortal achievement, the art of printing. Others advanced him more cash, as well as buying him paper, parchment and ink, and paying his rent. Such are the problems of genius. By 1448 this impoverished inventor had invented a typecasting machine and was using movable type cast in separate letters. His exquisite forty-two-line Mazarin Bible, probably the first book to be printed in Europe, appeared in 1456.

In 1442 he had borrowed eighty livres from the canons of St Thomas's church. Though Gutenberg soon after left Strasbourg, the church's register shows that he paid the interest regularly till 1457. Then the canons received no more. They were still recording that the interest remained unpaid six years after Gutenberg's death at Mainz in 1468.

A remarkable group of Alsatian humanists utilized the invention of the celebrated debtor to promote their own works. Beatus Rhenanus was one, the son of a Sélestat butcher, educated at a famous Latin school in his home town and later in Paris, where a leading Aristotelian scholar named Jacobus Fabius Stapulensis took the young man under his wing.

He then moved to Basel and there befriended not only the greatest humanist of the age, Erasmus, but also another noted printer, Johannes Froben. Froben was Erasmus's printer, a technician renowned for his accuracy and for the beauty of his work. Together these men set about a scholarly revival of the great texts of Christianity, many of them almost forgotten. The works of St Jerome, of St Cyprien, of St Ambrose, of St Hilary of Poitiers poured from Froben's press. His son Jerome produced a companion edition of the works of the Greek fathers of the Church. For a time Basel became the centre of German learning, and no less an artist than Hans Holbein illuminated the texts of the Froben press. When Froben died, Erasmus said he mourned him more than he lamented the death of his own brother. 'Every promulgator of learning must now weep,' he declared.

Beatus Rhenanus equally revered Erasmus. After his return to Sélestat he superintended the printing of his hero's works and corresponded with him. He became Erasmus's biographer. Neither he, nor Erasmus nor Froben wished to destroy Catholicism; yet their scholarship and humanist integrity impugned the unreformed Catholic Church of their day. In 1516 Froben published an edition of the

Greek New Testament which became the basis of Martin Luther's German translation. As for Luther himself, the printing-press was his propaganda-machine, and Alsace his inspiration. In 1518 he himself was seeing through the press the first printed edition of the *Theologia Germanica*, a mystical treatise written by the followers of Meister Eckhart, Johannes Tauler and Henry Suso.

The Alsatian humanists were patriots. Beatus Rhenanus's first published work was a biography of Geiler von Kaysersberg. He wrote a history of Germany. So did the Alsatian Jacob Wimpheling, whose *Stylpho*, written in 1480, severely criticized the laxity of contemporary clergy. The Alsatian who took these criticisms furthest was another son of Sélestat, Martin Bucer. In 1596 Bucer was a Dominican monk studying at the University of Heidelberg. There he began to read the works of Erasmus and Martin Luther, and there in April 1518 he watched Luther dispute with his Catholic opponents, who also happened to be Dominicans. Luther's views converted him.

In 1521 Bucer was still sufficiently Catholic to seek the Pope's dispensation when he resigned his vows as a monk. Next he married an ex-nun named Elizabeth Silbereisen. His zeal for the Reformation led to his excommunication, and in 1523 he arrived at Strasbourg. Already the views of Luther had been preached there by a canon of the cathedral named Matthäus Zell. Bucer succeeded him.

For twenty-five years he lived in Strasbourg, tirelessly preaching both the Reformation and Christian unity. He influenced John Calvin himself, who between 1538 and 1541 worked in the city as Bucer's lieutenant. What distinguished Bucer more than any other Reformer was his desire for peace not only within the Protestant Church but also with the Catholics. At Marburg in 1529 he tried in vain to reconcile Luther and Huldreich Zwingli. He brought the Basel reformer Andreas von Karlstadt to Strasbourg in 1536, in an unsuccessful attempt to bring together the Swiss followers of Zwingli and the German supporters of Luther. At Wittenberg in 1541 he was instrumental in bringing together Luther and the Upper German Protestants in a concord which, to his sorrow, the Swiss Protestants rejected.

At Regensburg in 1541 Cardinal Gasparo Contarini sought to devise formulas which might bring back moderate Protestants into the Roman fold. Bucer was there at his side. In that year his wife died of the plague, and a year later he married a distinguished widow. The following year Bucer worked out the rules of the abortive Protestant Church government which Archbishop Hermann of Cologne wished to bring into being in his own diocese. Soon, however, the continent of Europe became a dangerous place even for such an eirenic Protestant. Bucer fled to England. Such was his fame that the University of Cambridge made him Regius Professor of Divinity, and he was influential in the rewriting of the Anglican Book of Common Prayer.

Bucer died in 1551. His friend Archbishop Cranmer arranged a royal pension for his widow. When Bloody Mary acceded to the throne of England, his Protestant bones were dug up and burned in Cambridge market square. When Elizabeth I became queen, they were reverently reburied in the church of Great St Mary.

If Alsace for a century and more was a region of toleration between Protestants and Catholics, its attitude to Jews, as the pages of this book have revealed, was intermittently savage. In the first half of the sixteenth century a Jewish advocate from Rosheim named Joselin attempted to change things. Related to numerous martyred Jews, he sought to influence the courts of the Holy Roman Emperors Maximilian I and Charles V towards toleration. When the marauding peasants of 1525 attacked his own community at Rosheim, he cunningly bribed them to pillage his town only when they had done their worst elsewhere. By the time they had destroyed their other victims, the peasants were too sated and exhausted to attack Rosheim.

In 1520 Joselin of Rosheim presented Emperor Charles V with a memorandum refuting the charge that the Jews were allies of the Turks. He tried to have the business practices of his fellow-Jews approved by the Diet of Augsburg. Yet toleration was hard won. In 1613 the bishop of Strasbourg had inveighed against the building of synagogues. His successors did the same in 1700 and 1706. In consequence, the earliest Jewish synagogues in Alsace were semi-clandestine affairs. The one at Pfaffenheim, for example, is a half-timbered building, for all the world just another house in an Alsatian town. And although a ritual bath-house or *miqwah* was essential for any Jewish community, the oldest in Alsace, that at Bischeim, dates only from the end of the seventeenth century.

Toleration came only with the revolution, with the result that the noblest synagogues of Alsace date from the nineteenth century. That at Dambach-la-Ville boasts a fine Greek portico; that at Saverne is almost oriental in spirit. At Soultz the synagogue is neo-Romanesque. At Mulhouse it is more like a Protestant church – not surprisingly, since its architect also designed the church of Saint-

Étienne. By this time some Jewish congregations in Alsace, contrary to the long Jewish tradition, were installing organs in their synagogues – another architectural assimilation of Christianity. At Strasbourg, Ludwig Levy of Karlsruge, who designed the Catholic church of Saint-Pierre-le-Jeune, was commissioned in 1898 to build an immense synagogue which the Nazis destroyed in 1940. In 1958 it was replaced by the sole Alsatian synagogue built in the twentieth century, the so-called Strasbourg synagogue of peace.

Eighteenth- and nineteenth-century Strasbourg also nurtured a remarkable philanthropist who welcomed the revolution and became one of the great pioneers of education in the eighteenth and early nineteenth century. This extraordinary man, who started the world's first kindergartens, is another Alsatian whose influence still survives. He was a Protestant pastor named Jean-Frédéric Oberlin. Although Oberlin spent nearly sixteen years of his life ministering to peasants in one remote spot in the Vosges, his fame and example spread not only throughout France but also into the New World.

Born at Strasbourg in 1740, Jean-Frédéric Oberlin attended the Protestant gymnasium there and at the age of fifteen reached university. A bachelor of philosophy before he was eighteen, he had graduated as doctor of philosophy by the time he was twenty-three.

Oberlin has left us an account of what a university course at Strasbourg covered in the mid-eighteenth century. 'I had to study Latin, Greek, Hebrew, logic, rhetoric, metaphysics, mathematics, geometry, trigonometry, astronomy, ancient and modern geography, the history of the world, physics, natural history and the history of philosophy,' he tells us, followed by, 'law and jurisprudence, Egyptian, Greek, Roman and Hebrew antiquities, and finally theology.'

Thus equipped, at the age of twenty-seven after three years as a teacher he set out for the remote village of Waldersbach. Waldersbach lies in the valley of the Chergoutte some fifty kilometres south-west of Strasbourg and on the border between Alsace and Lorraine. The region is known as the Ban-de-la-Roche, dominated by the 830-metre-high rock on which once perched a twelfth-century château, until in 1469 several lords of Strasbourg (the bishop, the duke of Lorraine, the duke of Austria, the lord of Lichtenberg and Margrave of Baden) decided to attack and demolish it. All that remains today is a lonely ruined tower.

You can still see at Waldersbach the presbytery that Oberlin built for himself in 1787, helped by the donations of his friend Jean de

Dietrich, mayor of Strasbourg. Today it houses a small museum in his memory. (It opens from Easter to September from 14.00 to 18.00, except Mondays and Wednesdays.) Oberlin had the pious habit of putting a scriptural quotation over every door in the presbytery, so that as you enter the dining-room, for instance, you read the words, 'Blessed are those who hunger and thirst after righteousness, for they shall be filled.'

He found himself in charge of five villages altogether, Foudray, Neuwiller, Rothau, and Solbach, as well as Waldersbach. Although the Thirty Years' War had been over for almost 120 years, Oberlin discovered that none of these villages had recovered from its devastating effects. Some eighty wretched families lived here in utter poverty, unlettered and half-clothed. Their pastures produced coarse grass; the swollen mountain streams turned everything to marshland when the snows melted. Nothing the new pastor said seemed at first to make any difference to the way his flock lived and worked, so he decided instead to show them what could be done. On his own land he experimented with better kinds of grain and fruit trees. The contrast between his crops and those of his parishioners was so startling that they began to watch and listen. He taught them to graft better fruit trees on to the poor crab and wild apples. He persuaded the men to drain the marshlands.

Whereas the traditional Christian pattern was to devote one-tenth of one's wealth to charity, Jean-Frédéric Oberlin devoted three-tenths of his. Into a box he would put one-tenth for the church, in another one-tenth for what he called 'useful purposes', and in a third one-tenth to be given to the poor. But Oberlin was determined to help the poor to help themselves. To improve his parishioners' livestock, he gave an annual prize out of his own pocket to the farm that bred the finest ox.

He taught them to spin wool and manufacture ribbons. One day he called the peasants of Waldersbach together and said, 'My children, it is vital that we make a road through the valley, throwing a bridge across the River Bruche, so as to join the main highway to Strasbourg.' The people refused. The task was beyond their powers, they said, and in any case they already had enough to do. Oberlin put on an old jacket, took up his own pickaxe, and started work on the road himself. Picking up their axes, adzes and spades, the peasants joined him. Within a few months the road was finished, the Bruche bridged and the parish in communication with Strasbourg.

Its pastor next set about constructing paved roads to join up the other four villages. Now Oberlin could select young men and send them to the capital to train as carpenters, blacksmiths, glaziers, masons and wheelwrights. Young women went with them to train as midwives. They returned and applied their skills in their own villages, replacing the hovels of the families with stone homes that possessed cellars where wine and vegetables could be stored.

Pastor Oberlin was a son of the Enlightenment. He was determined to build a new schoolhouse for his parishioners. The benches he made himself; his trained workers built the rest. Once a week he himself taught every child from every village in a general class. The best children were taught agriculture and horticulture. Oberlin even taught them drawing and painting. Then came his remarkable innovation of kindergartens for the under-sevens, five such schools in a room in each village. Oberlin appointed two intelligent peasant women as teachers for each of these infant schools. They taught the children religion, the Bible, morals and manners, but also singing, some natural history, botany, drawing and colouring, as well as knitting, sewing and spinning. This education continued after the age of seven. And Oberlin set up an itinerant library to serve his five separate flocks.

As Oberlin's fame grew, other more valuable livings were offered to him, but invariably they were turned down. Oberlin had married a woman called Margaret Witter in 1768. She bore him nine children and died sixteen years later. For another eight years, Oberlin claimed, she would appear and converse with him. Then she told him this was over. They would meet again in the hereafter.

Meanwhile the French Revolution had occurred. Jean-Frédéric Oberlin welcomed it enthusiastically, even going along with the theories of some of the more extreme revolutionaries about what they dubbed empty religious ceremonies and unfruitful dogmas. Oberlin had never been a dogmatic man. He preferred to be called a Catholic-Evangelical than a Protestant pastor. He offered Holy Communion to Catholic, Calvinist and Lutheran alike, and when he discovered that they would not partake of the same kind of bread, he provided on the same plate wafers, unleavened and leavened bread. Now, when the National Assembly prohibited public worship and church rites, Oberlin blithely changed his service into club meetings, instructing his flocks on the duties of good citizenship, though always ending these meetings with prayers.

Oberlin was kinder to the revolution that it was to him. On its first anniversary, 14 July 1790, he gathered his flocks together on an open hill-top and held a patriotic festival around an 'altar of the fatherland'. The following year his son volunteered to fight for France against Austria, and Pastor Oberlin led a special service in honour of all such volunteers. Yet the revolutionaries still doubted his patriotic ardour. On 28 July 1794 he was summoned to Sélestat, roughly handled by a mob, and imprisoned. Happily, Robespierre fell a few days later, and Oberlin was released.

Now the National Assembly changed its tune, formally thanking Pastor Oberlin for his services to education. Never again was he reviled. When the allied armies entered France, Tsar Alexander himself issued Oberlin with a special letter of protection for himself and his parishioners. In 1818 the Royal Agricultural Society awarded him its gold medal. A year later Jean-Frédéric Oberlin received the cross of the Legion of Honour. When he died, amidst torrential rain on 1 June 1826, it was said that even the heavens were weeping.

His fame and influence lived on. Among countless biographies, one was written by the great English reformer Josephine Butler. Under Oberlin's inspiration two American missionaries in 1833 founded Oberlin College, Ohio. There Jean-Frédéric Oberlin's pioneering spirit continued. Oberlin College was the first co-educational college in America, and the first degrees ever granted to women were given there in 1841. In 1847 Oberlin College admitted the first two women ever to be accepted for training in theology. And this institution, inspired by the Alsatian pastor, was the first in America to admit students regardless of race or colour, standing up too, in the face of savage opposition, for the abolition of slavery.

Catholic Alsace too had its saints. Charles de Foucauld was like Oberlin in his love for the poor (and like Goethe in leaving behind a good number of broken-hearted women as he passed by). Like Oberlin, de Foucauld's fame outlasted his death, and like the leaders of Oberlin College, Ohio, he too hated slavery.

Born at Strasbourg in 1858 to a noble family whose ancestors came from the Dordogne, Charles Eugène, vicomte de Foucauld was an unlikely candidate for sanctification. He joined the French army and by his own account became so gluttonous that his features resembled those of a pig, his eyes sunk in layers of fat. At the Saint-Cyr military academy he would lie in bed at night spooning into his mouth chunks of the *foie gras* of his native Alsace.

His conquest of women was both charming and ultimately heartless. At one point his excessive amours forced his regiment to send him back to Paris. He joined the cavalry at Saumur and even

there was frequently disciplined by his superiors for wildness. When
he was transferred to the 4th Chasseurs d'Afrique and sent to Africa,
he took his current mistress with him, passing her off as his wife.
When the colonel discovered the deception, he demanded that de
Foucauld either repudiate the woman or temporarily quit the
regiment. De Foucauld chose the latter course.

The young officer had acquired this mistress at Nancy and
nicknamed her Mimi. There when the Meuse was frozen over, he
once gave a winter party for her, with sledges and skates, red lanterns
on every tree and blazing torches and fires. It was a party such as an
Alsatian with Périgordin ancestry would especially relish.

A sleigh in the shape of a swan drew up, and out of it de Foucauld
lifted his sable-coated mistress. His biographer Margaret Trouncer
describes the feast that followed:

The orderlies brought up a buffet table on which were caviare and *foie gras*
and truffled ortolans. Also, two specialities invented by Charles, coffee
brewed with old Kirsch instead of water, and his favourite chestnut mousse
frozen into an ice cream and covered with hot chocolate sauce.

The *foie gras* bespeaks not just Charles de Foucauld's Strasbourg
upbringing but also the earlier origins of his family – and that dish –
in Périgord. So do the truffled ortolans. I have to disagree with his
biographer about who invented the two extra treats. Kirsch drunk in
every conceivable fashion was, and remains, native to Alsace; and
chestnut mousse is still a speciality of the Dordogne. A gourmet
inheriting the twin traditions of the two regions had little need to
invent new dishes.

He soon enough abandoned his Mimi. Learning in 1881 that his
regiment was off to Algeria to quell an insurrection against the
French, de Foucauld successfully pleaded with the War Office to let
him rejoin the 4th Chasseurs. This time he acquitted himself like a
soldier and struck up a lifelong friendship with his general. Now he
fell under the spell of Africa, and two years later he was leading an
important exploration of Morocco, the first ever by a European.
Later he would map out the oases of southern Algeria. In between he
fell passionately in love again, this time with a girl of whom his
parents disapproved, for she was no aristocrat. He even became
engaged to the young bourgeoise, and then bowed to his parents'
wishes. The girl was heartbroken, and de Foucauld began to realize
the continual heartache his callous behaviour caused others.

He now began to brood about the virtues of chastity. Conversion was near, and was brought about by the remarkable Abbé Huvelin, priest of the church of St Augustine, Paris. A visit to the Holy Land confirmed de Foucauld's new vocation. He returned to France, and the former gourmand was received into the austere order of Trappist monks. Even this was not severe enough for the converted rake, and for a time he became a ragged servant of the Poor Clare Sisters of Nazareth and Jerusalem.

Charles de Foucauld was ordained priest, and decided to become a hermit in North Africa. Soon he was living entirely on bread and water. He did not remain entirely solitary, for Africa was beset with a problem which he felt he must try to remedy. At the beginning of 1902 he started to buy slaves and set them free. The Moslems saw him as a holy man who, strangely, was not Moslem like themselves. De Foucauld, for his part, believed that all the missionary problems of the Church in Africa could be put down to the fact that the French, who were supposed to be Christians, spent their time there despising the natives, getting drunk and visiting brothels. For his part, he said, 'I admire the amazing detachment of the Arabs, who do not even mend their tents when they are dropping in pieces. They simply enjoy existing, basking in the sun.' As a young man, he confessed, 'I thought I enjoyed myself hugely, but certainly I never did so much as those Arabs.'

Charles de Foucauld desperately wished to form an order of Christians who would share his own intensely austere life. Not a single person came forward to join him. He died a martyr, or perhaps, like so many Alsatians, merely a victim of World War I. The German policy of inciting the native Tuaregs to turn against their French masters was a success. In his rough stone hermitage on the peak of Mount Assekrem, de Foucauld's hope was to persuade them to stay loyal to France. On 1 December 1916, after night had fallen, Tuareg rebels surrounded his house. De Foucauld came out and was forced to sit against a wall, his hands tied behind him, while the rebels ransacked his home. After half an hour a sentry warned that Arabs loyal to the French were approaching. The rebels began firing, and the Tuareg nearest to de Foucauld put a gun to the hermit's head and fired. After a few moments blood began to flow, and Charles de Foucauld slipped gently on to his side. His body was stripped and thrown into a ditch, where camel-drivers discovered it some days later. There he lies buried.

The legacy of this Alsatian who never in his lifetime managed to persuade a single disciple to join him in the desert was extraordinary.

In 1933, inspired by the example of de Foucauld, a monk named René Voillaume founded in southern Oran, Algeria, the Little Brothers of Jesus. Six years later the Little Sisters of Jesus were founded at Touggourt in Algeria. These two contemplative orders, living in the strictest poverty, have spread throughout much of the world, earning their living amongst those who have been forsaken by others – in prisons, amongst poor labourers and indigent farmers – hoping, as de Foucauld did among the Arabs, that their companions will be converted not by preaching but by example.

Charles de Foucauld was no theologian. When a young soldier asked him for a little history of St Paul, Charles replied, 'I would much have liked to write this for you, but I cannot. I have other urgent things to write just now.' Instead he offered the soldier 'his very tender, very brotherly affection and his profound devotion to the heart of Jesus'. By contrast with de Foucauld, another great Alsatian Christian, Albert Schweitzer, again a man devoted to the welfare of the poor of Africa, managed to combine profound theological contemplation with a life of incessant, devoted action on behalf of the oppressed of the world.

'I was born in the little town of Kaysersberg, in upper Alsace, on January 14, 1875, in the small house with the turret which you see on the left as you leave the upper end of the town,' wrote Albert Schweitzer in his autobiography. Even though Kaysersberg was savagely bombed in World War II, Schweitzer's birthplace still stands, a handsome half-timbered house, with dormer windows, an archway leading into its courtyard and a little tower rising from the roof. Such was the substantial home of his father, Louis-Théophile Schweitzer, Lutheran pastor of Kaysersberg.

Kaysersberg, the 'mount of Caeser', takes its name from the nearby hill on which the Romans built a fort to control a route across the mountains into Gaul. Down the years this route remained important and so the town prospered. In the thirteenth century the Emperor Frederick II built a castle, virtually on the site of the Roman fort. Its ruins still stand. Happily, after World War II almost every war-damaged building in Kaysersberg was meticulously restored, so that today the exquisite little town looks much as it did on the day Albert Schweitzer was born. (See Kaysersberg in the index to this book.)

For the young pastor's son, the old houses and streets of Kaysersberg were redolent of a different kind of history. It was a matter of pride for Schweitzer that it was from Kaysersberg that

Geiler von Kaysersberg, the famous medieval preacher, took his surname. Born at Schaffhausen in Switzerland, Geiler was brought up in Kaysersberg, after his father's death, by his grandfather. He made his name as a preacher in Strasbourg cathedral in the years immediately preceding the Reformation, and died in 1510, just before the immense split in Western Christendom between Catholic and Protestant occurred. That the Protestant Albert Schweitzer could so revere one who lived and died a Catholic tells us something about the unusual religious complexion of late-nineteenth-century Alsace, as well as shedding light upon Schweitzer's own temperament.

The Schweitzers did not stay long in Kaysersberg after the birth of Albert. 'A few weeks after I was born,' Schweitzer recalled, 'my father moved to Gunsbach in the Munster valley. There with my three sisters and one brother I experienced an extremely happy childhood, troubled only by the frequent illnesses of my father.' Later, Schweitzer continued, 'his health improved. As a sturdy septuagenarian he cared for his flock during the [First World] War, when the French artillery fire raked the valley from the heights of the Vosges mountains, claiming as victims many a house and native of Gunsbach.'

In Kaysersberg, where Protestants were in the minority, Albert Schweitzer's father taught Lutheran Christianity to a tiny congregation set amidst a majority of Catholics. When he became pastor of the predominantly Protestant village of Gunsbach a year after Albert's birth, Catholicism, as a result of Louis XIV's decree of 1861, still had a presence in the Protestant parish church. For Louis-Théophile and later for his son Albert Schweitzer (as for most Alsatians) this was no burden. Quite the contrary – to Albert's youthful gaze the Catholic chancel of Gunsbach church was:

the *ne plus ultra* of magnificence. There was first an altar painted to look like gold, with huge branches of artificial flowers upon it; then tall candlesticks of metal with majestic wax candlesticks in them; on the wall, above the altar and between the two windows, was a pair of large gilt statues, which to me were Joseph and the Virgin Mary; and all these objects were flooded with the light which came through the chancel windows.

The entrancing Catholic chancel at Gunsbach never ceased to be part of a lifelong romantic dream – a diffused fantasy that was by no means specifically religious. Through the stained-glass window he gazed in his imagination upon 'trees, roofs, clouds, and blue sky', upon a world 'in short, which continued the chancel of the church into an infinity of distance, and was, in its turn, flooded with a kind of transfiguring glory imparted to it by the chancel'.

Gunsbach brought Schweitzer security, so much so that when he won the Goethe prize in 1928 he used the money to build a permanent home there, a square, solid, rather ugly house facing towards the mountains. Today it is a major Schweitzer archive (see Gunsbach in the index to this book). And in his father church there he first learned to play the organ. When his son was only five, Louis-Théophile Schweitzer began teaching Albert on the old square family piano. The boy was but nine years old when he first substituted for the organist at his father's Gunsbach church. Soon this gifted child was working out harmonies of his own. 'I did not play much from notes,' he remembered: 'my delight was to improvise, and to reproduce songs and hymn tunes with an accompaniment of my own invention.'

At Mulhouse at the age of fifteen he found a yet greater teacher, Eugen Münch. With a passion for the works of Bach, Münch had just arrived from the Berlin music high school to take up the post of organist at the Calvinist church of St Stephen. At first he could scarcely bear teaching his curmudgeonly pupil. 'Albert Schweitzer is a thorn in my flesh,' he would cry. One day the teacher reacted with justified anger when Schweitzer played a badly practised Mozart sonata. The irate Münch opened a copy of Mendelssohn's E natural 'Song without Words', commenting, 'You really have no right to be asked to play such beautiful music. You'll now come and spoil this "Song without Words" for me, just as you have spoiled everything else.' Eugen Münch ended his tirade with the insult, 'If a boy has no feeling, it's certain that I can't give him any.'

The technique worked. 'Oho,' thought the nettled Schweitzer, 'I'll show you whether or not I have any feeling.' Throughout the following week he practised the piece again and again. Although no one had yet taught him fingering, he worked out the best way of playing it, noting it above the score. When his next lesson with Münch took place, Albert Schweitzer patiently sat through the finger exercises and scales. Then he braced himself and played Mendelssohn's E natural 'Song without Words' from the depths of his soul.

At the end Eugen Münch hardly spoke. Placing his hands firmly on Schweitzer's shoulders, he moved the boy from the piano and sat down there himself. Then he played for the boy another Mendelssohn 'Song without Words' which Albert had never heard.

A year later Münch allowed his sixteen-year-old pupil to take his place at services in Mulhouse. Not long afterwards Schweitzer was trusted by his distinguished teacher to play the organ accompaniment to Brahms's *Requiem*, sung by the choir of St Stephen, Mulhouse. 'Then, for the first time, I knew the joy – which I have so often savoured since – of letting the organ send the flood of its own unique tones to mingle with the powerful music of the choir and the orchestra,' Albert wrote.

Albert Schweitzer was to become a world-famous organist and an authority on the works of Johann Sebastian Bach. Together with the celebrated Paris organist Charles-Marie Widor he was to edit a brilliant edition of Bach's works. As Widor later put it, 'One cannot fully understand Bach without Schweitzer, nor in fact Schweitzer without Bach.'

Alsace is a country of magnificent organs. This inheritance derives above all from one family, the Silbermanns (see Silbermann in the index to this book). The founder of the dynasty, Andreas Silbermann, was born in Saxony, but he died in Alsace in 1734. One of his own masters, the Strasbourg organ-builder Friedrich Ring, brought him commissions, and soon he was repairing organs for numerous Alsatian monasteries. He moved to Paris, to learn the skills of a master organ-builder named François Thierry, but soon he was back at Strasbourg, though keeping up a lively professional correspondence with his colleagues elsewhere, including such masters as Louis Marchand of Paris and Johann Christoph Egedacher of Salzburg.

Thus combining French and German expertise with his own genius, Silbermann built in all thirty-four organs. Not all of them survive to this day, but you can see his masterpieces at, for instance, Marmoutier abbey (a two-manual organ with twenty-one stops, built in 1710), Altdorf abbey (built in 1730 with two manuals and sixteen stops), at the church of Saints-Pierre-et-Paul, Rosheim (three manuals with twenty-two stops) and at Ebersmunster abbey (an organ with three manuals and twenty-nine stops, built in 1732).

Soon Andreas Silbermann was being assisted in Strasbourg by his brother and partner Gottfried. Gottfried was also celebrated for his clavichords. C. P. E. Bach played on and prized one for half a century. Gottfried made grand pianos for Frederick the Great, and it is said that Johann Sebastian Bach himself, criticizing their heavy action and weedy treble registers, persuaded Gottfried to bring in numerous technically brilliant improvements.

Andreas Silbermann taught his two sons Johann Andreas and

Johann Daniel. Of the two, Johann Andreas was equally brilliant and innovative as his father. He toured central Germany in 1741, studying every important organ he could find. His fifty-four organs include the one he built with three manuals and twenty stops for the Dominican nuns at Colmar in 1736, another three-manual organ built for the Catholic parish church at Soultz in 1750, and the lovely three-manual organ with forty stops on which Albert Schweitzer played at St Thomas's church, Strasbourg.

When the Germans annexed Alsace in 1870 they were determined to make their new province a show-case of musical excellence. A chair of music was founded at the university in 1875. An association of Minnesingers was set up. Eugen Münch was encouraged to revive the works of J. S. Bach. Émile Rupp, organist at the church of Saint-Paul from 1896, revived the art of organ-building, in collaboration with the organist at Strasbourg cathedral, F. X. Mathias. Albert Schweitzer relished the whole scene. In 1909 he, Rupp and Mathias published jointly their *International Rules for Organ Building*, inaugurating a return to the traditions of the Silbermann dynasty.

Alongside this tradition of organ-music and organ-building in Alsace, the religious heritage of the province and of his own home bequeathed to Schweitzer another priceless legacy: a passion for theology. At the age of nine he had left Gunsbach village school and entered a secondary school in Munster, where he was taught Bible stories by a pastor named Schäffler who evidently possessed a remarkable talent for making the tales of the ancient Jews as real as if they had happened only a day before. As he told the entrancing story of Joseph being recognized by his brothers, Pastor Schäffler would himself weep as he sat at his desk. As he wept, every child sitting on its own form would sob with him. Schweitzer sat entranced. The boy was learning to become the brilliant theologian of the future.

The secondary school at Munster offered Schweitzer the delightful bonus of being four kilometres away from Gunsbach. The walk through beautiful countryside from his own village to school and back again enchanted him. Suddenly all this came to an end – at the age of ten, his parents decided that he should be educated in far away Mulhouse, to be taught by his married godfather, great-uncle Louis. Louis and his wife Sophie offered to feed and lodge the growing boy for nothing. This is where he met the organist Münch (see Mulhouse in the index to this book). Ten years later, after a brief interlude in Paris studying the organ under Charles-Marie Widor, Albert Schweitzer followed in his father's footsteps and entered the theological faculty of the University of Strasbourg.

He studied under the foremost theologians of the age, became a professor himself and in 1906 wrote a book, *The Quest of the Historical Jesus*, which stunned the Christian world. Many acclaimed him. Others regarded him as a heretic. But by now Schweitzer had found a new calling. 'Between the ages of sixteen and eighteen I found battling within myself a dispute over whether my calling should be in the field of music or of theology,' he confessed. Neither won. Instead, without abandoning either music or theology, Schweitzer determined to become a servant of the outcast.

Curiously enough, what drove him to this conviction was an Alsace statue sculpted by a man whose work is better known even than Michelangelo's. Frédéric August Bartholdi was born in Colmar in 1834. He became famous in 1880 for sculpting in Vosges sandstone the 'Lion of Belfort', symbol of that city's invincibility. In the next decade the people of France raised 250,000 dollars for a colossal statue in New York Harbour commemorating the birth of the United States and her deep friendship with France. Bartholdi suggested that its site be Liberty Island (known at that time as Bedloe's Island). In the United States 350,000 dollars were collected for the statue's granite and concrete pedestal, which rises 305.5 feet from the ground. Bartholdi created the figure of a woman raising a torch in her right hand. The height of the statue, covered with over 300 copper sheets, is 151 feet from the pedestal. In her head there is an observation platform. An inscription on the pedestal reads:

> Give me your tired, your poor,
> Your huddled masses yearning to breathe free,
> The wretched refuse of your teaming shore,
> Send these, the homeless, tempest-tossed, to me:
> I lift my lamp beside the golden door

(part of a sonnet by Emma Lazarus called 'The New Colossus').

For Colmar, Bartholdi was commissioned in 1864 to create a memorial statue to Admiral Bruat, who had commanded the French fleet on its expedition to the Crimea. It stood in the public park, surrounded by four bronze figures, one of them a noble negro. The Germans destroyed the statue in 1940, the four bronze figures were melted down, and Admiral Bruat's present memorial is surrounded by four stone ones sculpted by Cérard Choain in 1958. At the turn of the century Albert Schweitzer contemplated Bartholdi's negro with awe and remorse. He became determined to found a missionary hospital in French Equatorial Africa, 'not out of benevolence', as he declared, 'but in atonement' for all that the white nations had cruelly imposed on the blacks. In 1905 the musician and theologian began studying medicine in preparation for his work. In 1913, an expert in tropical medicine, he set up his first jungle hospital.

Its future was uncertain. In 1914 the French put him under house arrest as an enemy German. In 1917 both Schweitzer and his wife Hélène were interned in France in a concentration camp at Saint-Rémy-de-Provence. After the war he paid off his debts and returned to found another hospital, further up the Ogowe River at Lambaréné. For the rest of his life he wrote brilliant books, gave acclaimed organ concerts and raised money for his jungle hospital. He was awarded the Nobel peace prize, made a knight of the French Legion of Honour and given the peace prize *pour le mérite*. Like his fellow-Alsatian, Alfred Kastler, who in 1966 won the Nobel prize for physics, Albert Schweitzer passionately campaigned against atomic warfare and the atomic bomb.

'All I have to say to the world and to mankind,' wrote Schweitzer five years before the end of his long life, 'is contained in the notion "Reverence for Life".' He was returning to an insight of his childhood. As a child he had deeply empathized with the sufferings of others. This identification extended even to the animal world. It was to prove the whole basis of the mature Albert Schweitzer's ethics. 'So far back as I can remember I was saddened by the amount of misery I saw in the world around me,' Schweitzer recalled of his childhood. 'One thing that specially saddened me was that the unfortunate animals had to suffer so much pain and misery. The sight of an old limping horse, tugged forward by one man while another kept beating it with a stick to get it to the knacker's yard at Colmar, haunted me for weeks.'

So, even before he became a schoolboy, he began to add to his evening prayers petitions for animals as well as for his own family. As soon as his mother had prayed with him and kissed him good-night, he silently added a prayer of his own composition: 'O heavenly Father, protect and bless all things that breathe; guard them from all evil; and let them sleep in peace.'

This simple prayer brought him into terrible moral conflict, for his daily childhood life involved some innocent hunting. One spring day when Schweitzer was scarcely eight years old he and a boy named Heinrich Bräsch armed themselves with catapults and set out to kill birds. The leaves had barely returned to the trees. The birds were visible and vulnerable. Heinrich Bräsch took aim. So did Albert. And then the church bells began to ring and the child, remembering his prayer, shooed the birds away from the reach of his own catapult and Heinrich's. Thenceforth, every time the bells of Lent rang out, he remembered with gratitude how on that day they had driven deep into his heart the law 'Thou shalt not kill.' Later he was to confess that, beside the dawning of this conviction that he must not kill or torture his fellow-creatures, every other childhood experience was utterly insignificant. Heinrich Bräsch, we may surmise, was less pleased.

Was this the initial impulse towards Albert Schweitzer's later rigorous and costly philosophy of reverence for life? There are numerous other instances in his *Memoirs* of a revulsion for harming or tormenting mute animals. Twice other boys persuaded him to fish with rod and line, but the simple acts of screwing the hooks into the mouths of the worms that were used for bait, not to speak of wrenching open the mouths of fishes he caught, revolted him. Schweitzer was so affected by this revulsion that he even set about dissuading other boys from going fishing altogether.

He came to see that suffering was an unavoidable element in the struggle for existence. Yet as he later wrote, 'The husbandman who has rightly mowed down a thousand blooms in his meadow in providing fodder for his cattle must not on his homeward way *wantonly* switch off the head of a single flower.'

Schweitzer died in 1965. He is buried not in Alsace but at Lambaréné. Twenty years after his death an authoritative German research institute produced a list of the thirty-two persons most admired by West Germans. At the top of the list came the name of the Alsatian Albert Schweitzer.

Information about Alsace

In Britain a most useful centre for the wines of Alsace is L'Alsacien, 105 Old Brompton Road, London SW7 3LE (telephone 01 589 3320). L'Alsacien not only organizes regular wine tastings and sends out a newsletter, but will also deliver cases of wine to those unable to collect them personally. This enterprising firm also arranges Alsatian dinners at selected restaurants, at which are featured throughout the meal, for example, wines of the Tokay-Pinot gris variety, with the diners offered wines varying from the style of a light dry apéritif through a *vendange tardive* (served with the *foie gras*) and ending with a luscious selection of *grains nobles* served with the dessert.

For more information on the wines of Alsace, try the Centre d'Information du Vin d'Alsace, BP 145, Colmar, 68003 France. Alsatian wine growers and merchants are far too numerous to list here, and in any case in most wine villages you can find vintners as well as *caves coopératives* without any pretence at international fame who are ready to sell you excellent and far from expensive wines. One exception would be to mention Hugel et Fils of Riquewihr, whose stock of different wines and vintages seems inexhaustible.

Useful addresses for prospective tourists include the Association des 'Fermes-Auberges', 4 rue de l'Est, Mulhouse, 68100 France (telephone 89 45 84 25), for information on rooms to let in the Vosges farmhouses. Other information on rural *gîtes* can be obtained (for Bas-Rhin) from the Relais départemental du tourisme rurale,

Maison de l'agriculture, 103 route de Hausbergen, 67300 Schiltigheim (telephone 88 62 45 02) and the Relais at 47 rue du Maréchal Foch, Strasbourg (telephone 88 35 17 60). For Haut-Rhin enquire at SVA Tourisme et propagande, Chambre d'agriculture, 4 rue de l'Est, 68055 Mulhouse Cedex (telephone 89 45 84 25). Youth hostellers should obtain details and prices of Alsace youth hostels from the Féderation Unie des Auberges de la Jeunesse, 6 rue Mesnil, 75116 Paris (telephone 261 84 03).

Lists of hotels, as well as *gîtes*, and much other information can be found at the Strasbourg departmental tourist office, 9 rue de Dôme, Strasbourg (telephone 88 22 01 02) and the Colmar departmental tourist office, Hôtel du Département, 68006 Colmar (telephone 89 23 99 51). Haut-Rhin also has a couple more centres for such information: in Colmar at the CCI, 2 rue Georges-Lasch (telephone 89 23 99 40) and in Mulhouse, at the CCI, 8 rue du 17-Novembre (telephone 89 46 01 14).

In the capitals of France and Britain, for general information about Alsace, enquire at the Maison d'Alsace, 39 Champs-Élysées, Paris (telephone 42 56 15 94), at the Féderation Nationale des Gîtes Ruraux, 34 rue Godot-de-Maury, Paris (telephone 073 25 43) and at the French Government Tourist Office, 178 Piccadilly, London W1V 0AL (telephone 01 499 6911). In Alsace itself even the smallest towns often have their own *syndicats d'initiative* or information offices.

Skiers should first make contact with the Comité des Vosges, 39 avenue du Président-Kennedy, 68100 Mulhouse (telephone 89 43 25 50). Major winter sports centres are to be found at le Champ du Feu (the best known and probably the best equipped, its slopes reaching a height of 1,100 metres), le Hohwald (its slopes also reaching a height of 1,100 metres), le Schlucht (reaching a height of 1,120 metres), le Grand Ballon (a small ski centre at a height of 1,424 metres, the peak of the Alsatian Vosges), Grendelbruch (with slopes reaching a height of 900 metres), le Donon (reaching a height of 1,000 metres), Saales (reaching a height of 800 metres), Wangenbourg-Engenthal (reaching a height of 1,000 metres), Brézouard (reaching a height of 900 metres), and in the region of Munster. See also the index to this book.

After suffering on the ski-slopes you can recuperate at the health centres of Merkwiller-Pechelbronn (telephone 88 80 52 14), Niederbronn-les-Bains (the most famous, with its casino and cultural life, telephone 88 09 60 55), Morsbronn-les-Bains (telephone 88 09 31

91) and in the parc Albert-Schweitzer, Munster (telephone 89 77 36 40).

The Alsatian fishing federation has its main offices at Strasbourg (2 rue de Nomeny, telephone 88 34 51 86) and at Mulhouse (29 avenue de Colmar, telephone 89 59 06 88). In Alsace, as elsewhere in France, hunting game is strictly regulated. If you do want to try your hand at shooting wild animals, the departmental federations of hunters are at 2 avenue Auguste-Wicky, 68100 Mulhouse (telephone 89 45 20 28) and at 5 rue Staedel, Strasbourg (telephone 88 79 12 77).

You can hire bicycles at the railway stations of Colmar, Mulhouse, Strasbourg and Saverne, as well as in Sainte-Marie-aux-Mines at the Groupement d'intérêt touristique de la Moyenne-Alsace (telephone 64 58 80 50). The Ligue Alsace de cyclotourisme is based at 1 rue Frédéric Kulmann, Colmar. A less strenuous and delightful way of exploring two small regions of Alsace is to take first the tourist train which runs along ancient tracks for fourteen kilometres between Cernay and Sentheim at 15.00 every day between 1 July and 10 September (except Sundays and Mondays) and then the yet more antiquated train that runs between Ottrott and Rosheim (see Ottrott in the index to this book).

The main sailing association of Bas-Rhin has its headquarters at 9 rue du Général-Gouraud, Strasbourg (telephone 88 35 68 68). That of Haut-Rhin is at 1 rue Principale, Houssen, Colmar (telephone 89 23 59 02). There are aero-clubs at Rixheim (telephone 89 44 01 41), Saverne (telephone 88 91 11 41), Sarre-Union (telephone 89 00 11 96), Strasbourg (telephone 88 34 00 98) and Sélestat (telephone 88 92 88 48). The chief aero-club of Haut-Rhin is at Colmar (telephone 89 41 15 25).

For horseback-riding in Bas-Rhin, enquire first at the Ligue d'Alsace, 1 rue Sainte-Élisabeth, Strasbourg (telephone 88 36 10 13). Riding clubs have been established in Bas-Rhin at Wissembourg (telephone 88 80 40 76), Sarre-Union (telephone 88 00 15 59), Molsheim (telephone 88 38 10 99) and Haguenau (telephone 88 73 03 12). To ride in Haut-Rhin enquire first at 78 rue Oberhardt, Colmar (telephone 89 79 33 48), or at the Association Alsacienne de Tourisme équestre, 8 Grand'Rue, 68600 Neuf-Brisach (telephone 89 71 41 36). At Ensisheim (telephone 89 81 10 10), Metzeral (telephone 89 77 68 62), Guebwiller (telephone 89 76 93 35), Neuf-Brisach (telephone 89 72 56 56) and Munster (telephone 89 60 26 20) there are well established Haut-Rhin riding clubs.

To my mind the Alsace temperatures scarcely encourage naturism, but there are nudist clubs at 27 rue des Vosges, Illzac, at 5 rue de Dahlias, Mulhouse, and at the Centre gymnique d'Alsace, Strasbourg.

Potholers should apply to the Groupe spéléo d'Alsace, 3 boulevard d'Europe, Mulhouse, or to the Amis des Anciennes-Mines, 70 rue Wilson, Sainte-Marie-aux-Mines.

Bibliography

Jean-Pierre Beck and Dominique Harster, 'Recensement des synagogues', in *Monuments Historiques No. 135*, Caisse nationale des monuments historiques et sites, Paris, Octobre-Novembre 1984, pp.33–9.

Albert Bielschowsky, *The Life of Goethe*, tr. William A. Cooper, Haskel House, New York, 1969.

Jean-Marc Biry, 'L'habitat ouvrier et les usines de Dietrich', in *Monuments Historiques No. 135*, Caisse national des monuments historiques et sites, Paris, Octobre-Novembre 1984, pp.54–7.

Patrice Boussel, *Guide des champs de bataille en France*, Éditions Pierre Horay, Paris, 1981.

James Brabazon, *Albert Schweitzer, A Comprehensive Biography*, Victor Gollancz, London, 1976.

Sebastian Brant, *The Ship of Fools*, tr. Edwin H. Zeydel, Columbia University Press, N.Y., 1944.

Jean-Claude Brumm and Jean-Claude Gilbert, 'Parc naturel régional des Vosges du Nord', in *Monuments Historiques No. 135*, Caisse nationale des monuments historiques et sites, Paris, Octobre-Novembre 1984, pp.27f.

Jean Defrasne, *L'Occupation Allemande en France*, Presses Universitaires de France, 1985.

Jacques-Louis Delpal, 'L'Alsace de la Route des Vins', in *Cuisines et Vins de France*, No. 369, Paris, October 1981, pp.60–6.

Die Kleinen Blauen, *Elsaß Lothringen*, Verlag Molden, Freiburg im Breisgau, 1983 edition.

Karlheinz Ebert, *Das Elsaß*, DuMont Kunst-Reiseführer, Cologne, 1979.

Pierre Gaertner and Robert Frédérick, *The Cuisine of Alsace*, tr. J.F. Bernard and Helen Feingold, Barron's, Woodbury, New York, n.d.

Sylvie Girard, *Alsace Lorraine*, Librairie Larousse, Paris, 1987.

Gottfried von Strasbourg, *Tristan und Isolde*, ed. and tr. E. H. Zeydel, Princeton University Press, N.Y., 1948.

Marc Grodwohl, 'Ecomusée de Haute-Alsace', in *Monuments Historiques No. 135*, Caisse nationale des monuments historiques et sites, Paris, Octobre-Novembre 1984, pp.29–32.

Jean-Louis Gyss, *Le vin et l'Alsace*, Berger-Levrault/Jean-Pierre Gyss, Rosheim, 1978.

Paul and Jean-Pierre Haeberlin, *Les recettes de l'Auberge de l'Ill*, Éditions Flammarion, Paris, 1982.

Hans Haug, *L'Art en Alsace*, Arthaud, Mulhouse, 1962.

Hans Haug, 'Le style Louis XIV, essai sur la transition entre la "manière allemande" et le "goût français", in *Archives Alsaciennes d'histoire et de l'art*, Strasbourg, 1924, pp.65–111.

Fernand L'Huillier, *Histoire de l'Alsace*, Presses Universitaires de France, Paris, 1965.

Garms Jörg, 'Le plan d'urbanisme de Strasbourg dressé par J.-F. Blondel en 1764–1769', in *Cahiers Alsaciens d'archaeologie, d'art et d'histoire*, tome XXI, Strasbourg, 1978, pp.103–40.

Benedict Leclerc, 'L'embellissement de Strasbourg au XVIIIe Siècle', in *Monuments Historiques No. 135*, Caisse nationale des monuments historiques et sites, Paris, Octobre-Novembre 1984, pp.40–6.

Jacques Legros, *Le Mont Sainte-Odile*, Éditions Alsatia, Strasbourg, 1974.

Alexis Lichine, *Encyclopédie des vins et des alcools de tous les pays*, revised edition, Robert Laffont, Millau, 1985.

Frédéric Luckel, 'L'architecture viticole, spécifité de la construction et insertion dans le paysage du vignoble', in *Monuments Historiques No. 135*, Caisse nationale des monuments historiques et sites, Paris, Octobre-Novembre 1984, pp.10–15.

Henry McNulty, 'Bitten by the Alsatian', *Departures* magazine, July/August 1986, pp.112–15.

Michel de Montaigne, *The Complete Works*, tr. Donald M. Frame, Hamish Hamilton, London, 1958.

Denis Mougeot, 'La bière a un pays', in *Cuisines et Vins de France*, No. 387, Paris, June 1983, pp.50–4.

Wolfgang and Franziska Müller-Härlin, *Elsaß und Vogesen*, Robert Pfützner GmbH, Munich, 1985.

Klaus Nohlen, 'Baupolitik im Reichsland Elsaß-Lothringen 1871–1918', in *Kunst, Kultur und Politik im Deutschen Kaiserreich*, series I, vol.5, Berlin 1982.

Klaus Nohlen, 'Strasbourg au temps de l'annexation', tr. Marie-José Nohlen, in *Monuments Historiques No. 135*, Caisse nationale des monuments historiques et sites, Paris, Octobre-Novembre 1984, pp.47–53.

Julien Nussbaum, 'Regards technologiques sur l'architecture rurale', in *Monuments Historiques No. 135*, Caisse nationale des monuments historiques et sites, Paris, Octobre-Novembre 1984, pp.5–9.

The Baroness d'Oberkirch, Countess de Montbuisson, *Memoirs*, Colburn, 3 vols, London, 1852.

Nikolaus Pevsner and Michael Meier, *Grünewald*, Thames and Hudson, London, 1958.

Roger Pilkington, *Small Boat to Alsace*, Macmillan, London, 1961.

Pierre Prunet, 'La tour de Klotz à la cathédrale de Strasbourg', in *Monuments Historiques No. 153*, Caisse nationale des monuments historiques et sites, Paris, Octobre 1987, pp.45–9.

Denis de Rougemont, *Passion and Society*, tr. Montgomery Belgion, Faber & Faber, London, 1940.

E. Ruhmer, *Grünewald, The Paintings*, Phaidon, 1958.

Pierre Schmidt, *Alsace: Enchantements de la route des vignes*, with colour lithographs by Jean-Pierre Rémon, Éditions d'Art des Heures Claires, Paris, 1981.

Albert Schweitzer, *Aus meiner Kindheit und Jugendzeit*, Verlag Paul Haupt, Bern, 1979 edition.

Charles H. Sherrill, *Stained Glass Tours in Germany, Austria and the Rhine Lands*, John Lane/The Bodley Head, London, 1927.

Sacheverell Sitwell, *Gothic Europe*, Weidenfeld & Nicolson, London, 1969.

Louis Spach, *Oberlin, Pasteur du Ban-de-La-Roche*, Éditions Berger Levrault & Fils, Paris and Strasbourg, 1866.

Margaret Trouncer, *Charles de Foucauld*, Harrap, London, 1972.

Jean Jacques Waltz ('L'Oncle Hansi'), *Le Paradis tricolore*, Éditions H. Floury, Paris, 1918.

Jean Jacques Waltz ('L'Oncle Hansi'), *Mon Village: images et commentaires par l'Oncle Hansi*, Éditions H. Floury, Paris, 1914 edition.

Edwyn H. Zeydel, *Sebastian Brant*, Twayne Publishers, N.Y., 1967.

Index